CONTENTS

KU-647-683

TABLES, FIGURES AND CHARTS

Tables

Figures

Tables, Figures and Charts

Charts

PREFACE

There are a number of ways of approaching the study of social policy. Perhaps the most common is the division by 'service', which means that students take courses in areas such as income maintenance, health, housing or education policy. But there are other ways of cutting the social-policy cake. One is by 'group': the disabled, for example, or the old, or women. Another is first to isolate a concept — for example, social justice or equality — and then to relate it both to policies in a particular area and to particular groups. This book has opted explicitly for an amalgam of these strategies. Although its primary focus is women as a group, most of the contributors, who work from a wide variety of disciplinary perspectives, take a particular policy area and try to see what is happening to women within it, concentrating chiefly on women's experience in the family and in paid employment.

It is hoped that the book will prove helpful, above all, to students, whose opportunities for reading about women and social policy have to date been limited. Indeed, it was the desire of a group of students at the London School of Economics to discuss the subject of gender roles in relation to social policy which gave rise to the seminars on which this book is based. Special thanks are due to them, and to Irene Bruegel, Miriam David and Dulcie Groves for stepping in to join the project at a later stage.

1 INTRODUCTION[1]

Jane Lewis

Few would disagree that sexual divisions have always existed in all areas of human activity in all cultures, although they have certainly not always taken the same form and have changed markedly over time. In Britain, the emergence of a rigid separation of public and private spheres came about with the removal of the workplace from the home during the late eighteenth and early nineteenth centuries as a result of industrialisation.[2] The public sphere of paid employment, public office and citizenship remained with the male, and the private and familial with the female. The separation was, of course, more complete in terms of public office and citizenship, and in the case of paid employment, more complete for middle than for working-class women.[3]

Women achieved political citizenship in most western countries during the second quarter of this century, and since the Second World War we have seen an acceleration in the move away from separate spheres. A majority of adult women now engage in both reproduction and production. But this has not been accompanied by a breakdown of sexual divisions, either at home or in the workplace. Women have retained responsibility for housework, and the care of children and other kin within the home, and the segregation between men's jobs and women's jobs has intensified. In our society it is still generally assumed that women will take primary responsibility for house and children, which means that they are defined in terms of the family (and, in particular, in relation to a male wage-earner), and that their work outside the home is considered to be of secondary importance.

Until very recently there has been no need for policy-makers to articulate these assumptions, and the construction of social policies has reflected the idea that 'normally' adult women will be economically dependent on men, and that there will be a division of labour between them. In the case of social insurance, for example, although there has been extensive debate over what might be considered fair and equitable contributions and benefits for women, the discussion has been premised on implicit assumptions as to the nature of women's responsibilities and patterns of dependency within the family. Thus social policies have tended to reproduce sexual divisions.

An examination of the nature of sexual divisions shows that women

1

relate to a more complicated set of structures than men, because of their role within the family. They are mothers, housewives and carers of children and elderly or otherwise incapacitated relatives, as well as waged workers, and their experience in one role structures their experience in the others. This is important, because it is possible for policies to effect greater equality in one area of women's lives, yet to remain unchanged or actually to reinforce traditional sexual divisions in another. Changes in policy must therefore be considered in regard to their effect on the totality of women's experience.

In seeking to promote greater equality between the sexes, the feminist movement has historically campaigned most vigorously to gain entry to the public world of paid employment, and it is here that we have seen the most rapid changes, culminating in the equal-rights legislation of the 1970s, which was aimed primarily at equalising pay and employment opportunities. In both Britain and the USA the results of the legislation have been disappointing. As well as raising doubts as to the efficacy of legislating equal rights, this begs the larger question as to how far action on one issue has the power to change the totality of women's experience. The question becomes more pressing when it is realised that policies touching women's position in the family have often reinforced sexual divisions.

Looking at the problem from the opposite direction, when equal opportunities are extended to individuals, who, because of the additional burden of their family responsibilities, are not in a position to start equal, the rights gained are likely to be formal rather than substantive. Moreover, the equal treatment of men and women as autonomous individuals within the family (in regard to their claims for state benefits, for example), without any corresponding commitment to encourage the equal division of work within the family, may well result in diswelfares for women.

By examining the nature of policies affecting various aspects of women's lives, the contributors to this book explore the mechanisms by which policies reproduce sexual divisions, the way in which the issue of equality for women has been defined by policy-makers, and the effect of measures designed to achieve greater equality between the sexes. In large part, the pursuit of a narrowly defined equality has been confined to the area of paid employment; little has been done to encourage the sharing of work done within the family. Indeed, as many of the contributors point out, recent changes in the political climate in both Britain and the USA have led to calls for a strengthening of the traditional sexual division of labour in the home, and it is by no means certain as to how successful the feminist movement will be in countering them. This introduction aims to draw together some of the major issues and themes addressed in the book: first, by looking at the relationship between social policy and sexual divisions, and by directing attention to the links between the effects of policy changes on women's position in the family and their position in the labour-market; second, by considering possible policy directions in the light of this analysis; and third, by outlining the political obstacles women currently face in promoting further change.

Social Policies and Sexual Divisions

Women's reproductive function has meant that there has always been a school of thought which considered all sexual divisions to be naturally founded on biological facts. It is argued that because women bear children, it follows that they should also rear them and that their sphere of activity should be home-based. During the nineteenth century, the claims of women to higher education were denied on the basis that their reproductive systems would be irreparably harmed, their claim to the vote was rejected on grounds of biological inferiority and incapacity resulting from the need to attend to home duties, and their claim to equal job opportunities was declared incompatible with their primary role of motherhood.

The tendency to tie the biological roles of child-rearing and home-making together as 'natural' finds constant expression from the earliest differential experiences of girls and boys in schools – divided into separate groups, and choosing between woodwork and domestic science – through to the anti-sex-discrimination legislation, with its 'genuine occupational difference' clause, where the concept of 'genuine' employs both social and biological definitions, as for example in the reference to jobs that call for 'authentic male characteristics'. Underneath this lingering biological determinism we must read a deeper desire for a particular kind of order. Christopher Lasch's recent book mourning the passing (as he sees it) of the patriarchal family – the haven in the heartless world and the guardian of the inner life, imagination and self-discipline – is perhaps typical in this respect.[4]

The assumption that the family should consist of a male breadwinner and a woman, who makes the welfare of her husband, children and other dependent kin her first responsibility, has persisted, chiefly because of the belief that this is the best way of maintaining male work

incentives and hence social stability. Women who do not fit
this pattern have tended to be classed as problems. The next essay in
this book looks at the notion of female economic dependency and at
the way in which social policies have treated a particular group of
women – married women workers – who did not wholly conform to
prescribed roles; it shows the tensions and contradictions that have
arisen in the past from the conflict between policy-makers'
assumptions and the reality of women's experiences. For it is not the
case, as one early commentator argued, that 'the feminine is a social
problem'.[5] Indeed, it is this sort of formulation that can still so easily
lead to a 'blame the victim' approach, as Ann Oakley shows in this
volume. Rather, the problem lies in the structures to which women
must relate.

In fact, women experience a basic contradiction between their
labour in the home and in the workplace, which has been reflected in
and reinforced, rather than resolved, by social policies. Oakley draws
attention to the evidence which suggests that women's traditional
work in the home may generate both personal dissatisfaction and
conflict between husband and wife, especially when combined with
the expectation, desire, or reality of paid employment. At worst this
may result in wife assault. A large percentage of married women also
appear to suffer from depression. Oakley argues that these conditions
are exacerbated by the absence of policies (to provide more day-care
facilities for example), which would ease the burden of women's double
load.

Policies providing financial support to families have also ignored the
real needs of women who combine a number of roles. The policies
have operated on a set of assumptions which have treated women's
paid employment as secondary, ignored the question of the division of
power and resources within the family, and taken for granted the
sexual division of labour within the home.

Both the social-security and the tax systems take the family as
the basic unit of assessment on the assumption both that marriage
(and, in the case of the social-security system, cohabitation) make
women dependent and that money coming into the family is shared
equally. Both assumptions are problematic. Notions of female economic
dependency and the family wage have persisted, despite evidence that
has always existed to show both the crucial contribution made by
married women to the family economy, and the inability of a majority
of working-class husbands to earn a wage that would enable their
wives to be completely dependent.[6] In regard to the division of

resources within the family, studies have shown repeatedly that wives often do not know how much their husbands earn, and that money controlled by the wife (which often takes the form of a housekeeping allowance paid by the husband) frequently fails to keep up with either inflation, increases in the husband's pay, or increases in family size.[7]

The persistence of assumptions regarding the economic dependency of women is crucial to Dulcie Groves's interpretation of the development of pension provision for women. From the beginning, the social-security system as a whole was set up to cater for the male breadwinner. Women workers have never been easy to fit into the system because of their low pay, part-time hours and tendency to have interrupted work careers. Thus, in general, provision for women has been made through their husbands. Pensions are no exception, and schemes have been designed in the main for dependent wives.

Recently, more recognition has been accorded women's claim to financial independence in pensions legislation, and in many other policies affecting the financial position of family members. For example, the changes in the administration of supplementary benefits and family-income supplement, scheduled for 1983, will allow either partner (rather than the man alone, as at present) to claim benefit as long as he or she has been engaged in full-time work for a specified period. But the Department of Health and Social Security rejected the idea of assessing need on an individual rather than a family basis on grounds of expense, and what it considered to be the unwarranted inequalities of paying benefits to the partners of prosperous husbands or wives.[8] This decision was defended on the grounds that it reflected 'the assumptions of the overwhelming majority of the people of Britain'.[9] Policy-makers often use the argument that decisions affecting the private sphere must not do violence to public opinion to justify their conservatism. But such an argument does not explain the often dramatic lags between changes in mores and changes in policy. For example, the use of contraceptives was not accorded formal recognition until 1967, one hundred years after the birth-rate had begun to show signs of steady decline. Nor does it explain the fact that one area of state policy may be much more resilient to change than another. Indeed, the idea of treating couples as individuals, rather than aggregating their resources, has made greater progress in the area of family law — in regard to the question of maintenance after divorce — than in social-security law.

However, as Hilary Land argues, there is a grave danger inherent in policies that move towards treating couples as autonomous individuals for economic purposes, when it is clear that there is no intention of either equalising the burden of parenting and caring, or of ensuring a fairer distribution of resources within the family. For example, the Family Law Commission has recommended that the courts pay more attention to the wife's capacity to earn when assessing her claim to maintenance, without giving due consideration to the fact that the work of caring for the young, the old and husbands effectively reduces women's leverage on the labour-market. Indeed, as Land also shows, the recent changes (proposed and already made) in income maintenance and taxation have tended to reduce women's claims to maintenance on men, but at the same time have tended to reinforce their work of caring in the home. Thus, two new benefits included in the 1975 legislation—the invalid-care allowance and the non-contributory invalidity pension—perpetuated assumptions regarding the 'normal household duties' of married women and hence their unequal treatment. In the case of the tax system, the government's recent discussion of changes necessary to achieve equity between the sexes has centred in large part on proposals to abolish the married man's tax allowance, which was introduced in 1918 to ease the burden imposed by a dependent wife on her husband's taxable capacity, but which has always been paid to all married men regardless of whether their wives actually stay at home.[10] The government favours a solution which establishes formal equality in terms of transferable tax allowances to each partner, but which in practice protects the position of the childless, single-earner couple and the family where the wife stays at home, as compared to couples where both work.

The reluctance of policy-makers to tackle the problem of inequalities within the family is just as clear in regard to the question of the division of resources between family members. Land has shown elsewhere that the introduction of the child benefit (which replaced the child tax allowances claimed by husbands, and effectively increased the cash allowance paid in the form of family allowances to mothers) almost foundered because of the transfer it represented from 'wallet to purse'. Barbara Castle, the secretary of state who steered the legislation through Parliament in 1975, commented that 'only by the father giving up tax relief was it possible to finance the mother's need properly', but both trade unions and politicians resisted transferring money from the father's wage-packet to the mother.[11] In this connection, it is worth noting that recent arguments from both right and left in favour of equalising the ability to buy services, rather than increasing their provision by the state, tend to pass over the problems of first, the unequal division of power and resources within the family, and second, the unequal division of labour particularly in regard to the work of caring, which accompanies it.[12]

Women's participation in production[13] cannot be divorced from the constraints they experience in terms of their family responsibilities. In periods when the demand for labour has been great, this has been recognised and policies have been framed to facilitate women's entry in to the workforce. During both world wars state provision of day-care facilities increased dramatically, and at the end of the Second World War, when it was feared that there would be a labour shortage, a wife's tax allowance on her earned income was raised to the level of that for a single person and the Royal Commission on Population advocated giving women greater access to birth-control information in order to encourage married women to work. As Oakley's chapter shows, women's struggle to take control of all aspects of reproduction, including childbirth, is still a major issue.

Despite the periodic, deliberate encouragement that has been given to women to take paid employment, the burden of women's wife/mother/career role and the notion of the family wage has ensured that the wife's earnings have for the most part remained secondary, and this in turn has reinforced traditional gender roles. In particular the absence, in peacetime, of adequate day-care facilities has meant that women have shouldered a double burden. Any woman who adds paid work to her familial responsibilities must under-take to work out her own salvation. Thus it is that married women are more likely to take paid work that is part-time, requires little training and which is usually poorly paid. Irene Bruegel's chapter shows that the expansion in the female labour force since 1951 has been largely due to an increase in the number of low-paid, low-status workers; and, as Hilary Land points out, these workers are not eligible for insurance benefits and fall outside employment-protection legislation. They therefore comprise a cheaper and more flexible workforce from the employers' point of view, which in turn helps to explain the increase in their numbers. Moreover, women's unequal status in the labour-market will tend to be reflected in their unequal status in old age. As Dulcie Groves demonstrates, occupational pension schemes are rarely the same for all categories of worker within an organisation, and women often find themselves offered an inferior pension plan by virtue of their lower job status rather than on grounds of sex *per se*.

Neo-classical economists have analysed the connection between women's restricted participation in the workforce and their home responsibilities, but because they assume that sexual divisions are natural, they argue that women's low-paid and low-status jobs are a matter of individual choice. Like the biological arguments supporting sexual divisions, these economic arguments become circular: taking the division of labour within the household as given, women will acquire less training and will earn less in the labour-market, or, taking the wage differential as given (because the likelihood of interruption of work due to pregnancy and family responsibilities make women of inferior value to employers), the division of labour in the household logically follows.[14] However, as Bruegel argues, only a more structural view of the labour-market can elucidate the systemic processes which trap women as a group, rather than as individuals, within certain grades and kinds of work. Women's earnings will never equal those of men as long as they are confined to women's jobs (stereotypically located in the service sector) or to the lower categories of work.

Women's experience of paid employment is structured by their responsibility for childbearing, parenting and caring. Work and the family cannot therefore be neatly compartmentalised; the domestic division of labour and the segregation of male and female paid work are mutually reinforcing.

Policy Directions

The failure of the equal-rights legislation of the 1970s to make any significant change in the position of women might, therefore, have been predicted, in so far that it aimed only to correct the inequalities experienced by women in the public sphere. For example, the Sex Discrimination Act does not cover discriminatory practices in the areas of social security, pensions, taxation and family law, which directly affect the way in which women experience the family. Equal-rights legislation has always concentrated on equalising opportunities in the public sphere on the terms set by men. For example, the Equal Opportunities Commission (EOC) has recently adopted the traditional egalitarian position on the issue of protective legislation, calling for its abolition on the grounds that what women need is 'a fair field and no favour'. This is but the latest development in a long argument amongst feminists over this question (see Chapters 2 and 7). Trade union women, in particular, see no reason why protective legislation should not be extended to men, rather than women be forced to conform to male work practices.

This argument throws into sharp relief the assumption inherent in equal-rights legislation that the struggle for equality is an individual one, waged by a woman abstracted from her familial relations and responsibilities. Both the Equal Pay and Sex Discrimination Acts rely on the ability of an individual to recognise discrimination and bring a charge, but as Bruegel argues, in a society where women's economic dependency and secondary status in the labour-market are taken for granted, recognising (let alone proving) discriminatory treatment may be problematic.

A much broader concept of equality is therefore needed, if women's choices are to be expanded. Two anthropologists have contended that, if the public sphere is ever to belong to more than an elite of women, men must be brought into the private sphere.[15] In other words, the aim must be to equalise the division of responsibilities and tasks between the sexes in the home as well as in the workplace. The notion of equality inherent in most social policies, particularly those affecting women's position in the family, has been rather different. As Brian Abel-Smith points out in the case of the social-security system, policies have been concerned more with achieving equal benefits than equal roles. (In practice, of course, women's benefits have usually been unequal because they have been judged to pose greater risks and have lesser needs than men, and because it is assumed that, if married, they will be able to depend on their husbands.)

If we consider the interrelation of the structures that form the unity of women's condition, the goal of equality between men and women must lead logically to a call for policies to counter the inequalities experienced by women in all aspects of their lives. This would mean not only treating men and women as autonomous individuals, but also promoting policies that would, first, ensure a fairer distribution of resources between family members (both Abel-Smith and Land recommend using the married man's tax allowance to provide a cash benefit for those involved in parenting and caring) and, second, encourage the equal division of household tasks and greater female participation in the labour force. The latter must involve the implementation of positive-action programmes, the importance of which is briefly indicated by a number of contributors.

Elizabeth Meehan's chapter shows that differences in the judicial and political system in the USA have given positive or affirmative-action programmes a much larger place in that country's equal-opportunity policy than they have achieved in Britain. There are many types of positive-action programme. In the USA, programmes are not supposed to be mere quota systems, which may involve the hiring of less-qualified women in order to fill the quota (a practice commonly referred to as reverse discrimination). Rather, they are supposed to expand the pool of qualified applicants through active recruitment campaigns. However, as Meehan points out, in time of recession the line between the two types of programme is easily blurred.

Women in the trade union and feminist movements in Britain have argued that neither programme is sufficient, if it applies only to the public sphere and mainly to opening up hitherto male jobs to women.[16] They argue that programmes should also include equal employment rights for part-time workers, more possibilities of job sharing, and a shorter working day, as well as more opportunities for education and training. They also call for the whole programme to be backed by much greater day-care provision. In other words, policies should encourage both the sharing of household responsibilities and the improvement of women's position in the workforce. There is, for example, little point in campaigning for parental rather than maternity leave (such as is granted in Sweden), if women workers are to remain in the low-paid jobs which make it impossible for their husbands to afford to give up work and share child care.

Unequal practices to achieve equality have a logic when the burden of past discrimination is considered, but the idea of positive discrimination sits uneasily with liberal political philosophers.[17] The most thoroughgoing form of positive discrimination – the quota system – raises the most acute concern, because the burden of adjustment falls on individuals, who may themselves never have been guilty of discriminatory behaviour.

The dilemma arises from pitting right against right: the right of individuals against the rights of minority groups or women. But it is difficult to defend the *status quo* in the name of individual liberty. The evidence that the market is not blind and that there is both direct and indirect discrimination against certain groups of people is indisputable. Janet Radcliffe Richards has argued that although the practice of reverse discrimination undoubtedly means that individual men will suffer, this is only because men as a group have historically expected and received more than their fair share. She therefore claims that reverse discrimination can be justified as long as it is clear that what is being defended is the choice of a candidate for the purpose of achieving social justice, rather than the more usual one of finding the best person for the job.[18]

Political Obstacles to Further Change

Progress towards a policy of positive action must seem increasingly remote in the present economic and political climate. The breakdown in the post-war consensus has been marked in both the USA and Britain by an attack on the role of the state in the economy and by a reassertion of traditional values regarding the family and the role of women. New Right ideologies have perceived recent dramatic changes in family patterns as evidence of the 'dissolution' of the family (feminist writers see it more as a 'transformation'),[19] and hence a threat to the social fabric. The family is seen as a bedrock and yet fragile. In Britain, the number of single-parent families has increased from an estimated 620,000 in 1971 to 920,000 in 1980 (accounting for one in eight of all families) and the divorce-rate has increased 400 per cent during the last twenty years.[20] The response of the New Right has been to condemn the forces they believe to be responsible (particularly feminism, which they blame for encouraging women to neglect their home responsibilities in favour of paid employment), and to call for policies to strengthen the family; for example, when Secretary of State for Social Services, Patrick Jenkin, expressed fear at the prospect of the family losing more of its functions, which he attributed to the changes in the position of women: 'There is now elaborate machinery to ensure [that women have] equal opportunity, equal pay and equal rights; but I think we ought to stop and ask—where does this leave the family?'[21]

The essay by Miriam David shows the way in which family-policy rhetoric leads to policies which aim to limit women's choices. She looks at the example of education, particularly at recent policy documents on the curriculum, and finds that great importance is being attached to the more traditional aspects of feminine socialisation, such as preparation for motherhood. This is reminiscent of the reaction of the government in the early twentieth century to the publicity accorded to the fear of racial deterioration attendant on the decay of family life and the high infant-mortality rate, which resulted in a curriculum for girls giving priority to the study of domestic subjects and infant care.[22] But in the more recent past this sort of explicit sexual differentiation in the curriculum has been muted, and socialisation into traditional gender roles has been largely confined to the 'hidden curriculum', for example, to textbooks showing girls in traditional roles, or to teachers who consciously or unconsciously promote sex stereotypes.[23]

Several contributors also show the way in which recent social policies have tended to limit the participation of married women in the labour force and to promote their traditional role of carer. As David points out, although the right of equal opportunities in the workplace is still being admitted for single women and married women with no maternal responsibilities, women with small children have recently been actively discouraged from taking paid employment. Having witnessed major retreats from the provision of day care after both world wars, we seem to be witnessing a third. Even the provision of nursery education, which has always been justified in terms of the child's welfare rather than the assistance it provided the mother, has been threatened by the 1980 Education Act, which removed the legal responsibilities of local education authorities to provide nursery education for children aged 3-5 years. Similarly, the 1980 Employment Act eroded the rights to maternity leave afforded women under the 1975 Employment Protection Act. Land also refers to the way in which some women now applying for unemployment benefit are being asked to satisfy officers that their family responsibilities will not interfere with their availability for work, a tightening of administrative procedures that is strikingly similar to those of the 1930s described in my own chapter. In keeping with this trend, the government's proposal to replace the married man's tax allowance by transferable personal allowances would, in all probability, reverse the present tendency of the tax system to encourage married women's work. A wife staying at home could transfer her personal allowances to her husband to set against his income, thus giving husbands an incentive to discourage their wives from re-entering the labour force. All these restrictions (actual and contemplated) on married women's right to take paid employment will result in greater pressure on women to choose between either the role of wife/mother/carer *or* that of a childless career woman.

Running parallel to this trend is the priority being given to community care. Land and Parker have suggested that governments have always perceived the sense of family responsibility for kin to be in a state of 'precarious balance' and have therefore tended either to define their help with the care of dependent family members as exceptional, or to disguise it as 'something not easily'generalisable to a wide spectrum of family roles and tasks'[24] (nursery education provides a good example). There is in fact a crucial distinction between care by, and care in, the community. In practice, the concept of community care tends to mean care by the family and by women in the family.[25] In this volume, Oakley comments on the way in which women's traditional work of caring for sick and infirm relatives is being stretched. Policy-makers have always tended to regard women as the natural guardians of the national health because of their central role in the family.

Two of the leading proponents of a family perspective on policy define the concept of family policy neutrally to encompass 'what the state does by action or inaction to affect people in their roles as family members or to influence the future of the family (families?) as an institution'.[26] But most proponents of family policy have a clear idea of the kind of family relationships and responsibilities they wish to promote and these assumptions will be necessarily reflected in their policy proposals. Evidence suggests that whenever policy-makers have talked of 'mothers' needs' in the past, they have done so in relation to a precise concept of motherhood as a social function, thereby creating an inflexible notion of need. Thus at the end of the Second World War, for example, day-care centres were closed, mothers were paid family allowances and women received a new insurance status on marriage in recognition of their important work in the home, which served to reinforce their economic dependency.[27] The rhetoric of 'mothers' needs' was entirely prescriptive.

It is impossible to make family policy politically neutral.[28] Today, for example, both the pro-choice and the pro-life lobbies on abortion can claim to be pro-family. There is no guarantee that those promoting family policies to whatever end will consciously consider the realities of women's experience at all. The New Right ignores women's economic need for jobs and their desire for work that is personally satisfying; lobbyists interested in the welfare of children may well pursue their rights to the exclusion of those of women; and those interested primarily in the redistribution of income between rich and poor may not consider the need to redistribute resources within the family.[29] At present, the New Right seems to be the strongest group pressing the cause of the family, and in the absence of strong pressure to the contrary, family policy may well become more firmly the province of those desiring the kind of 'new moral economy' described by David.

It is logical to expect the strongest opposition to such a development to come from the women's movement. However, women's pull on the political system has never been great. Their relative lack of power in the home, at the workplace and in public office has made articulation of their needs difficult, and their lack of economic power has also tended to thwart satisfaction of wants. For example, there is certainly evidence to suggest that because of their relation to the structures of production and reproduction, women might be as interested in fighting for shorter hours, and in particular for a shorter working day, as for more pay, but this has tended to go unrecognised by the male trade union leadership.[30] Women's relationship to unions, as to any other public institution, has historically been mediated by men.[31] Moreover, as David Donnison has pointed out, the women's movement is fragmented: a demand for equal opportunities is not the same as a demand for liberation and personal autonomy, and a demand for equal rights in an unequal society is not the same as a demand for equal rights for all.[32]

In addition, US studies have shown that women who do achieve political office tend to prefer not to be identified with promoting the interests of women.[33] Representation of women's policy interests has depended more on the strength of the women's lobby at an early stage in the policy-making process. The abortion issue provides a good, albeit rare, example. Meehan believes that the stronger links of the American Equal Employment Opportunities Commission with the grass-roots women's movement (which has exhibited greater involvement in elective politics than its British counterpart), together with the greater access provided to the issue of women's equality by the American political and judicial system, have been crucial in making women's rights a more serious issue in the USA than in Britain.

This is a view that must be considered alongside gloomier accounts of a right-wing backlash. In the USA, *both* the women's movement and the New Right coalition on the family are strong, and it is by no means clear who is most threatening to whom. In concentrating on pointing out how much further women have to go to achieve equality, there is a danger of appearing over-pessimistic. After all, the rhetoric regarding women's proper duties and place is greatly at odds with the realities experienced by a majority of adult women in the 1980s. The very fact that traditional assumptions are having to be made explicit is a sign that those articulating them have already lost ground.

Nevertheless, the essays that follow make it clear that there are great difficulties involved in making an effective break in the web that structures inequality between the sexes. There is a good cause for arguing that the equal-rights legislation of the 1970s provided formal, but not substantive, rights. If women are to achieve a full and real equality, it cannot be on men's terms because they start unequal. Nor can women be treated as equal but different, because this will only reinforce sexual divisions. When the complex structure of inequality is considered, it becomes apparent that in the long run 'women's issues' cannot easily be added on to a list of policy goals. Equality between men and women involves changes in all the structures that form the unity of women's condition and therefore demands a radically different set of social-policy priorities. For example, Anna Coote has recently suggested that an alternative economic analysis might start from the question: '"How shall we care for and support our children?"', which immediately leads to a consideration of fundamental issues regarding the division of labour and resources within the family, the function and source of the wage, and the way in which work is defined.[34] Such an analysis seems utopian, especially in view of the history of unequal treatment and recent partial reversals chronicled in the essays which follow, but radical restructuring is the logical implication of thinking about women's rights and women's welfare.

Notes

1. I would like to acknowledge the helpful criticisms given by Celia Davies and Hilary Land on earlier versions of this introduction.

2. Leonore Davidoff and Catherine Hall, 'The Architecture of Public and Private Life: English Middle Class Society in a Provincial Town, 1780-1850', forthcoming in A. Sutcliffe (ed.), *The Pursuit of Urban History* (1982).

3. For an introduction to these points see: Martha Vicinus (ed.), *Suffer and Be Still* (1974); and Sarah Delamont and Lorna Duffin, *The Nineteenth Century Woman: Her Cultural and Physical World* (1978).

4. Christopher Lasch, *Haven in a Heartless World* (1977).

5. Alva Myrdal, *Nation and Family: The Swedish Experiment in Democratic Family and Population Policy* (1941).

6. Joan Scott and Louise Tilly, 'Women's Work and the Family in Nineteenth Century Europe', *Comparative Studies in Society and History*, vol. 17 (1975), and *Women, Work and Family* (1978).

7. Jan Pahl, 'Patterns of Money Management within Marriage', *Journal of Social Policy*, vol. 9 (1980). See also: Linda Oren, 'The Welfare of Women in Labouring Families: England, 1860-1950' in Lois Banner and Mary Hartman (eds.), *Clio's Consciousness Raised* (1974).

8. Department of Health and Social Security, *Social Assistance: A Review of the Supplementary Benefit Scheme in Great Britain* (1978).

9. Department of Health and Social Security, *Response of the SBC to Social Assistance: A Review of the Supplementary Benefit Scheme in Great Britain*, paper no. 9 (1979), p. 32.

10. Equal Opportunities Commission, *Income Tax and Sex Discrimination* (1978).

11. H. Land, 'The Child Benefit Fiasco' in K. Jones (ed.), *The Year Book of Social Policy in Britain, 1976* (1977).

12. For example: J. Le Grand, *The Strategy of Equality* (1982); and Edward West, *Education and the State* (1970).

13. In using the term 'production' to mean work outside the home, I am ignoring the important but difficult debate as to whether housework is productive work. For an introduction to this literature, see: Eva Kaluzynska, 'Wiping the Floor with Theory: A Survey of Writings on Housework', *Feminist Review*, no. 6 (1980).

14. A. Amsden, 'Introduction' in A. Amsden (ed.), *The Economics of Women's Work* (1980).

15. Michele Zimbalist Rosaldo and Louise Lamphere, 'Women, Culture and Society: A Theoretical Overview' in M.Z. Rosaldo and L. Lamphere (eds.), *Women, Culture and Society* (1971).

16. See Sadie Robarts with Anna Coote and Elizabeth Ball, *Positive Action for Women. The Next Step* (1981).

17. D.D. Raphael, *Justice and Liberty* (1980).

18. J. Radcliffe Richards, *The Sceptical Feminists* (1980).

19. See, for example, V. Beechey, 'Some Notes on Female Wage Labour in Capitalist Production', *Capital and Class*, no. 3 (1977).

20. Lesley Rimmer, *Families in Focus* (1981).

21. Jean Coussins and Anna Coote, *Family in the Firing Line* (1981), p. 7. See also Anna Coote and Patricia Hewitt, 'The Stance of Britain's Major Parties and Interest Groups' in P. Moss and N. Fonda (eds.), *Work and the Family* (1980).

22. See Carol Dyhouse, *Girls Growing up in Late Victorian and Edwardian England* (1981).

23. Glenys Lobban, 'The Influence of the School in Sex Role Stereotyping' in J. Chetwynd and O. Hartnell (eds.), *The Sex Role System: Psychological and Sociological Perspectives* (1978).

24. H. Land and R. Parker, 'United Kingdom' in S. Kamerman and A.J. Kahn (eds.), *Family Policy. Government and Families in Fourteen Countries* (1978).

25. Janet Finch and Dulcie Groves, 'Community Care and the Family. A Case for Equal Opportunity', *Journal of Social Policy*, vol. 9 (1980).

26. Kamerman and Kahn, *Family Policy*, p. 495. On family policy in Britain, see P. Moss and Don Sharpe, 'Family Policy in Britain' in M. Brown and S. Baldwin (eds.), *The Year Book of Social Policy in Britain, 1979* (1980).

27. Denise Riley, 'The Free Mothers: Pronatalism and Working Mothers in Industry at the End of the Last War in Britain', *History Workshop Journal*, no. 11 (1981).

28. Gilbert Steiner, *The Futility of Family Policy* (1981).

29. For example: Margaret Wyn, *Family Policy* (1970) is concerned primarily about children; and Myrdal, *Nation and Family*, about income maintenance. Many of the publications issuing from the recently established (British) Study Commission on the Family have also failed to differentiate between the interests of family members.

30. H. Land, 'The Changing Place of Women in Europe', *Daedalus*, vol. 108 (1979); and Sheila Lewenhak, 'Trade Union Membership amongst Women and Girls in the UK, 1920-65', unpublished PhD thesis, University of London, 1971.

31. Joanna Bornat, 'Home and Work: A New Context for Trade Union History', *Radical America*, vol. 12 (1978).

32. David Donnison, 'Men, Women and Social Security', the Fawcett Lecture, 1978.

33. Irene Diamond, 'Women Representatives and Public Policy: Reflections for the Future' in D. McGuigan (ed.), *Women's Lives: New Theory, Research and Policy* (1980). On Britain, see: Elizabeth Vallance, *Women in the House. A Study of Women Members of Parliament* (1979).

34. Anna Coote, 'The AES: A New Starting Point', *New Socialist* (November/December 1981).

DEALING WITH DEPENDENCY: STATE
PRACTICES AND SOCIAL REALITIES, 1870-1945

Jane Lewis

The typical life experience of adult women in the recent past has
included marriage and motherhood. Between 1871 and 1951, the
percentage of women aged 35-44 who were married never fell below
74.6 per cent (a low reached after the First World War) and in 1951
reached a high of 82.1 per cent. In 1871 the average woman married at
the age of 24 and subsequently gave birth to six children. She would
also typically have experienced three or four years widowhood. By
1901, a woman at marriage would, on average, have been a year older,
would have given birth to three or four children and would have
experienced four years of widowhood; and the woman marrying in
1931 would have been roughly the same age, the number of her
children would have dropped to two and the period of her widowhood
would have increased to five years. These are 'average' experiences.
They assume first and foremost that the woman survived infancy and
childhood and reached her mid-twenties; life expectancy at birth for
males and females was low in the late nineteenth and early twentieth
centuries, due to the high infant-mortality rate. And, in looking at the
typical experience, we mask important class and regional variations; for,
example, the wife of a manual worker might expect a greater number
of years of widowhood, due to her husband's greater occupational
mortality risk.[1]

Census data show that the typical married woman did not work
outside the home. The census figures before 1911 do not break down
the female labour force by civil status,[2] but between 1911 and the
Second World War, it appears that only 10 per cent of married women
worked. In fact, this aggregate figure conceals a substantial increase
in the percentage of married women aged 18-34 who were working
and a decline in the older age-groups (probably reflecting increased
state provision for the elderly). There are problems in relying on
census data. Catherine Hakim has pointed out that not until the 1881
census was unpaid household work excluded from the definition of
those economically active. This change in definition caused a dramatic
drop in the female activity rate. The category of domestic service, in
particular, was progressively narrowed between 1881 and 1901 and

more and more married women were thereby defined as not being involved in productive work.[3] The census also missed the extent to which married women engaged in part-time work. Women's auto-biographies, interview data and attempts to document the number of home-workers in the early twentieth century as well as today tell us that married women have always contributed to the family economy as and when necessary, whether by taking in washing, hawking goods, making matchboxes or tailoring at home, taking in lodgers, or, more recently, by working the 'twilight shift' or taking in typing.[4]

Nevertheless, it could be argued that the typical experience of adult women in the early twentieth century has included dependency, first, during marriage, due to fewer opportunities for paid employment and more time spent in childbearing and rearing, than has been the case since the Second World War and, second, in widowhood. And it is often argued that this justifies locating all adult women in the family and defining them in terms of the familial relationships which provide them with legal assurance of maintenance. For example, Professor Kahn-Freund has argued that social security and maintenance law are more 'realistic than property law because they address the needs of the family rather than the individual'. Prior to the married women's property acts of the last quarter of the nineteenth century, property could be given, willed to or settled on a married woman for her separate use through the expensive resort to equity. The idea was to protect the property of the wife's kin group from both the woman's husband and the woman herself, for she could use the income from the property but was not permitted to alienate it. Kahn-Freund argues that the principles of separate property and equal status, which were developed in the married woman's property acts between 1870 and 1935, represented the unfortunate extension of what had been merely 'a technical conveyancing device invented by equity'.[5] As a legal principle, separate property has caused most difficulty in cases involving possession of the matrimonial home and its effects. If these were registered in the husband's name, the wife was legally judged (until after the Second World War) to have no claim.[6] How much more realistic then, argued Kahn-Freund, was the law of family maintenance, which recognised the right of a married woman to be maintained by her husband, or social-security law whereby, from 1911, national insurance recognised married women's inferior earning powers and dependency on their husbands by requiring smaller contributions, paying lower benefits and changing their insurance status on marriage.

Kahn-Freund was concerned to make the law treat the social reality, but, in so doing, law may also sustain it.[7] Furthermore, there is a problem regarding the perception of that social reality. Beveridge was perhaps the most open and the most influential policy-maker to state his views on the special problems women posed for social security. In his 1942 plan, which provided the model for the law of family maintenance so admired by Kahn-Freund, he made certain assumptions about women's role and place: a married woman, regardless of whether or not she had children, was to be regarded as dependent, and Beveridge made her benefits payable through her husband's insurance. But in fact this assumption did not correspond to wartime realities. In 1943, 40 per cent of married women were in paid employment. At best, it may be argued that Beveridge took as his social reality the number of married women who were dependent during the inter-war period. It may also be argued that Beveridge projected his own values regarding morals, marriage and the family on to his report.[8] In which case, Beveridge's perception of the 'is' also became the 'ought'. Beveridge's conviction that adult women were normally dependent became embodied in legislation which then had a prescriptive effect, leaving little room for changes in gender roles. Both Kahn-Freund and Beveridge, like many policy-makers before and after them, gave serious consideration to the real problem posed by dependency. But their solutions to those problems were premised on normative ideas of gender roles and family formation.

At the time, Beveridge was criticised strongly by two feminists, Elizabeth Abbott and Katherine Bompass, who condemned the way in which he located married women in the family and defined them in relation to their husbands: 'denying the married woman, rich or poor, housewife or paid worker, an independent personal status'.[9] What we have here are different notions of equality. Beveridge talked of marriage as a partnership of equals, but obviously in the sense of 'equal but different'. Abbott and Bompass, on the other hand, came out of the feminist tradition which had fought for the married women's property laws, demanding that women be granted equality before the law and be secured 'a fair field and no favour' at work. This may well have been unrealistic in terms of the typical experience of the adult woman as wife, mother and dependant (had they addressed the issues raised by matrimonial property law concerning the matrimonial home in the 1950s and 1960s, they would have had to have defended the continued existence of separate property in order to be consistent), but Abbott and Bompass were aware that, in the case of the Beveridge Report, the recognition accorded women's reproductive role had turned into prescription.

The idea that under normal circumstances adult women would be dependants used the social reality of the dependency of a majority of women as its justification, but, as the first part of this paper shows, it gained its strength from the desire to emphasise the desirability of an economic dependence that was accompanied by distinct and separate roles for husband and wife. The family reliant on a male breadwinner was regarded as the bedrock of society and deviations from that norm were therefore perceived as potentially threatening to the social fabric. But not all women fulfilled the typical role envisaged for them. Policy-makers regarded all married women as dependants, presumably in anticipation of their becoming mothers, but some married women, especially those without children, chose to continue to go out to work, and others were forced to do so, whether because the wage earned by the male breadwinner was too small to support a wife and family, or because there was no male breadwinner to support them. In order to see more clearly the way in which normative ideas of adult women's role as dependants have structured policy, this paper focuses on the way in which policy-makers have defined and responded to the needs of married women workers. This chapter shows that attempts were made to limit the work of married women using a variety of policy instruments, and that married women who continued to work were treated as a class apart for the purposes of insurance benefits. Finally, the extent to which early feminists came to grips with problems of dependency, motherhood and work is considered.

Assumptions regarding the Maintenance of Married Women

Policy-makers in the late nineteenth and twentieth centuries assumed that all married women would be dependent on their husbands and that the husbands would fulfil their legal obligation to maintain. The desirability of such assumptions was stressed by social investigators such as Helen Bosanquet, who drew eagerly on the work of the French sociologist Frederic Le Play to argue that the 'stable family' with its male breadwinner was 'the only known way of ensuring with any approach to success, that one generation will exert itself in the interests and for the sake of another'.[10]

Policy-makers at once expected and assumed the existence of a family wage, ignoring the reality of Booth's findings that 30 per cent of the population was unable to rely on a man's wage in 1889, or Bowley's 1921 estimate that only 41 per cent of working-class families were dependent on a man's wage alone.[11] In fact it was not just wives but also children who either assisted their mothers' labours if they made boxes, paper flowers, brushes or shirts at home, or who left school as soon as possible at the age of 13 with the aid of the labour certificate (which required a high level of attendance, but which in practice seems rarely to have been refused).[12] As late as the 1930s, as Anne Crowther has pointed out, the working-class family economy was still often complicated by erratic contributions from wives and children, which made implementation of the means test for public assistance difficult.[13]

Normally, it was believed, women would be protected from the world beyond the home: married women could not be held personally liable in law, and their ability to enter into contracts was tied to the extent of their separate property until 1935. A woman without resources of her own and living with her husband, or living apart from him where the fault was not her own, was entitled (until the 1970 Matrimonial Proceedings and Property Act) to pledge her husband's credit for 'necessaries', the nature of which was defined by the husband. Thus, in an 1884 case, it was held that an artisan, whose wife had bought blankets at the door worth 22s 6d when he had given her permission to spend but 17s 6d, could not be held liable for the extra sum.[14]

In fact the legal obligation to maintain has never been a good guarantee of a married woman's security, especially if the husband was a low or irregular wage-earner. During the late nineteenth and early twentieth centuries the courts increasingly tried to make the working-class husband live up to his legal obligations in order to prevent the wife coming into the poor law,[15] and middle-class legislators became increasingly aware of and ready to blame the failure of some working-class men to maintain their wives.

In order to make provision for those working-class wives who were placed in what was assumed to be the abnormal position of not receiving adequate maintenance from their husbands, the Married Women's Property Act of 1870 was passed. Witnesses before the Select Committee of 1867 argued strongly in favour of an Act that would extend the principle of equity to working-class women and allow them to keep control of their own earnings, which by virtue of common law legally became the property of their husbands.[16] Social investigators at the turn of the century were agreed that the wife was the 'pivot' of the working-class family and manager of the household economy, although it was hoped that the father rather than the mother would be the provider.[17] But the 1870 Act was obviously designed to encourage women, whose husbands had failed in their duty to maintain, to go out to work themselves. Legislators were in fact endlessly ambivalent about the rightful place of the working-class wife. Better for her to work and the family remain self-supporting than for it to draw on state resources via the poor law, but there remained the alternative danger of providing incentive to male idleness.

A 1906 investigation of 6,000 women workers in Birmingham found that out of the married women in families where earnings totalled less than 25s a week, 62 per cent of the unoccupied women's husbands were sober and industrious, as against only 39 per cent of those whose wives worked. The authors warned that such figures were capable of two interpretations: either 'the women are compelled to work because the husbands are unsteady, drunken or idle, or the husbands develop bad habits because their wives remove the burden of responsibility from them'.[18] It was the removal of that responsibility and the threat to incentives it represented that attracted particular attention whenever married women's work came under scrutiny. Women factory inspectors, for example, had no hesitation in labelling situations where the wife was the chief breadwinner as 'damaging to morale' and 'evil'.[19] The problem of maintaining the male incentive to work caused MPs much heart-searching during debate on the introduction of legislation to provide school meals for children in 1906.[20] Advocates of family allowances also had to meet arguments about incentives before the 1937 report of the Unemployment Assistance Board revealed that 6 per cent of male earners were better off drawing unemployment benefits than working. Most of these were men with low pay and large families. After 1937, it was the turn of proponents of allowances to argue their case in terms of maintaining the incentive to work.

The existence of the married working woman, with her dual reproductive and productive role, strained the assumptions of policy-makers regarding the family wage and the dependency of married women as the dominant family form. Moreover, it was very difficult to define those situations in which the work of married women was necessary, and those in which it posed a threat to family life. Policies directed specifically towards the married woman worker tended to revolve around the perceived need to limit the extent of married women's work. This was done in part by defining work considered suitable for women using a variety of policy instruments. Protective legislation and, after 1911, national insurance both effectively controlled working-class women's job opportunities and the marriage bar was widely used during the inter-war period to exclude middle-class women from employment.[21] During the early twentieth century, the strengthening ideology of domesticity and motherhood also played a part in limiting the extent of married women's work. Policies which acknowledged the existence of the married woman worker as part of the labour force, such as national insurance, dealt with them as a class rather than by occupational group and used the problems raised by their reproductive role to justify punitive action against them as workers.

Limiting the Extent of Married Women's Work

From 1833 onwards, protective legislation was passed to restrict the nature and hours of women's work. The legislation was most severe in the case of jobs requiring heavy physical labour, because these provided the greatest contrast to the prevailing sex-role standards among the middle and upper classes. The statements of commissioners, investigating the work of women in the mines or of women chainmakers operating the sledge hammer used to cut cold iron, show that their main preoccupation was with the indecency and immorality of a woman performing a man's task in male company.[22]

Male workers showed a similar concern with the impropriety of such labour for women, but also revealed more pragmatic, economic fears: married women represented a threat to male wages. Thus a male chainworker commented to a Commission in 1876: 'I should advocate their [women's] time should be so limited as neither to interfere with their own health and morals nor with our wages.'[23] During the late nineteenth century, trade unions could not decide whether to exclude women entirely or include them and fight for equal pay to stop them undercutting the male wage.

During the early twentieth century the case for protective legislation was argued more in terms of the need for married women to devote themselves wholeheartedly to home and family, than of morality. Medical officers of health, sanitary and factory inspectors drew attention to what they perceived as a connection between the domestic ignorance of the working mother and the high infant-mortality rate.[24] At the 1906 National Conference on Infant Mortality, John Burns MP, the President of the Local Government Board, called for stringent restrictions on all married women's work.[25] Although the ideology of domesticity and motherhood thus received powerful reinforcement, efforts to place a more general legislative ban on married women's work were not successful, and during the First World War, married women entered employment in unprecedented numbers. However, government officials feared the possible repercussions of war work on women's reproductive systems and in 1919, the Women's Employment Committee of the Ministry of Reconstruction, set up to advise on the opportunity for women's employment at the end of the war, expressed the hope that 'every inducement, direct or indirect, will be given to keep mothers at home'.[26] Similar attitudes were expressed during the Second World War, when the continued decline in the birth-rate gave additional force to the argument that married women should stay at home. Even when the demand for manpower was at its height, women with children under 14 years old were never conscripted.

The most stringent limitations on women's work opportunities were imposed on the professions, where a marriage bar was introduced during the 1920s. In London, where 25 per cent of teachers were married women, the bar was imposed on the profession in 1923.[27] During the course of a court case, brought on behalf of 57 married women teachers by Elizabeth Price against the Rhondda Urban District Council, a councillor testified that it was the 'periodical temporary absences' of married women that proved educationally harmful and that justified their dismissal.[28]

Similarly, in the Civil Service, both the 1915 MacDonnell Commission and the Treasury Committee Report of 1919 agreed that family responsibilities were incompatible with devotion to public service.[29] Although economic reasons for the marriage bar were strong (local education authorities, for example, faced the problem of large numbers of unemployed newly-trained teachers), there is strong evidence to suggest that it was the ideology of domesticity which legitimised the policy. In the debate on a motion to abolish the bar in 1927 MPs expressed feelings of revulsion at the 'travesty' of nature presented by the image of a working mother and, in the last instance, possibly a father at home looking after the baby.[30]

The attempt to impose severe limits on middle-class married women's work was thus far more successful than was the case with working-class women and was achieved in the absence of fears regarding the threat to male work incentives or to middle-class women's virtue (although there was, of course, extended debate over the propriety of men and women working together in offices). It was, after all, middle-class men, for whom the conventional sexual division of labour involved the separation of spheres, who naturally located married women in the family. Thus it is perhaps logical that their hand was firmest in the case of women of their own class. The work of working-class women was only prohibited when its nature gave offence. As the feminist writer, Olive Schreiner, commented, in his private life no man, no matter how great his concern about the future of race, said to his domestic servant: 'Divine child bearer! Potential mother of the race! Why should you clean my boots or bring up my tea while I lie warm in bed?'[31] Certain forms of employment, such as domestic work, were considered quite appropriate for single working-class women or for married women forced to work by economic necessity.

During the inter-war years, national insurance provided a means of channelling women into 'suitable' work. In 1919 the Ministry of Labour became convinced that out-of-work donation was being widely abused and that the chief offenders were married women who had been munitions workers and were therefore entitled to the dole, even though they had no intention of going on working. Feeling against women drawing donation was fuelled by the need to find work for returned soldiers and the idea that the middle-class demand for domestic servants meant that alternative work existed for any woman who desired employment. Correspondents writing to *The Times* showed how vividly these ideas gripped the public imagination and the leader writers echoed their sentiments: 'If they refuse employment that lies open to them because it is not exactly to their taste, they ought not to be paid out of the public purse and so enabled to live a life of idleness.'[32] In fact, when the 1923 Committee appointed to inquire into the supply of domestic servants and, in particular, to investigate the effect of insurance on domestic service looked at specific cases of abuse reported to them, it found the vast majority of the claims to have been genuine.[33] During the 1920s and 1930s all women who applied for benefit under the Unemployment Insurance Acts could be required to train as a domestic servant; and grants for women's training schemes administered by the Central Committee on Women's Employment during these years came to focus exclusively on training for domestic work.

As a form of social-security provision, national insurance protected the worker from loss of earnings in a way that posed least threat to work incentives. Beveridge believed that a national-insurance scheme allowed the state to provide security for its casualties without demoralising them.[34] All workers were included in national-insurance provisions, but in the case of married women this was achieved only with difficulty.

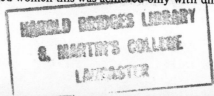

Married women were always considered as a separate class for insurance purposes and the terms of their inclusion were hotly debated. This must be explained, first, in terms of the conceptual difficulty policy-makers experienced in treating married women as workers and, second, in terms of the fact that the insurance system was formulated to cater for male employees in regular work. Thus if married women persisted in working, they would have to be fitted into this system with some 'appropriate' financial adjustment to take account of their fewer economic responsibilities. But no further recognition was accorded married women's two roles of worker and wife/mother. Women faced particular difficulties when their reproductive experience impinged on their working lives. However, if they chose to combine motherhood and work, they could expect to be penalised rather than assisted by the insurance system.

The Treatment of Married Women Workers

Not only was national insurance used to direct women into certain types of employment, but the regulations were also manipulated to the point of excluding married women altogether, the assumption being that they should seek support from their husbands. As the report of the Royal Commission on Unemployment Insurance stated in 1931:

> It is clear that it is the exception rather than the rule for women after marriage to earn their living by insured employment. It *follows* that in the case of married women as a *class*, industrial employment cannot be regarded as the *normal* condition. (My italics).[35]

Both the 'genuinely seeking work' clause, imposed as a test on persons drawing uncovenanted unemployment benefit in 1921, and the individual-means test, imposed on certain groups of claimants in 1922, were designed primarily to stop married women abusing the insurance system. Alan Deacon has argued that it was because the 'genuinely seeking work' clause was thus perceived as 'a legitimate defence of public funds' against the married-woman scrounger, that the Labour Party saw no problem in extending it in 1924.[36] Throughout the period 1925-8, two and a half times as many women as men were dis-allowed benefit under the 'genuinely seeking work' and means-test clauses. Few studies of what happened to those disallowed benefit were undertaken. One carried out in 1931 for the Royal Commission on

Unemployment Insurance reported that 31.8 per cent of men, 43.8 per cent of single women and 18 per cent of married women subsequently found work, which confirmed the commissioners' view that married women had a 'different attitude towards wage earning'.[37] This was true in so far as married women often assessed their need to earn in terms of the dictates of the family economy. But this did not justify the conclusion that their contributions were unnecessary.

With the abandonment of the individual means test in 1928 and the 'genuinely seeking work' clause in 1930, the number of married women drawing benefit increased, such that stories about married women abusing the system began to prey on the mind of the Prime Minister, Ramsay MacDonald. According to Robert Skidelsky: 'he began to picture married women driving up in fur coats to draw benefit and the retailing of such tales became a staple part of his conversation'.[38] Thus the Royal Commission was appointed to inquire into the workings of unemployment insurance. The commissioners identified certain 'anomalies' in the insurance system, particularly striking in the case of married women, but present also in the claims made by seasonal and short-time workers. It was possible for these groups to possess sufficient contributions to qualify for unemployment insurance benefit and yet not be genuinely unemployed. The Commission declared itself satisfied that many married women were receiving benefit when they had never worked in an insured trade after marriage and thus recommended that married women should have to satisfy a Court of Referees that they had not withdrawn from employment as a result of marriage and that they could reasonably expect to get insured employment in respect of their experience in their district (the assumption being that married women were constrained in their search for employment by their inability to relocate).

The commissioners' desire to judge women's intention to work by their ability to get it posed difficulties. Married women were, after all, often the first to be fired in time of economic downturn, and increasingly firms and public-service employers were refusing to hire married women at all. The Anomalies Act of 1931 assumed that any married woman who had left the labour force for whatever reason had effectively retired. If a woman showed that she had been seeking work and thus satisfied the first clause of the Act, she could automatically be disqualified under the second clause, which required that she have 'reasonable expectation' of finding work. As a result of the Act, 48 per cent of women's claims were disallowed between 13 October 1931 and 3 December 1931 as against 4 per cent of those of men.[39] Textile workers (a traditional area of employment for married women) were particularly hard hit. Between 1931 and 1933 almost one-third of applications for benefit from married women came from north-west England, where the introduction of the 'more looms' system (increasing the number of looms each weaver was responsible for from four to six) forced many married women out of work.[40]

Married women who did remain in insurable occupations were eligible for national health insurance (under the 1911 Act) and this also proved problematical. For reasons of cost and in keeping with attitudes regarding family responsibility, married women who did not work and children were excluded from the Act.[41] Very soon questions were also being asked as to whether the inclusion of married working women could be justified. Apart from anything else, by 1932, married women were found to be experiencing 140 per cent more sickness than had been calculated for, unmarried women's sickness rates were 25 per cent higher than expected, whereas those for men were actually lower than anticipated.[42] These statistics immediately raised the issue of malingering on the part of married women. In the 1916 report of the Departmental Committee it was suggested that because women's rate of benefit at 7s 6d was so much closer to the average earnings for women (10s) than was the men's rate, women were more tempted to claim. It was also alleged that women were more ignorant of the principles and practices governing insurance and so expected to get out as much or more than they paid in. Worse still, it was pointed out that it was very difficult to supervise the behaviour of women drawing benefits. When men felt better, boredom would drive them back to work, but a married woman could always usefully employ herself catching up on household tasks.[43]

The difficulties arising from the attempt to contain women in an insurance system that made no allowance for their dual productive and reproductive roles was best exemplified by the problems encountered by pregnant women. Under the 1911 statute, sickness benefit was payable to an insured person while he/she was 'rendered incapable of work by some specific disease or by bodily or mental disablement'. However, as pregnancy was a natural physiological process, it was widely felt by the approved societies, who administered benefits under the Act, that 'if a woman is disabled by pregnancy alone, if such an expression is permissible, she cannot thereby be entitled to sickness benefit'.[44] Only if the incapacity was due to a complication of pregnancy did benefit fall due. Needless to say, the actual practice of the approved societies when faced with this problem varied considerably.

Moreover, because the rate of sickness benefit was lower than that of unemployment benefit, women preferred to try and draw unemployment benefit for as long as possible, whereupon the question of their capacity for genuinely seeking work was immediately raised.[45] Suggestions that the costs incurred on behalf of pregnant women by the approved societies should be shouldered by the Treasury were vetoed by the Government Actuary on grounds of cost and also because he felt that any move which might give married women an incentive to work should be avoided.[46]

The problem was that married working women genuinely suffered more sickness than men, not least because they combined paid work with motherhood and household tasks.[47] They were low paid and therefore their contributions could not be raised to meet the burden they imposed on the insurance system. Women trade unionists, in particular, asked that this system be restructured to meet married women's needs.[48] Instead, it was decided in 1932 that the risks posed by married women were too great to be carried by the scheme and married women's benefits were cut accordingly.[49] As Eleanor Rathbone and Mrs Pritchard pointed out in the House of Commons, no other high-risk group with excessive claims (for example, miners) were singled out for similar treatment.[50] When married women's reproductive experience impinged on their working lives, it was taken as vindication of the view that work and motherhood were incompatible and, because wife and motherhood were assumed to take priority, then, logically, it was the woman as *worker* who was penalised. When combined with an immediate need for economy measures, the call to reduce married women's benefits became irresistible, despite the publicity accorded the high maternal-mortality rate during the inter-war years and the promise of the government to improve maternity services.

The discriminatory treatment of married women was not questioned until the Second World War, when the issue was brought into sharp focus over the question not of unemployment or health insurance but of compensation for civilian injuries. When the civilian compensation scheme was extended in 1940 to the non-gainfully employed (in the main, housewives), the scales for women were set lower than those for men. The Treasury defended this:

The principle of sex differentiation, whether it is right or wrong, is at present a matter of government policy and it runs right through a large part of the social structure. It appears in all the social services, with the exception of old age pensions.[51]

One Member of Parliament maintained that to give an equal return to the man and to the woman would 'do away with the principle that men are responsible for the family. Once that principle has gone, many men might repudiate that responsibility . . .'[52] This principle had sustained the treatment meted out to married women under unemployment insurance. However, in evidence to a Select Committee on Equal Compensation, witnesses as various as Beveridge, the TUC and the National Council of Women agreed that in the case of compensation for injury, there was no differentiation of risk to justify the difference in scale between men and women[53] (as was the case in health insurance). Equal compensation was granted in 1943.

The witnesses appearing before the Select Committee on Equal Compensation were particularly concerned that the burden shouldered by the housewife during the war should be given due recognition. This conviction, together with his anxiety about the falling birth-rate, made Beveridge especially sensitive to the status of the housewife in his Report on Social Insurance and Allied Social Services, published in 1942. He wrote: 'In the next thirty years housewives as mothers have vital work to do in ensuring the adequate continuance of the British race and British ideals in the world.'[54] He refused to call housewives 'dependants', referred to marriage as an equal partnership, and wrote grandly of women assuming a new and important insurance status on marriage. In fact, as Abbott and Bompass pointed out, it was only the rhetoric that changed. In the case of the housewife, she was rendered totally dependent on her husband's contributions and the benefits he received on her behalf.[55]

In the case of married working women, Beveridge continued to believe that the 'claims by women who, on marriage, had practically retired from industry' were a real problem, but because he also believed that the numbers of married women stating a desire to work or actually working after marriage would be small, he felt that a scheme whereby all women assumed a new insurance status on marriage would meet the problem. He maintained that the case for lower benefits for the married woman was strong 'both on practical grounds and in equity',[56] because the husband would provide for her needs and her expenses were therefore less. As Abbott and Bompass commented, this was to confuse insurance with assistance principles.[57]

Feminist Views

Feminist opinion was not united on any of the issues under discussion
in this chapter. Nineteenth-century feminists such as Josephine Butler,
campaigner against the Contagious Diseases Acts, Mrs M.G. Fawcett,
the suffragist leader, and Mrs Emma Patterson, founder of the Women's
Trade Union League, mounted a strong campaign against protective
legislation, which they regarded as part of male trade unionists' strategy
to restrict the number of jobs open to women, and which in turn led
to the crowding of women into unskilled, low-paid jobs.[58] Their
analysis may be questioned and the spectre they held out to working-
class men of legislative interference in the home following hard on the
heels of intervention to restrict women's hours at work, could only be
termed scare-mongering. But their protest that 'this doctrine of
Reproduction is not the essential aim of existence for either half of the
human race'[59] struck, albeit obliquely, at the crux of the issue. Were
women to be protected because of their reproductive capacity at the
expense of their right to work? This line of egalitarian feminist thought
persisted, challenging the strengthening ideology of motherhood which
accompanied the concern over infant mortality. For example, Cicely
Hamilton, actress and suffragist, joined the Open Door Council when it
was founded in 1926 by Elizabeth Abbott and Chrystal Macmillan
because 'its aim was to correct the tendency of our legislators to be
overkind to women who earn their livelihood; to treat them from youth
to age as if they were permanently pregnant, and forbid them all manner
of trades and callings in case they might injure their health.'[60] The
Council claimed the freedom of women to work on the same terms as
men and reacted to the government's desire to limit women's work
opportunities by denying that the woman worker had any needs that
were different from those of men.

On the whole, working-class women trade unionists did not take
this position, being conscious of the double burden imposed by
work outside and in the home. They preferred to campaign for
legislation that would ease the load imposed by women's reproductive
and productive roles: for example, the six weeks' paid maternity leave
advocated by the International Labour League's Washington Convention
of 1919. This was unacceptable both to egalitarian feminists, who saw
maternity provision as a species of protective legislation, and to the
government. The Government Actuary rejected the request for six
weeks' paid maternity leave because he questioned the wisdom of
usurping the father's responsibility and, more decisively, maintained

that it would mean increasing male and female national health insurance contributions by 4d per week.[61]

To ignore the economic needs resulting from childbearing put the egalitarian feminists into the kind of box identified by Kahn-Freund, when he criticised matrimonial property law. On the other hand, how were feminists to avoid the trap of defining the needs of women who happened to be mothers solely in terms of their reproductive function? Prior to the First World War, the Fabian Women's Group perceived the essential issue to be the economically dependent status of the married woman and believed that the solution to the problem lay in economic individualism.[62] They conducted inquiries into the extent to which women with children suffered disabilities as workers and how many women were sole supporters of families. As a result, they asked that economic recognition be given the mother for her services in the form of family endowment (no mention was made of the married woman who had no children). Paying the mother for her services directly questioned the principle of the husband's obligation to maintain. The family allowance campaign that was started by Eleanor Rathbone in 1917 began similarly by emphasising the need to remunerate mothers for mothering, as well as providing maintenance for the children.[63] Family endowment and allowances were intended to cut the Gordian knot of dependency in much the same way as the advocates of wages for housework argue that these would today. However, neither campaign was accompanied by any call for changes in gender roles, thus the way was left open for other groups and individuals to argue for similar policies with very different ends in view, or to couch very different policies in similar rhetoric.[64] Thus Beveridge, for example, promoted family allowances as a means of eliminating child poverty and raising the birth-rate, and he talked of raising the status of the mother when introducing his insurance scheme for married women.

Conclusions

We have been looking only at some of the blunter policy instruments which either directly or indirectly erected institutional boundaries in respect of a particular group of women. It should be remembered that policies crucial to women's welfare which were *not* pursued, such as day nurseries or birth control, also repay careful study. Policies towards adult women in the recent past must be understood in the context of policy-makers' assumptions regarding the family, which were grounded in the idea of a family wage, the separation of spheres (the public/male from the private/female), and the sexual division of labour within the home and at the workplace. Normative concepts of the role of adult women as dependent by virtue of marriage and their capacity for motherhood were reinforced by economic and moral imperatives, and dictated the framework within which policy-makers worked. To a large extent these were unarticulated assumptions, forming as they did part of the fabric of the political culture to which women had only been formally admitted in 1918.

Some recognition was accorded the fact that assumptions might not hold true in all cases, particularly amongst the working class, but the problem of married women workers could not but strain the framework of social policy. This group defied normative classification in terms of (a) its pattern of family maintenance and (b) its practice of combining motherhood and work. All married women were treated as a separate class for policy-making purposes, regardless of whether or not they were mothers. It was assumed that married women would confine themselves to the home. Such a belief was clearly reflected in something like the marriage bar, but fitting the widow and the working mother into a system of insurance also proved difficult. The interruption caused by the pattern of women's reproductive lives made it hard to impose insurance discipline and raised problems regarding the financing of women's benefits. According to Beveridge, social insurance was designed to maintain 'individual freedom and responsibility and the family as the unit of the state'.[65] In view of his assumptions regarding the family wage, it is likely that he had the responsibility of the individual male breadwinner in mind. Obviously, the position of the married woman worker cut across these assumptions.

The nineteenth-century feminist campaign for equality before the law, including equal citizenship rights, was conducted on terms already defined by men. This meant that it was not possible to consider the needs of women arising out of their role as mothers. Egalitarian feminists demanded that women choose between marriage and motherhood and a career, and their campaign for equal treatment concerned only the woman who chose the latter course, and thus retained her individual identity before the law. Such 'negative' egalitarianism was not sufficient to ensure equal opportunity for married women workers, as the married women teachers' failure to overcome the marriage bar showed. Meeting women's needs within the family was implicitly defined as the responsibility of the husband, and Beveridge made it explicit in his insurance plans for married women. Proposals for family endowment were intended to get around the problem of dependency by extending economic individualism to the family. This did not affect assumptions regarding women's responsibility for home and children; women were still seen as either mothers or workers. Thus even those who produced practical proposals to end the economic dependency of married women still implicitly expected them to choose between a career and marriage and a family.

The notion of dependency was premised on a set of beliefs regarding sexual divisions and structured policies, which in turn reinforced them. It was assumed that married women would be dependent on their husbands because they would devote themselves to wife and mother-hood. Recognition of married women's two roles as mothers and workers was first given by the Royal Commission on Population in 1949, when fear of a shortfall in the labour force led the Commission to recommend both easier access to birth-control information and an increase in the availability of part-time work for women. Since 1949, the reality of married women doing two jobs has tended to receive more sympathetic recognition, and there have been moves to reform policies which penalise the married woman as worker. But very little has been done positively to ease the continuing tensions and strains they experience, or to encourage the sharing of household responsibilities, both of which are necessary if women are to be given a wider set of choices. Social policy still carries with it precise notions of social role, based on normative ideas as to the legal, economic and moral aspects of family responsibility.

Notes

1. These statistics are drawn from the *Census of England and Wales 1951*, 'Fertility Report', tables 4.1 and 4.2, p. lxv; and 'General Tables', table 22C; con-ventional abridged life tables; and the *Annual Reports* of the Registrar General.

2. The 1901 census does give a breakdown by civil status, but combines the categories of married and widowed women in the labour force. Margaret Hewitt, *Wives and Mothers in Victorian Industry* (1959), pp. 9-20; and Louise Tilly and Joan Scott, 'Women's Work and the Family in Nineteenth Century Europe', *Comparative Studies in Society and History*, vol. 17 (January 1975), pp. 36-64, show that a greater percentage of married women worked during the period 1850-90.

3. C. Hakim, 'Census Reports as Documentary Evidence. The Census Com-mentaries 1801-1851', *Sociological Review*, vol. 28 (August 1980), pp. 556-8.

4. On this general point, see Sally Alexander, 'Women's Work in 19th Century London — A Study of the Years 1820-1850' in Ann Oakley and Juliet Mitchell (eds.), *Women's Rights and Wrongs* (1976), pp. 59-111; and Louise Tilly

and Joan Scott, *Women, Work and Family* (1978).

5. Otto Kahn-Freund, 'England' in W. Friedmann (ed.), *Matrimonial Property Law* (1955), p. 277.

6. Otto Kahn-Freund, 'Matrimonial Property Law – Some Recent Developments', *Modern Law Review*, vol. 22 (May 1959), pp. 241-72.

7. Judith Walkowitz, *Prostitution and Victorian Society* (1980), p. 5, makes a similar point.

8. A revealing book regarding Beveridge's attitudes towards sex and gender is his *John and Irene, An Anthology of Thoughts on Women*, (1912).

9. Elizabeth Abbott and Katherine Bompass, *The Woman Citizen and Social Security* (1943), p. 3.

10. Helen Bosanquet, *The Family* (1906), pp. 199 and 222. The work of Frederick Le Play was popularised in England by Patrick Geddes, biologist, sociologist and town planner, and Victor Branford, editor of the *British Journal of Sociology*.

11. Hilary Land, 'The Family Wage', *Feminist Review*, no. 6 (1980), p. 60.

12. Adelaide Anderson, *Women in the Factory* (1922), p. 173; and Joanna Bornatt, 'The Home and Work: A New Context for Trade Union History', *Radical America*, vol. 12 (September-October 1978), pp. 53-69.

13. Anne Crowther, 'Family Responsibility and State Responsibility in Britain before the Welfare State', *Historical Journal*, vol. 25 (March 1982), p. 135.

14. *Walter* v. *Aldridge*, 1884, 1 TLR 138.

15. C.A. Morrison, 'Contract' in R.H. Graveson and F.R. Crone, *A Century of Family Law* (1957), p. 125.

16. 'Special Report from the Select Committee on the Married Women's Property Bill', *Parliamentary Papers* (1867-8) (441), *VII*, 330, Q. 1154.

17. For example, Bosanquet, *Family*, p. 277; and Charles Booth, *Life and Labour*, vol. I (1889), p. 476.

18. Edward Cadbury, M. Cecile Matheson and George Shann, *Women's Work and Wages* (1906), p. 216.

19. 'Report of the Select Committee on Homework', *Parliamentary Papers* (1907) (290), *VI*, 55, Qs. 803 and 1024.

20. B.B. Gilbert, *The Evolution of National Health Insurance in Great Britain* (1966), deals with this measure in detail.

21. There are many other important policy areas, such as job training and education, which it has not been possible to consider in this paper.

22. Jane Humphries, 'Protective Legislation, the Capitalist State, and Working Class Men: The Case of the 1842 Mines Regulation Act', *Feminist Review*, no. 7 (Spring 1981), p. 28.

23. 'Report of the Commissioners appointed to inquire into the working of the Factory and Workshop Acts with a view to their Consolidation and Amendment', *Parliamentary Papers* (1876), C 1442, *XXIX*, 1, p. lxvi.

24. G. Reid, 'Infant Mortality and the Employment of Married Women in Factories', London School of Economics, Papers of the British Association for the Advancement of Science, Committee on the Effect of Legislation regarding Women's Labour', Coll. Misc. 486, Box 1/9; and 'Report of the Inter-Departmental Committee on Physical Deterioration, Vol. I', *Parliamentary Papers* (1904), Cd 2175, *XXXII*, 1, p. 57.

25. *Report on the Proceedings of the National Conference on Infant Mortality* (1906).

26. 'Report of the Women's Employment Committee on the Ministry of Reconstruction', *Parliamentary Papers* (1918), Cd 9239, *XIV*, 783, p. 51. On welfare supervision generally, see Noelle Whiteside, 'Industrial Welfare and Labour Regulation in Britain at the Time of the First World War', *International Review of*

Social History, Pt 3 (1980), pp. 307-31; and on its effects on women in particular, see Gail Braybon, *Women Workers in the First World War* (1981), pp. 132-40; and Marion Kosak, 'Women Munitions Workers in the First World War', unpub. Ph D. thesis, University of Hull (1976), pp. 255-94.

27. 'Report of the Royal Commission on Equal Pay', *Parliamentary Papers* (1945-6), Cmd 6937, *XI*, 651, pp. 153-6; 'Report of the Civil Service National Whitley Council Committee on the Marriage Bar in the Civil Service', *Parliamentary Papers* (1945-6), Cmd 6886, *X*, 871; and Alison Oram, 'The Introduction of the Marriage Bar in Teaching in the 1920s', unpublished paper, 1980.

28. *Price* v. *Rhondda UDC*, 1923, 2 Ch. 372. The bar against married women teachers was not lifted until the passing of the 1944 Education Act.

29. 'Final Report of the Treasury Committee on Civil Service Recruitment After War', *Parliamentary Papers* (1919), Cmd 164, *XI*, 191, p. 7; and Cmd 6886, p. 3.

30. House of Commons, *Debates*, vol. 205 (1927), col. 1175.

31. Olive Schreiner, *Woman and Labour* (1978) (1st edn, 1911), p. 20.

32. *The Times*, 3 March 1921, p. 12.

33. Ministry of Labour, *Report of the Committee Appointed to Enquire into the Present Conditions as to the Supply of Female Domestic Servants* (HMSO, 1923), pp. 6 and 27.

34. See W.H. Beveridge, *Insurance for All and Everything* (1924).

35. 'First Report of the Royal Commission on Unemployment Insurance', *Parliamentary Papers* (1930-1), Cmd 3872, *XVII*, 885, p. 43.

36. Alan Deacon, *In Search of the Scrounger*, Occasional Papers in Social Administration no. 60 (1976), p. 26. The 'genuinely seeking work' clause required applicants to prove they were 'genuinely seeking whole time employment but [were] unable to obtain such employment'.

37. Deacon, *In Search of the Scrounger*, p. 65.

38. R. Skidelsky, *Politicians and the Slump* (1970), p. 266.

39. 'Final Report of the Royal Commission on Unemployment Insurance', *Parliamentary Papers* (1931-2), Cmd 4185, *XIII*, 393, p. 472; and Deacon, *In Search of the Scrounger*, p. 109.

40. Sheila Lewenhak, 'Trade Union Membership Amongst Women and Girls in the UK 1920-65', unpublished PhD thesis, University of London, 1971, pp. 24 and 222.

41. 'Report of the Royal Commission on National Health Insurance', *Parliamentary Papers* (1926), Cmd 2596, *XIV*, 311, p. 142.

42. 'Report by the Government Actuary on an Examination of the Sickness and Disability Experience of a Group of Approved Societies in the Period 1921-1927', *Parliamentary Papers* (1929-30), Cmd 3548, *XXV*, 825, p. 10, table C.

43. 'Report of the Departmental Committee on Sickness Benefit Claims under National Insurance Act', *Parliamentary Papers* (1914-16), Cd 7687, *XXX*, 1, pp. 47-8.

44. Ibid., p. 49.

45. 'Final Report on Unemployment Insurance', Cmd 4185, pp. 460-1.

46. Public Record Office, ACT 1/65, Memo by Alfred Watson on the Proposed Special Maternity Benefits, 2 December 1918.

47. See, for example, M. Llewellyn Davies (ed.), *Maternity: Letters from Working Women* (1915); M. Spring Rice (ed.), *Working Class Wives, Their Health and Conditions* (1939); and Jane Lewis, *Politics of Motherhood* (1980), pp. 41-51.

48. 'Report on Sickness Benefit Claims', Cd 7687, evidence of Mary MacArthur, p. 78; and Women's Industrial Council, 'Memo on the National Health Insurance Bill as it Affects Women', typescript, 1911.

49. Public Record Office, ACT 1/448, Alfred Watson's Memo on Women's Insurance, 19 January 1932.

50. House of Commons, *Debates*, vol. 267 (1931-2), col. 255.

51. 'Report from the Select Committee on Equal Compensation', *Parliamentary Papers* (1942-3), (53), *III*, 41, pp. 307.

52. House of Commons, *Debates*, vol. 371 (1941), col. 653-4.

53. 'Report on Equal Compensation', *Parliamentary Papers*, (53), Qs. 1019, 1679, 1881.

54. 'Report by Sir William Beveridge on Social Insurance and Allied Services', *Parliamentary Papers* (1942-3), Cmd 6404, *VI*, 1, p. 53.

55. Abbott and Bompass, *The Woman Citizen*, p. 7.

56. 'Report on Social Insurance', Cmd 6404, p. 51.

57. Abbott and Bompass, *The Woman Citizen*, p. 11.

58. M.G. Fawcett, 'Equal Pay for Equal Work', *Economic Journal*, vol. XXVIII (March 1918), pp. 1-6.

59. J. Butler, (ed.), *Legal Restrictions on the Industrial Work of women from the Women's Point of View* (1872), p. 18.

60. Cicely Hamilton, *Life Errant* (1935), pp. 288-9.

61. 'Memo by the Government Actuary on the Washington Draft Convention Concerning the Employment of Women before and after Childbirth', *Parliamentary Papers* (1921), Cmd 1293, XXXI, 583.

62. See Sally Alexander's Introduction to Maud Pember Reeves, *Round About a Pound a Week* (1979) (1st edn, 1915).

63. The focus of the family allowances campaign soon switched to the politically acceptable focus of child poverty; see John McNicol, *The Movement for Family Allowances 1918-1945* (1980).

64. See Anna Davin, 'Imperialism and Motherhood', *History Workshop Journal*, no. 5 (Spring 1978), pp. 9-65; and Denise Riley, 'The Free Mothers: Pronatalism and Working Mothers in Industry at the End of the Last World War in Britain', *History Workshop Journal*, no. 11, (Spring 1981), pp. 59-118.

65. Beveridge, *Insurance for All and Everything*, p. 31.

3 MEMBERS AND SURVIVORS: WOMEN AND RETIREMENT-PENSIONS LEGISLATION

Dulcie Groves

In 1978, major changes in the legislation governing both statutory and occupational retirement provision came into force.[1] These changes incorporated measures designed not only to improve the status of women as beneficiaries in their own right of state and occupational retirement-pension schemes, but also their entitlement, if married, to widows' benefits. Thus, at one and the same time, such measures advanced the position of women as generators of their own financial independence in retirement, while yet confirming them in their traditional role as the financial dependants of their husbands. Herein lies the continuing paradox of retirement-pension provision as it relates to women.

Both major political parties, in the course of the 'pensions debate' which culminated in the Social Security Pensions Act 1975, promised a new deal to women in the light of incontrovertible evidence that poverty in old age was, to a very considerable extent, a matter of female poverty.[2] However, although such poverty undoubtedly did stem from inadequacies in pension provision, such inadequacies were but a reflection of wide and persisting inequalities of income among men and women during their working lives. Women, in particular, tend to occupy lower-paid jobs and to suffer from interruptions to their earnings; they also continue to be designated as the major providers of unpaid domestic labour in the home.[3]

As Hilary Land has argued, the British income maintenance system is predicated on this unequal sexual division of labour, which also designates men as 'main breadwinners'.[4] It is, in consequence, an easier political exercise to bring about improvements in widows' pensions, or even to institute 'home responsibilities' credits towards eventual pension entitlement, than to radically improve the position of women (especially if married) as members of pension schemes in their own right. For this latter goal cannot be achieved without a fundamental improvement in the position of women in the labour-market, which in turn raises fundamental questions about the traditional division of labour in the home. It is their position as low-paid and part-time workers, with periods of employment interrupted by domestic

duties, which still severely limits the access of many women to the
benefits arising from contributory membership of state and, in
particular, occupational pension schemes.

The above considerations can usefully be held in mind when
examining issues of female access to retirement-pension provision, and
they are faithfully reflected in parliamentary debates over three decades
since the Second World War. The pivotal theme which recurs with
regard to women and retirement pensions is that of marital status,
since married women have, traditionally, been designated in family
and public law, as well as by custom and practice, as the financial
dependants of their husbands.[5] It is only in cases where a husband is
incapacitated as a 'breadwinner' that a wife is, and then unusually,
expected to maintain her husband. Thus, pensions legislation and
practice tends to confirm married women in this financially dependent
status, while yet attempting to come to grips with the fact that in
reality the majority of married women have at least modest earnings
of their own.

Both state and occupational pension schemes are run on a
contributory basis, such contributions being derived from status as a
wage-earner. In this context, issues relating to female economic activity,
again linked to marital status, have been much debated. The House of
Commons, an overwhelmingly male body of MPs, has struggled for
years to fit employed married women into pension schemes indubitably
designed for men with dependent wives, and 'incipient' widows. The
debates reflect a widespread view of economic activity on the part of
married women as deviant behaviour, or, at the least, behaviour
requiring justification. The legislation eventually enacted by the
Labour government in 1975 was an advance on previous attempts to
accommodate married women within statutory pension provision as
contributors in their own right. However, this same legislation further
confirmed married women in their position as financial dependants by
making it compulsory for 'approved' occupational pension schemes to
offer widows' pensions.

Another recurrent issue in all post-war parliamentary pensions
debates is that relating to the rule which decrees that women may
claim their state retirement pensions at 60, whereas men may not do so
until 65. This regulation has its origin in considerations arising out of
marital status. It causes complications with regard to female pension
entitlement and is currently a very live issue in the face of trends
towards earlier retirement for both sexes (see Chapter 4).

The differential age of entitlement to state retirement pension is an example of permitted sex discrimination in pension schemes. Although some of the more blatant discrimination against women in the occupational pension sector has now been removed, there has been extreme reluctance to regulate either state or occupational schemes so as to eradicate sex discrimination as practised against both men and women. To this day, both state and occupational retirement-pension provision remains exempt from equal-pay and sex-discrimination legislation, a situation which is beginning to be challenged in the European courts.[6]

This chapter offers perspectives on the access of women to retirement-pension provision, covering contributory membership of state and occupational pension schemes and access to survivors' benefits. Before the issues outlined above are discussed in more detail, with a major emphasis on the overarching theme of marital status, an account will be given of the development of pension provision up to the Second World War, with particular reference to women.

Early Development of British Pension Provision

State pension provision dates from shortly before the First World War, whereas occupational pension provision has a much longer history, with its modern origins lying in the development of public-sector schemes, notably in the Civil Service, in the nineteenth century.[7] After a lengthy period of public debate on the rights and wrongs of statutory pension provision, a non-contributory, means-tested state pension scheme was introduced under the Old Age Pensions Act of 1908. This must have been a potentially useful measure for elderly women, since 'throughout the history of the New Poor Law, from its introduction in 1834, women were a majority of adult recipients of Poor Law relief. Almost certainly they were a majority of the much larger number of the very poor'.[8] Both men and women, over the age of 70, could, on proof of industrious habits, qualify on the same terms for this small weekly pension awarded to 'the very old, the very poor and the very respectable'.[9] Any person who had been on poor relief in the recent past, or currently, was initially disqualified from receipt of pension, although these regulations were quite soon modified.

In terms of the access of women to pension provision, it is interesting to note that in the discussions which preceded the eventual introduction of non-contributory pensions, it was argued that a contributory state pension scheme would be problematic for women

workers, among others. The arguments set out as evidence against
contributory pension provision for women by Amy Hurlston of the
Womens Trade Union League in 1895, have a curiously modern flavour:

> (1) Intermittent employment; (2) low rate of wages now current;
> (3) marriage; (4) actual inability of married women to contribute
> anything during the earlier years of marriage and the upbringing of
> children, save only in exceptional cases; (5) the frequent cessation
> of work through physical or domestic necessities.[10]

The first state contributory pension scheme was introduced after
the First World War via the Widows', Orphans' and Old Age Contributory Pensions Act of 1925. The former means-tested non-contributory
old-age pension continued to be available to non-insured persons over
the age of 70. The new contributory scheme introduced certain
principles of importance for women. Employed women could build
up, via contributions, an eventual entitlement to an old-age pension
in their own right at 65, provided that they were working within an
occupation covered by the scheme and were not receiving a wage or
salary sufficiently high to disqualify the earner from membership. This
latter rule would have endangered comparatively few female earners in
the inter-war period. Married women were to become entitled to a
pension by virtue of their husband's contribution record, provided that
he was already drawing his pension and they themselves had reached the
age of 65. Married women of any age were to be entitled to a widow's
pension on the death of an insured husband. Single-women
contributors qualified for a pension at 65.[11]

Between the wars there were more single women than single men in
the mature adult population, and increasingly such single women
supported themselves by paid work with a consequent need for pension
provision in their old age. Women employed in the public sector,
the overwhelming majority of whom would have been teachers, with
some Civil Servants and the occasional local government employee,[12]
were able to join occupational pension schemes and were thereby
excluded from the state contributory scheme. A government survey
published in 1936 showed just under 300,000 women in membership
of private occupational pension schemes. There were 200,000 women
in public-sector schemes. Roughly one in five members of occupational
pension schemes was a woman.[13] She would, typically, have been single.

Married women, by virtue of the 'marriage bar', were widely
excluded from employment in the public sector (see Chapter 2). The

Civil Service awarded a 'marriage gratuity' to 'established' single women employees who left to get married,[14] and local authority teachers commonly withdrew their accrued employees' pension contributions on thus being forced to resign their posts. Private-sector employers were likewise at liberty to operate a 'marriage bar'.[15] An 'insured' married woman could, under the state scheme, continue to make contributions if she carried on working after marriage, although a contemporary estimate stated that only one in seven women thus continued in paid employment.[16] Married women were not permitted to make voluntary contributions until the rules were changed shortly before the Second World War. Nor was a married woman allowed 'double benefit' in old age – she could get no more by contributing in her own right once she became 65 than she could as the 'dependent wife' of an insured husband, or if widowed at any time.[17] If by withdrawal from employment, a woman ceased to contribute after marriage, she got no credit for her earlier contributions as a single woman.[18]

An Act of 1937 set out to extend the possibility of voluntary contributions towards old-age-pension provision to certain classes of self-employed persons and to those with modest levels of unearned income. Men and women were, for the first time, treated differentially as regards income limits on membership, and for the first time the test of income was not merely on the income from paid employment. A man could contribute voluntarily if his income did not exceed £400, of which not more than £200 was to be unearned. Women, by contrast, could not have a total income of more than £250 (the same level as the current 'ceiling' for employed contributors of both sexes), of which not more than £125 could be unearned. Since women in the private sector of employment had more restricted access to occupational pension provision, even if earning a comparatively high salary, their continued exclusion from the contributory state scheme was not helpful to those wishing to make provision for their old age. All this, however, had nothing to do with sex discrimination, as contemporary commentators were at pains to point out:

> Differentiation in this matter, for the first time, between men and women, occasioned a good deal of controversy. Whether it was right or wrong must always be a matter of opinion. It had nothing to do with sex discrimination, and simply recognised facts. The scheme was intended to appeal mainly to married men whose income provided for at least two persons – the incomes of husbands and wives being aggregated – and possibly more including children,

whereas a woman could insure for an old age pension only.[19]

And lest the crafty single woman thus excluded should attempt to secure a pension for herself via a late marriage, no woman was entitled to an old-age pension by virtue of her husband's insurance unless three years had elapsed from the date of marriage, although if a woman was already receiving a widow's pension, she could receive a wife's pension immediately, provided that she had reached the age of 65. The same commentators carefully explained that this regulation existed so as 'to discourage marriage late in life with the object of securing pension for the bride'. With reference to this unseemly prospect of unsuspecting insured elderly gentlemen being seized upon by predatory spinsters they comment: 'It is doubtful whether a deterrent of this character is really necessary.'[20]

In 1940, following the recommendations of a government committee in response to pressure for statutory pensions for unmarried women at 55, the age at which women were to become eligible for contributory state pensions was lowered to 60. In addition, wives of contributory male pensioners became eligible for pension benefit at 60.[21] When supplementary pensions were also introduced in 1940 as a form of means-tested social assistance, these were also payable to women at 60.[22]

Housewives and Solitary Women

Land[23] has commented on the extent to which the values and assumptions which underpin a society's social-security system reflect the wider values and assumptions of that society, including those relating to the position of women. The post-war national-insurance legislation was largely informed by the recommendations of the Beveridge Report (1942).[24] It can be argued that the more recent attempts made to offer women a 'better deal' in retirement-pension provision represent efforts to alter principles incorporated in the report. Beveridge was criticised at the time for his categorisation of married women as *de facto* 'dependent' housewives, regardless of their employment status.[25] Certainly, the ideologies contained in the Beveridge Report had become increasingly anachronistic by the mid-1970s, based as they were on particular notions about marriage and a consequent perceived need to reinforce the position of married women as the financial dependants of their husbands. For although Beveridge argued for social-insurance provision, which treated husband and wife as a 'team', the team was in fact assumed to be one in which the paid labour of the husband was promoted by the unpaid labour of the wife.

The National Insurance Act 1946 introduced a funded scheme, with contributions from employers and employees, which included provision for the payment of a pension, conditional on actual retirement from full-time paid work, to men at 65 and women at 60.[26] The Beveridge Report had made a clear distinction between the insurance position of single women, on the one hand, and married women, on the other, designating the former group as 'solitary' women, responsible for their own financial support, whereas married women were firmly categorised as financially dependent 'housewives'.[27]

Beveridge argued that whereas 'most married women have worked at some gainful occupation before marriage: most who have done so give up that occupation on marriage or soon after' and that 'on marriage a woman gains a legal right to maintenance by her husband as a first line of defence against risks which fall directly on the solitary woman'.[28] Women's earnings were viewed as being 'in general – a means not of subsistence but of a standard of living above subsistence, like the higher earnings of a skilled man as compared with a labourer'. 'In the national interest'[29] such earnings should cease as soon as possible on pregnancy, nor should there be financial pressure on mothers to return to work. In Beveridge's view, expressed in the middle of a world war, marriage had everything to do with maternity since 'In the next thirty years housewives as mothers have vital work to do in ensuring the adequate continuance of the human race'.[30]

In his blueprint for post-war social insurance, Beveridge treated married women as 'a special insurance class of occupied persons' 'occupied on work which is vital though unpaid', for whom retirement benefits would eventually be payable in such a way as 'treats man and wife as a team'. A husband's social-insurance contribution was defined as 'made on behalf of himself and his wife, as for a team, each of whose partners is equally essential'. In the next breath comes an admission that housewives' benefits were not only to be paid for by husbands, but also to be funded 'partly by contributions made by men and women before and after marriage'. All this must have brought a wry smile to the faces of single women, who were obliged to engage in paid employment without the back-up of that unpaid domestic support without which 'husbands could not do their paid work'.[31]

Old-age pensions as such were to be replaced by pensions which were conditional on retirement from all but a modicum of paid employment.

The aim was a flexible retirement age, which assumed full employment, since 'the age to which men [*sic*] can go on working with satisfaction to themselves and advantage to the community varies with each individual and from one occupation to another'.[32] The female half of the 'team' was to become eligible for a retirement pension at the point where her insured husband took his retirement pension. Not surprisingly, the report is silent on the point at which the wife might retire from her unpaid work.

Although Beveridge assumed, erroneously in the event, that the 'great majority' of married women would not engage in paid work, he did set out conditions for their inclusion as contributors in the proposed social-insurance programme. The flat-rate contributions required of employees were to be at a lower rate for women, since it was men who were to provide 'part of the benefit for housewives'.[33] Persons 'depending for their maintenance upon remuneration received under a contract of service'[34] were to be liable for Class 1 contributions. A married woman in paid employment of a like nature was to have the right to elect to pay no such contributions, since her employment was likely to be of an intermittent nature. She would, in consequence, get no retirement benefit other than an imputed share of a retirement pension 'in partnership' with her husband.

For a married woman contemplating paying full contributions in order to qualify in her own right for a full retirement pension at the age of 60, there was in fact a disincentive built into the proposed scheme. The sickness and unemployment-benefits entitlement for those same contributions was to be at a permanently reduced rate, since 'the needs of housewives in general are less than those of single women when unemployed or disabled, because their house is provided either by their husband's earnings or by his benefit'.[35]

Yet the eventual reward proposed for a married woman who did continue to pay contributions was better than that eventually embodied in legislation. Beveridge recommended that a married woman should be able to earn a single person's retirement pension, at a rate which would be increased if she stayed in employment to 65, *in addition* to her 'share' of the higher-rated married man's pension payable to her husband on his retirement from work, again with a 'bonus' if he worked on past 65. The wife's share of her husband's pension would not be payable while she herself was still in paid employment. Should the couple separate, the 'joint' retirement pension was to be divided equally.[36]

Beveridge recommended that widows' pensions should not be paid other than to women over the age of 60. He proposed that widows should receive a 'training allowance', unless caring for dependent children in which case a widowed mother's allowance would be payable, so as to help them return to full-time work.[37] There is a certain lack of fit between Beveridge's desire to propel married women into motherhood and out of the labour force at the first possible opportunity, and his firm objection to the payment of pensions to widows under retirement age, allied with generous proposed retirement-pension arrangements for married women. The woman widowed at 59 or younger was supposed to rely, in retirement, on her own earnings or pension entitlement, such financial provision as her husband had been able to make for her, and failing that, on 'social assistance'.

In the event, the post-war national-insurance arrangements for both married women and widows differed from the Beveridge proposals. The position of a married woman who wished to contribute towards her own retirement-pension provision was made more difficult, but the financial position of widows was eased. A married woman wishing to qualify for a retirement pension in her own right was obliged to contribute as an employed person for at least half the year of her married life, irrespective of the length of her contribution record before marriage. If she failed to pass this 'half-test', she lost her entire contribution record. This iniquitous ruling was particularly hard on women who married later in life, for instance women who married in their late thirties and then had children, or who married for the first time in middle age.[38]

It appears from the parliamentary debates which preceded the 1946 Act that the position of married women was simply not thought through and was dismissed as a triviality compared with other aspects of the legislation. The real issues involved in legislating for female pension entitlement on the basis of marital status were left unresolved. The detail of the new arrangements, as they were to affect married women, were in fact left to ministerial regulation.

Married women were faced with a 'choice'. If they opted to pay full national-insurance contributions, they could obtain in their own right at 60, a 'single person's' retirement pension. They also qualified for reduced-rate unemployment and sickness benefits. However, by opting instead to pay a very small contribution for national health and industrial injuries provision, and to forfeit the right to unemployment and sickness benefit, they could still at 60 (provided their husband had reached the age of 65 and was claiming a retirement pension), draw a dependent wife's pension at 60 per cent of the single person's rate. If a wife had qualified for a partial pension in her own right, having not entirely fulfilled the conditions for a full pension although passing the 'half-test', she could make her pension up to the single person's level by claiming a proportion of the pension payable to a married couple. Barbara Castle MP suggested that if working married women had contributed in their own right for at least ten years before marriage, they should be entitled to a full pension in their own right at 60, with only a reduced contribution record required of them after marriage.[39] This proposal was not adopted.

Although some MPs conceded that there was a case for improved access to state retirement-pension rights for married women, the outcome of the post-war legislation was to leave women with what was virtually a null choice. R.A. Butler offered a fatuous and representative comment on the married woman's position: 'If she is dependent, like certain married women we all know, she may well choose one path, and if of an independent type, she may choose the other. This is a fair offer.' Butler's idea of fairness is breath-taking.[40]

One explanation as to why the position of employed married women was not sorted out more satisfactorily would seem to lie in the fact that the new legislation treated widows more generously than the Beveridge Report had recommended. Widows over the age of 50 who had been married to their husbands for at least ten years, were to be entitled to a life pension (provided they did not cohabit or remarry), in recognition of their likely difficulties in attempting to re-enter the labour-market.[41] A pension was not payable to an employed widow. At 60 the widow's pension turned into a retirement pension. The ten-year marriage rule was reduced to three years in 1957 and the earnings rule was abolished in 1964.[42] These arrangements left the financial position of certain elderly women very dependent on the age at which they had been widowed and on the age at which they had ceased to have the care of dependent children, since a widowed mother who ceased her responsibility for dependent children over the age of 40, could immediately qualify for a widow's pension. As George comments: 'This differential age limit between two sub-groups created gross inequities in some cases'[43] and, from 1956, no widows' pensions were payable until the age of 50.

In the debates preceding the 1946 legislation, pleas were made for special consideration to be given to the insurance position of employed single women, designated by Beveridge as full female-rate contributors with a right to retirement pension at 60. Echoing the pre-war agitation for contributory pensions at 55 for 'unmarried' women, such a case was again made, and in vain. Mrs Ridealgh MP gave a pathetic picture of the 'spinster's' lot, her health typically broken by late middle age from a combination of low-paid employment and domestic cares, and childless withal.[44] Beveridge had also considered, and failed to solve, the insurance problems of the 'domestic spinster' who, typically, 'kept house' for relatives.[45] In the report, he recommended that such women should pay contributions unless qualified for exemption by virtue of low income, and that 'those who get unpaid domestic service from daughters or sisters who might otherwise be earning should pay the social security contributions of these persons'.[46] These recommendations, with provision for low-income exemption, were embodied in the post-war legislation and the unresolved issues remained dormant until revived again in the mid-1960s by the new National Council for the Single Woman and Her Dependants.[47]

Beveridge viewed the position of divorced women as a somewhat intractable problem, needing, at the least, further consideration. For separated wives he had, as previously mentioned, proposed an eventual two-way split of the 'joint' retirement pension, although he also envisaged some adaptation of widowhood provisions, indicating that he expected separated wives, if possible, to return to the labour-market with the aim of financial self-sufficiency. The problem with proposals for divorced wives was that, under existing legislation, they were invariably 'innocent' or 'guilty' with consequent implications for maintenance provision. Although Beveridge expressed the view that, for a woman, 'loss of her maintenance as a housewife without her consent and not through her fault is one of the risks against which she should be insured',[48] he made no practical proposals as to how this sentiment might be incorporated in social-insurance practice. In the event, divorced women were allowed to count their husband's insurance record during their married life towards their own basic state pension provision, and, later on, their own pre-marital insurance record. It is an interesting comment on the position of married women that this latter move was a concession.

In 1954 the Phillips Committee reported on the economic and financial problems of old age and, seemingly, viewed the position of women in the national-insurance system as unproblematic, since it was not discussed. Women were invisible among the 1,400,000 elderly people on social assistance, although they undoubtedly formed a large proportion of those with very low incomes who were claiming national assistance in addition to or because of lack of qualification for contributory national-insurance provision. No mention was made of the position of divorced women beyond retirement age, although a recommendation was made for the raising of that retirement age to 63 for women and 68 for men.[49] However, a major reconstruction of retirement-pension provision, including that for women, was on the far horizon.

The 'Pensions Debate' and Women

Current pensions provision is governed by the Social Security Pensions Act 1975. This legislation was preceded by lengthy parliamentary political debate over a six-year period, in which first the Labour Party proposed a scheme which relied heavily on earnings-related statutory provision, and then the Conservative Party opted for a massive extension of occupational pension provision. Finally, a Labour administration introduced a scheme whereby statutory and occupational retirement-pension provision was administratively interlocked.

The Labour Party, in opposition in the 1950s, had produced a policy document entitled *National Superannuation* (1957) which proposed full earnings-related insurance contributions from employed married women. All married women of retirement age were to be entitled to a minimum retirement pension of their own in lieu of a 'dependent wife's' allowance payable via their husband's insurance record, in deference to the married woman's characteristic withdrawal from the labour-market for reasons of full-time child care. Eventually the retirement age for women would rise to 65, the same age as for men, and employed women would be expected to contribute for earnings-related pensions.[50]

In 1959, the Conservative government introduced an earnings-related 'graduated' pensions scheme which required contributions from all better-paid men and women (including those married women paying reduced contributions to the basic national-insurance scheme), with an abatement in contributions for those who were 'contracted out' into occupational pension schemes. Women were to receive a lower pension benefit than men for the same amount of contribution, on the grounds that their pension was payable at 60, not 65. This much-criticised scheme also provided earnings-related widows' benefits.[51]

The Labour government's plan for national superannuation was published as a White Paper in 1969.[52] The goal was comprehensive state earnings-related retirement-pension provision 'in partnership' with occupational pension schemes. It promised a 'new deal' for women, in which married women would be required to pay full earnings-related contributions at a level which would not penalise those working part-time. The scheme was to favour low-paid workers, who were typically female, in that the full single person's pension was to 'be made up to 60 per cent of his or her (revalued) earnings up to half national average, and 25 per cent up to the scheme's ceiling', which was three times the base level. The scheme recognised that it would take time for married women to build up a contribution record over the twenty-year period proposed for the scheme to come to full maturity. Hence, as an alternative, a married woman would be able, if the arrangement was more favourable, to claim a flat-rate pension on her husband's record, plus an earnings-related 25 per cent of her own life average earnings.[53]

Similarly, a woman widowed over the age of 60 was to be able to take over her husband's retirement pension, if this would be more favourable than a pension based on her own record. Earnings-related widows' pensions would be granted to women widowed over the age of 50, with a reduced pension payable to widows aged between 40 and 49, on a scale rising with age. Divorced women were to be able to use their husbands' contribution records before, as well as during, marriage, towards entitlement to a basic flat-rate retirement pension.[54]

When the legislation was put before Parliament, a lengthy debate was held on the question of requiring full contributions from married women. The Labour administration argued for equal contributions from men and women in return for equal benefits. The Conservative opposition argued for 'choice'. 'By giving women the right of choice at this moment we are giving them not only justice in equality, but a sort of social justice, so that they may choose the sort of marriage partnership they themselves want.'[55] The debates offer an interesting perspective on the gamut of parliamentary views on the role of women. Arguments against requiring full contributions from married women included comment on their low pay, the propensity for their earnings to be subject to periods of interruption on account of domestic duties, their presumed reluctance to go out to work if liable for full contributions, their habit of moving on their husband's promotion and a somewhat strange argument around the alleged tendency of 'qualified women to retire at a relatively early age because their husbands were older'. A married woman, it seemed, was to be given moderate approval for going out to work when not required to fulfil 'responsibilities which it is proper for her to fulfil',[56] and more enthusiastic approval if she was to be paid for doing a job designated as 'caring' and useful. Not all MPs were as certain about the role of married women as the one who stated firmly 'She should be encouraged to stay at home and do her job at home.'[57]

The Labour government fell, leaving the passage of the legislation incomplete. A White Paper published by the Conservative government in 1971 proposed to retain a basic state pension scheme, but placed much greater reliance in future on occupational pension provision. Married women and widows were to have a choice as to paying full contributions if employed, since: 'Many wives and widows work for only a part, and often only a small part, of their adult lives and the scheme provides a wife with a pension on her husband's contribution.'[58] As will be shown later, the promised 'expansion and improvement' of occupational schemes was seemingly to be unaccompanied by any particular measures designed to increase female participation, though there was open acknowledgement of the fact that women would be prime candidates for inclusion in the earnings-related State Reserve scheme proposed as a compulsory fall-back for employed persons not in membership of occupational schemes.

The State Reserve scheme was to provide lower pensions for women on the grounds of greater female longevity. All employed women would be required to contribute. A widow's pension would be payable at the rate of half the late husband's entitlement. Assuming constant earnings, a man of 65 would get up to 41 per cent of his average earnings in pension, whereas a woman would get only 26 per cent at 60 with no opportunity to contribute more and defer payment.[59] This latter proposal was deleted during the passage of the legislation. These arrangements were described by Mrs Castle MP as 'an insult and an injury to the women of this country'.[60] She expressed the view that since the basic flat-rate retirement pension would be inadequate, it was all the more important for second-tier arrangements to be adequate, but 'only those who get into the occupational pension scheme will get really adequate cover at the second-tier stage'.[61] As Land later commented, 'a funded scheme of this kind is likely to pay a woman a very inadequate pension indeed as it is imparting the inequalities of the marketplace into retirement.'[62]

On its return to office in 1974, the Labour government swiftly issued another White Paper, once more with an emphasis on 'equality for women'. A basic state retirement-pension scheme was to be complemented, on the one hand, by an earnings-related State Additional pensions scheme and, on the other, by 'well-founded' occupational schemes. All employed women would be required to make full contributions to the basic scheme, with credit for time spent outside paid employment on specified domestic duties. The 'half-test' was to be abolished. The basic pension was to reflect a pound for pound replacement of earnings, and the second-tier State Additional scheme would provide a pension of 25 per cent of the contributor's earnings, averaged out over his or her 'best' twenty years, up to a ceiling of seven times the base level.[63]

Earnings-related widows' pensions were to be provided in full at the age of 50 under the basic scheme, with an age-reduction for women widowed between the age of 40 and 49. If over the age of 60 and widowed, a woman could take over her husband's contribution record, provided that her total basic pension did not exceed that payable to a single person. There was also to be provision for men widowed over the age of 65 to have the same facility. Widows' pensions were also to be payable under the State Additional scheme, with similar provisions for elderly widowers.[64]

When these proposals were debated in 1975, there were once again Conservative arguments that the scheme constituted a 'swindle' for married women and widows, and that they should retain the 'choice' to pay much reduced contributions, since they could or would get an eventual benefit by virtue of a husband's contribution. Seeking to retain the 'dependent wife's' pension as a major component of retirement provision for women, one Conservative MP argued that 'what is involved is, not the concept of the dependence of the woman on her husband, but family insurance'.[65] It was obvious that in these debates (taking place at a time when sex-discrimination legislation was also on its way to the statute book, with equal-pay legislation already in existence), MPs still had very mixed feelings as to the proper place for married women. As a Labour minister remarked wistfully, 'We are living half in one world and half in another – an old world in which the generality of married women did not go out to work and the present world in which perhaps half of them go out to work.'[66]

The proposals contained in the White Paper of 1974 were enacted. The 'married women's option' was duly abolished, with a proviso for retention for a woman who had been paying reduced contributions, so long as she did not leave the labour force for a period exceeding two years. Women retiring after 5 April 1979 were no longer to be subject to the half-test.[67] In future 'home responsibilities' credits could be included in the contribution records of persons who were drawing child benefit or responsible for the home care of frail or handicapped persons qualifying for the attendance allowance.[68]

This 'new deal', however, applied to state pension provision. The new legislation also encompassed occupational pension provision, a sector in which women had, traditionally, suffered disabilities. It is this aspect of provision which will now be discussed.

Women and Occupational Pension Provision[69]

When, in the early 1970s, the Conservative Party proposed pension reforms which were to give a major place to occupational provision, it became apparent that, despite greatly increased labour-force participation, it was still a minority of women who had access to membership of occupational pension schemes and that such access was even more restricted outside the public sector of employment. Occupational pension provision was typically associated with full-time salaried occupations, especially in the public sector: many women worked part-time and/or were in lower-grade non-manual, or manual employment not covered by scheme membership. Some private occupational schemes (those outside government or similar employment) did not admit women to membership, or, more commonly, admitted women at a later age than men. A small proportion barred married women from membership. Provision for the widows of male scheme-members was variable and provision for even the 'dependent' widower, uncommon.

The Government Actuary's survey of 1971 had shown a total of 11.1 million employees covered in the United Kingdom, of whom 2.4 million were female. However, a survey of 33 organisations in the private sector covering half a million employees, showed that only 56 per cent of non-manual women were found to be eligible for membership of occupational schemes, as compared with 87 per cent of men. Only 18 per cent of manual women, but 56 per cent of manual men were so eligible.[70] Employees in occupational schemes are advantaged by receiving tax relief on their contributions and commonly, though not invariably, by obtaining a lump-sum benefit on retirement or having the option to 'commute' part of a pension into a lump sum. They may be able to 'buy in' missing years of service. Such provision is subject to Inland Revenue rules.

The 1969 national superannuation plan had emphasised the role of good statutory pension provision for women, but had anticipated some increase in female membership of occupational pension schemes.[71] Occupational pension benefits for women became a live issue in the early 1970s. With Conservative pensions policy committed to an expansion and improvement of occupational pension provision, the government acknowledged that, none the less, 'adequate occupational cover for everyone is not . . . in sight'.[72] It was proposed to strengthen greatly preservation rights to occupational pension benefits and to require approval from a new Occupational Pensions Board where employers wished to contract pension schemes out of the proposed State Reserve arrangements. One criterion for approval would be the availability of an inflation-proofed occupational widow's pension, payable on the death of a husband in retirement, at half his pension rate. For death-in-service it would be sufficient to pay the widow a lump sum.

There was substantial parliamentary debating exchange on the subject of female access to occupational pension-scheme membership, with the Labour opposition insistent that if the government was putting a major emphasis on occupational provision, then women should have equal rights to membership with men. Arguments were adduced to the effect that since such pensions are deferred pay, they should be included under legislation for equal pay. (In point of fact, the previous Labour government had feared to delay the passage of its equal-pay legislation by insisting on the inclusion of pension provision under equal pay.) There was Conservative support for an equal age of qualification for entry to scheme membership, for both men and women. However, the government feared that insistence on equal treatment for women with regard to occupational pension schemes would act as a major deterrent to employers, and especially to small employers, who might otherwise be willing to expand pension provision: 'There is no doubt that many employers who at present are prepared to set up occupational pension schemes for men alone would not . . . be prepared to set them up at all'[73] were statutory rights of membership for women required.

Thus the 1973 Social Security Act (which never became operative) did not contain measures to end discrimination against women in occupational pension schemes. The Labour White Paper (1974) did, however, commit the new government to 'the principle that women should have a fair deal in occupational pension schemes'. It was proposed to legislate for equal access to schemes for men and women doing comparable work.[74] In due course the newly constituted Occupational Pensions Board (the initial membership of which had been entirely male) was asked by the government to advise on what further action was needed to ensure equal status for men and women in occupational pension schemes. The Board reported in 1976.[75]

Under the terms of the Social Security Pensions Act 1975, schemes must be open to men and women 'on terms which are the same as to the age and length of service needed to become a member, irrespective of whether membership is voluntary or obligatory'. It is the responsibility of the Occupational Pensions Board to determine whether or not equal access requirements are being met. However, as Ellison notes,[76] certain discriminatory practices remain permissible, such as delayed admission of women to schemes, with retrospective benefits if they remain in employment to a certain age. This practice has recently been challenged under European law.[77] Rules of entry may still be based on marital status. A further allowable discriminatory feature of occupational provision, to be discussed subsequently, is mandatory employers' retirement rules, which can legally be applied to women at an earlier age than they are applied to men.

Where an employer wishes to contract a pension scheme out of the second-tier state pension arrangements, the alternative occupational pension scheme must provide benefits which are at least as good as the State Additional scheme.[78] The employer is under obligation to consult appropriate trade unions on this 'contracting-out' decision. However, scheme coverage need not be, and seldom is, the same for all categories of employees within an organisation. Hence, a majority of women can be excluded from pension coverage on grounds of job classification, not sex. All schemes must preserve benefit for members who have completed at least five years' service and reached the age of 26. People who fulfil this requirement and leave or change their employment, without transfer of pension rights, cannot now obtain or be made to take a refund of contributions. Those with less than five years' service retain their benefits in their occupational scheme or the employer may transfer their benefits to the State Additional scheme.

Occupational pension schemes are established under trust law and trustees, who are usually individual rather than corporate, commonly have discretion under this law to pay money to beneficiaries after a member's death. This particularly affects any discretionary payments to 'dependent' relatives such as widowers or elderly parents or to common-law or ex-wives. Trustees of pension schemes may include trade union representatives: they are usually persons with financial and business experience and, other than exceptionally, men. They are legally responsible for some major decisions regarding the financial welfare of the beneficiaries under their schemes. This can include the withdrawal of widows' pensions from women declared to be cohabiting or remarrying.[79]

The Occupational Pensions Board made a number of comments and recommendations for 'legislation to help to achieve equality of status for men and women besides drawing attention to other desirable changes which might be achieved by voluntary action'. However, it felt that any legislation for equal status, although 'right in principle', could not reasonably precede legislation to equalise pension ages.[80] The main areas of differential treatment of men and women were felt to be, in addition, an absence of general provision for the payment of benefits to survivors of women members (again a reflection of state pension provision), continuing permitted difference on age of entry to schemes, and the general exclusion of part-time workers, the majority of whom are women.

Among the large number of recommendations were a tightening up of the 'equal access' requirements to cover marital status, earnings requirements for entry and waiting periods for entry. It was felt that indirect sex discrimination in pension schemes should be made subject to legislative regulation analogous to that in the Sex Discrimination Act 1975, with additional provision for pension cover during maternity leave, and new powers for the courts in situations of divorce and separation involving occupational pension rights. It was argued that since 'contracting-out' arrangements were based on legislation which decreed a partnership between state and occupational pension sectors, both partners would have to assume any eventual requirements for equal pension ages. In the absence of such a move, it was felt by the Occupational Pensions Board that progress towards equal status would, for the time being, best be left to voluntary action.[81] Two consultative documents[82] were subsequently issued and in the second (1977) the government did propose legislation covering many of the Board's recommendations. However, nothing further had been done when the government fell in 1979.

The latest Government Actuary's report on occupational pensions shows a total membership of 11.8 million, of whom 3.3 million are women. In the public sector 90 per cent of men and 55 per cent of women are in membership, with 50 per cent and 25 per cent respectively in the private sector.[83] Over half of women working full-time are covered: those not in membership derive this status by virtue of the fact that their employer has no scheme (or no scheme for their particular occupational category), they are too young, have insufficient service or work part-time.[84] Women, as a class, are more likely to be affected by such exclusions than are men.

Widows' pension provision in the occupational pensions sector has greatly increased, in compliance with the regulations governing Occupational Pensions Board approval of 'contracted-out' schemes. The wives of male scheme-members who die in retirement are usually granted widows' pensions. (Some schemes require the marriage to have been of a certain duration and others will not grant a pension to the widow of a man in respect of a marriage which took place subsequent to his retirement.) The level of 'death-in-service' benefits are also relevant in the context of eventual retirement provision. All widows' benefits provided under occupational schemes must be at least as good as those which would be received under the State Additional pension scheme and there is provision for subsidy by the state, in certain circumstances, to ensure that this is so. Occupational widows' pensions provided on death-in-service can be considerably more generous than their state counterparts and in the private sector it is becoming increasingly uncommon for widows' pensions to be withdrawn on remarriage, let alone cohabitation. Public-sector widows, however, are even more strictly regulated than those women who rely on a state pension alone. The 94-year-old widow of a university professor can still, in theory, have her pension withdrawn on grounds of cohabitation. About 30 per cent of private schemes pay unconditional widowers' pensions, although in the public sector they are only granted to 'dependent' widowers.[85]

Thus there is still no legislation granting women 'equal rights' in the occupational pensions sector. Many working women are not covered by membership of such schemes. Hunt's survey of elderly people over 65 living in their own homes found, in 1976, that 51 per cent of husbands, and only 6 per cent of wives had a pension from a former employer.[86] These figures are virtually identical to those given by Layard *et al.* for 1975, who also found that 49 per cent of unmarried men, 32 per cent of never-married women and 19 per cent of widows were in receipt of occupational benefits. Many of these pensions were very small.[87] The 1979 Government Actuary's survey calculated the average ex-employee's pension at £20 weekly – £21 in the public sector and £14 in the private sector. Levels of occupational pensions paid for the first time in 1979 were, for men, £20 in the private sector and £28 in the public sector. Women received £11 and £26 respectively, with widows and dependants receiving £15 on average from the private sector and £10 from the public sector.[88]

Women's lower pension levels as ex-employees can be partially explained in terms of location within the occupational structure, level of remuneration and length of service. Crucial to the latter is the age at which women retire from work. In fact the rules of occupational pension schemes are so arranged that 90 per cent of schemes specify a 'normal' retirement age of 60 for women and 65 for men.[89] Scheme members may retire earlier or later with the permission of their employer, although the 1975 Social Security Pensions Act actually lays down that all female employees may retire (with reduced benefits) at 60 without their employer's permission, even if the 'normal' retirement age for both men and women in that employment is 65.

These rules relate to the fact that women become entitled to a state retirement pension (on their own contributions) at 60, whereas men are not so entitled until 65 (see Chapter 4). Arising from this situation, most employers do actually *require* their female employees to retire at a 'normal' retirement age which is five years earlier than that specified for their male colleagues. Thus, women typically have five years less than men in which to make occupational pension contributions, which further explains the lower occupational pensions (and lump-sum entitlements) which women characteristically receive in retirement.

It has been noted previously that the differential 'pensionable age' for men and women was viewed by the Occupational Pensions Board as a barrier to legislation requiring completely equal access to occupational pension schemes. Indeed, it can be argued that the paradoxes which arise from the differential 'pensionable ages' are second only to those which arise from entitlements deriving from marital status, the point at which this chapter began.

Conclusion

This chapter has outlined the development of pensions legislation as it relates to women as beneficiaries of pension schemes, both by virtue of their own contributions and as 'relicts' of male members of schemes. With increasing numbers of women typically achieving a substantial 'earnings record', albeit an interrupted one, both state and occupational pension schemes have been under some pressure to accommodate to such financially independent behaviour on the part of women. By contrast, provision for widows has increased, especially since recent legislation which requires occupational pension schemes to include widows' pensions as a condition of approval for 'contracting out'.

McIntosh has argued that 'provisions like widows' pensions and the custom of men taking out life insurance make it less necessary for a wife to be able to support herself alone'.[90] She has shown how state

policy appropriates the unpaid domestic labour of women, not only for
purposes of child care and the servicing of 'working' husbands, but
also for the care of the old and infirm. This account of pension policy
and legislation would seem to fit well with McIntosh's argument.
Provisions such as widows' pensions, home-responsibilities credits, the
'best twenty years' rule in the State Additional pensions scheme, all
serve to confirm women in their unpaid domestic role, although it can
also be submitted that they are some compensation for the 'two jobs'
undertaken by the vast majority of women and for the low, and,
arguably, deteriorating position of women in the labour-market.

It can further be argued that both women and men are confirmed
in their stereotyped roles as 'housewife' and 'breadwinner' by continuing
permitted sex discrimination in pensions legislation. Of particular
relevance here is the absence of general provision for widowers in state,
public occupational and many private occupational pension schemes.
Leaving aside arguments for an end to financial dependency in marriage
or like relationships, the current position as regards survivors' benefits
is patently unfair.

Pensions provision as it now stands rewards marriage, and especially
for women. This contributes to the paradoxes of current pension
provision and reinforces inequalities between the sexes. Within the
state retirement-pension system, a woman may not enjoy 'double
benefit'. If she has a full state retirement pension in her own right, she
may not claim a basic state widow's pension in addition. As a widow she
may claim on her husband's State Additional contribution record only
if it is better than her own. Nor may she claim a dependent wife's basic
(Category B) pension if she has her own larger Category A pension,
while her husband is alive and drawing a basic retirement pension
himself. The State Additional pension provides no dependent wife's
pension during a husband's lifetime — it is equivalent to a 'family wage',
though it does have the property, unique in state pension provision, of
being transferable from wife to husband where the husband is widowed
after the age of 65.

However, there is nothing to stop a woman drawing an occupational
pension by virtue of her own earnings and an occupational widow's
pension by virtue of her late husband's membership of such a scheme.
Occupational pensions are commonly viewed as deferred earnings and
these commonly transfer to a widow, more rarely to a widower. Their
potential loss, on divorce, can be a serious financial matter for women.
At the same time as occupational widows' benefits on death-in-service
are being improved, strong forces are at work arguing for early financial

independence for former wives whose marriages have ended in divorce.[91]

Access to retirement-pension benefits for women reflects the chances of the labour-market and the marriage-market. The system favours those women with good occupational pension rights (their own and/or their husband's), salaried occupational status (their own and/or their husband's) and the married over the unmarried.

There is no doubt that the front runners in the Female Retirement Pension Stakes are that very small minority of women who manage to combine a substantial retirement pension based on their own earnings with continuing marriage to a husband whose own substantial benefits include maximum widow's benefits. Indeed, the ultimate winners must surely be those women who precede the above scenario by serial marriage to husbands who conveniently predecease them, leaving each time an excellent widow's pension not subject to remarriage or co-habitation rules. Straggling last across the post come those unmarried women with little or no contributory record of their own and no entitlement to survivors' benefits. The consolation prizes in this case are means-tested 'supplementary pensions', subject to the cohabitation rule.

Notes

1. Social Security Pensions Act 1975.
2. See B. Abel-Smith and P. Townsend, *The Poor and the Poorest* (1965); D. Cole and J. Utting, *The Economic Circumstances of Old People* (1962); Ministry of Pensions and National Insurance, *Financial Circumstances of Retirement Pensioners* (1966); P. Townsend and D. Wedderburn, *The Aged in the Welfare State* (1965).
3. See P. Manley and D. Sawbridge, 'Women at Work', *Lloyd's Bank Review*, vol. 135 (1980), pp. 29-40; H. Land, *Parity Begins at Home: Women's and Men's Work in the Home and its Effects on Paid Employment* (1981).
4. H. Land, 'Women: Supporters or Supported?' in D.L. Barker and S. Allen (eds.), *Sexual Divisions and Society: Process and Change* (1976).
5. See K. O'Donovan, 'The Male Appendage' in S. Burman (ed.), *Fit Work for Women* (1979).
6. D.E. Boden, 'The Impact of Europe on Pensions', *Pensions World* (1980), pp. 373-7.
7. G. Rhodes, *Public Sector Pensions* (1965).
8. P. Thane, 'Women and the Poor Law in Victorian and Edwardian England', *History Workshop Journal*, vol. 6, (1978), pp. 29-51.
9. P. Thane, 'Non-contributory versus Insurance Pensions' in P. Thane (ed.), *The Origins of British Social Policy* (1978), pp. 103-4.
10. Ibid., p. 91.
11. Sir A. Wilson and G.S. Mackay, *Old Age Pensions* (1941).

12. *Census of England and Wales 1931*: Classification of Occupations (1934), table 5, pp. 39-62.

13. *Occupational Pension Schemes 1979: Sixth Survey by the Government Actuary* (1981), table 3.1 Numbers of pensions in payment, 1936-1979, p. 12.

14. H. Martindale, *Women Servants of the State 1870-1938*, (1939).

15. N.A. Ferguson, 'Women's Work: Employment Opportunities and Economic Roles 1918-1939', *Albion* (1963), pp. 55-68.

16. Wilson and Mackay, *Old Age Pensions*, p. 102.

17. Ibid., p. 168.

18. Ibid., p. 102.

19. Ibid., p. 178.

20. Ibid., p. 179.

21. P. Thane, 'The Muddled History of Retiring at 60 and 65', *New Society* (1978), pp. 234-6.

22. Wilson and Mackay, *Old Age Pensions*, p. 219.

23. Land, 'Women: Supporters or Supported?', p. 108.

24. Sir William Beveridge, *Social Insurance and Allied Services* (the Beveridge Report), Cmd 6404 (1942).

25. J. Harris, *William Beveridge* (1977), pp. 402-7; E. Wilson, *Women and the Welfare State* (1977), pp. 153-4.

26. V. George, *Social Security* (1968).

27. Beveridge, *Social Insurance*, Cmd 6404, paras. 107-11, pp. 49-50.

28. Ibid., para. 108, p. 49.

29. Ibid.

30. Ibid., para. 117, p. 53.

31. Ibid., para. 107, p. 49.

32. Ibid., para. 133, p. 59.

33. Ibid., para. 357, pp. 137-8.

34. Ibid., para. 314, p. 125.

35. Ibid., para. 112, p. 51.

36. Ibid., paras. 337, p. 139 and 343, p. 132.

37. Ibid., para. 346, pp. 133-4.

38. See A. Coote and T. Gill, *Women's Rights: a Practical Guide*, 1st edn (1974).

39. House of Commons, *Debates*, vol. 423 (1946), col. 1211.

40. Ibid., col. 1385.

41. George, *Social Security*, p. 137.

42. Ibid., pp. 139-40.

43. Ibid., p. 137.

44. House of Commons, *Debates*, vol. 418 (1946), col. 1792.

45. Harris, *William Beveridge*, p. 403.

46. Beveridge, *Social Insurance*, Cmd 6404, para. 121, p. 54.

47. D. Groves and J. Finch, 'Natural Selection? Perspectives on Entitlement to the Invalid Care Allowance' in J. Finch and D. Groves (eds.), *Women, Work and Caring* (forthcoming).

48. Beveridge, *Social Insurance*, Cmd 6404, para. 347, p. 134.

49. *Report of the Committee on the Economic and Financial Problems of Old Age* (Phillips Committee), Cmd 3333 (1954).

50. Labour Party, *National Superannuation* (1957).

51. Sir J. Walley, *Social Security: Another British Failure?* (1973), ch. XI, pp. 130-68.

52. Department of Health and Social Security, *National Superannuation and Social Insurance: Proposals for earnings-related social security*, Cmd 3883 (1969).

53. Ibid., paras. 72-4, pp. 25-6.

54. Ibid., paras. 75-81, pp. 26-7.

55. House of Commons, *Debates*, Standing Committee F, Official Report (5 February 1970), col. 66.

56. Ibid., cols. 129-30.

57. Ibid., col. 112.

58. *Strategy for Pensions: the Future Development of State and Occupational Provision*, Cmnd 4755 (1971), para. 47, p. 15.

59. Ibid., paras. 74-5, pp. 22-3.

60. House of Commons, *Debates*, 847 (1972), col. 227.

61. Ibid., col. 228.

62. Land, 'Women: Supporters or Supported?', p. 125.

63. *Better Pensions: Fully Protected Against Inflation*, Cmnd 5713 (1974), paras. 16-22, pp. 5-7.

64. Ibid., paras. 23-9, pp. 7-8.

65. House of Commons, *Debates*, Standing Committee A, Official Report (10 April 1975), col. 67.

66. Ibid., col. 98.

67. See M. Rowland (ed.), *Rights Guide to Non Means-Tested Social Security Benefits*, 4th edn (1981), section 7, 'The Contribution System', pp. 132-49.

68. Ibid., pp. 148-9.

69. Some material in this section derives from D. Groves, 'Women and Occupational Pensions', PhD thesis, University of London, in progress.

70. *Occupational Pension Schemes 1971, Fourth Survey by the Government Actuary* (1972).

71. *Better Pensions*, Cmnd 5713, para. 124, p. 137.

72. *Strategy for Pensions*, Cmnd 4755, para. 26, p. 9.

73. House of Commons, *Debates*, vol. 856 (1973), col. 258.

74. *Better Pensions*, Cmnd 5713, para. 75, p. 21.

75. Occupational Pensions Board, *Equal Status for Men and Women in Occupational Pension Schemes*, Cmnd 6599 (1976).

76. R. Ellison, *Private Occupational Pension Schemes*, vol. 1 (1979), pp. 102-10.

77. R. Ellison, 'The Worringham case: an interim report', *Pensions World* (May 1981), pp. 295-6.

78. For this and subsequent factual detail on the operation of occupational pension schemes, see TUC, *Occupational Pension Schemes: a TUC Guide* (1976).

79. See Occupational Pensions Board, *Equal Status*, Cmnd 6599, paras. 10.52-10.60, pp. 116-18.

80. Ibid., para. 15.37, p. 192.

81. Ibid., Summary of Conclusions and Recommendations, pp. 193-202.

82. Department of Health and Social Security, *Consultative Document on Equal Status for Men and Women in Occupational Pension Schemes* (1976); *Second Consultative Document on Equal Treatment for Men and Women in Occupational Pension Schemes* (1977).

83. *Occupational Pension Schemes 1979*, p. 4.

84. Ibid., pp. 10-11.

85. Ibid., pp. 59-69.

86. A. Hunt, *The Elderly at Home* (1978), table 6.4.3, p. 28.

87. R. Layard, D. Piachaud and M. Stewart, *The Causes of Poverty* (1978), table 10.13, p. 125.

88. *Occupational Pension Schemes 1979*, p. 14.

89. Ibid., pp. 39-40.

90. M. McIntosh, 'The Welfare State and the Needs of the Dependent Family'

in S. Burman (ed.), *Fit Work for Women* (1979), p. 165.

91. See the Law Commission, *The Financial Consequences of Divorce: the Basic Policy*, Cmnd 8041 (1980); and *The Financial Consequences of Divorce: the Response to the Law Commission's discussion paper* (1981).

4   WHO STILL CARES FOR THE FAMILY? RECENT DEVELOPMENTS IN INCOME MAINTENANCE, TAXATION AND FAMILY LAW

Hilary Land

> The world as it is at present is divided into two services; one the public and the other the private. In one world the sons of educated men work as civil servants, judges, soldiers and are paid for that work; in the other world the daughters of educated men work as wives, mothers or daughters . . . but the wives and mothers and daughters who work all day and every day without whose work the State would collapse and fall to pieces, without whose work your sons, sir, would cease to exist, are paid nothing whatever.[1]

So wrote Virginia Woolf nearly fifty years ago in her brilliant and witty, feminist polemic *Three Guineas.* Then women, especially married women, were less visible in the public world and were discriminated against in it in many more explicit ways than is currently the case. However, although women are no longer as exclusively confined to the private world of the family, it does not mean that their work within the family is valued any more highly or indeed that there is less of it. The rhetoric of the Right in recent years, as other contributors in this book demonstrate (see especially Chapter 9), is that women have acquired rights and opportunities in the public world, especially in the labour-market, but this, it is alleged, has been at the expense of their families. This is an undesirable state of affairs so women must once again be taught, persuaded and encouraged to give priority to their families, and in future social policies should be developed, or indeed not developed, with this aim in mind. Individualism is not a creed to be adopted by women. Such a view assumes that as wives, mothers and daughters, women care less for their families because they are more active outside the home. It also presupposes that the assumptions upon which social policies have been based in the past have changed in recent years in order to facilitate women's participation in activities outside the home. Neither supposition is correct. Not only do women still provide nearly all the care for the old, the sick and the young[2] (and most of it still unpaid), but also social policies are still framed, allocated and delivered on the assumption that they do so.[3]

In this paper I want to examine recent developments in three areas of social policy: income maintenance, taxation and family law, exposing the assumptions made about the division of responsibilities within the family on which debates and changes have been based. Although these three key areas of state activity were excluded from the Sex Discrimination Act 1975, as we shall see, the rhetoric surrounding the changes proposed, and already made, included greater concern than in the past to treat women as individuals rather than as dependants on men. However, this has been done in ways which least disturb the traditional division of labour between men and women within the family.

I shall therefore examine the assumptions about the economic relationship between men and women within the family, together with assumptions about the division of labour within it. These are intimately bound up together, not least because of the way in which the marriage contract is defined. The marriage contract still has different meanings for men and women and, although unwritten in Britain, it cannot be altered. Men take on an obligation to maintain their children and their wives, and refusal to take paid employment in order to do so can in the last resort lead to imprisonment. (It is an obligation therefore concerned as much with male work incentives as with the welfare of their families.) Women, however, take on an obligation to care for children, sick and elderly relatives and their able-bodied husbands. This is expected to take precedence over their paid employment and their leisure. Failure to provide this care will not lead to imprisonment unless there is evidence of criminal neglect, but may well reduce or remove their claim to maintenance on their husbands. This is very important, because married women still have fewer claims than men to maintenance from the state. Moreover, they have a much weaker foot-hold in the formal labour-market than men, not least because there is a conflict between their family responsibilities and their paid employment whereas for men there is no conflict.

Attempts to improve women's opportunities and pay within the labour-market can therefore only have a limited success as long as women within the family continue to undertake most of the work of caring. The processes of production and reproduction have to be analysed and understood in relation to each other. This has exciting theoretical consequences, for in trying to do this, feminist analyses are attempting to fill huge lacunae left by most economists and sociologists, including Marx. On the practical level, changes in social policies which reduce women's claims to maintenance on men but do not recognise that changes in the division of responsibilities for caring between men and women within the family and between the family and the wider community are also required, may in the end be counter-productive as far as women are concerned.

The history of the development of state systems of income maintenance for men is bound up with the development of wage-labour and the separation of men and women from direct and independent access to the means of subsistence. Formal labour-markets in capitalist economies have never been able to provide paid employment for everyone who needed it, and short of allowing wage-labourers and their families of future wage-labourers to starve, either individual capitalists or the state on their behalf had to provide alternative means of support. Paradoxically, this provided for the possibility of voluntary unemployment, an anathema to the capitalist class, and so the conditions under which men's claims to maintenance from the state were met were such as to weaken male work incentives as little as possible, and ideally to discourage men from making a claim at all, except in the direst circumstances. The subsequent development of state contributory systems of income maintenance, although to some extent building on the systems of mutual support developed by some trade unions and friendly societies, which were informed by a collective ideology and embodied the concept of the right to support, has also been constrained by the desire to maintain male work incentives.

Women's claims to maintenance from the state have been subject to different constraints. Although the old and the young have been gradually denied access to the formal labour-market and hence to wages, they have acquired increased rights to sources of income independent of their families. Since 1948, for example, the elderly have no longer been deemed to be the financial responsibility of their adult children or grandchildren. Women's claims to maintenance, however, are still derived less from their labour-market activities or the state and more from the men to whom they are married (or with whom they cohabit). The growth of individualism has weakened the economic relationships between the generations to a far greater extent than that between the sexes within the family. The conditions under which women, particularly married women, acquire maintenance from the state are determined not by a desire to maintain their incentives to take waged work, but by a concern that they will continue their unwaged work of caring for their families. This is still evident in the latest policy developments and debates.

Income Maintenance

The British social-insurance system was reformed in certain important respects in the legislation passed in 1975. Under the Social Security Pensions Act there was an attempt to change what Barbara Castle, then Secretary of State to the Department of Health and Social Security, described as a situation in which women were 'Second class citizens entitled to third class benefits'.[4] However, the changes were not a complete break with the past.

The Beveridge Report, which formed the basis of much of the post-war social-security legislation, contained certain features which in part led to the need to reform the pension system. These features profoundly affected the shape and priorities of the new scheme, although not all were carried over into it. They included different retirement ages for men and women; the choice offered to married women, including those in paid employment, of opting out of paying full contributions and relying instead on their husbands' contributions (this is known as 'the married woman's option'); and flat-rate benefits in return for flat-rate contributions.

The first — unequal retirement ages — has been incorporated into the new scheme. Since 1940, the retirement age for women has been 60 years, five years earlier than for men. Prior to that time retirement ages for men and women were the same and this meant that a man retiring at 65 often had to support himself and his wife on a single-rate pension, because on average women were younger than their husbands. This could cause considerable hardship. The 1946 legislation introduced dependency benefits for wives, irrespective of age, provided they were not earning. This removed one of the major justifications for different retirement ages; nevertheless they have remained. As a result the effects of differential mortality rates for men and women are exacerbated. Women currently outlive men by about six years, so that as they retire five years earlier they can expect on average to spend twice as long as men in retirement. The capital value of a flat-rate pension for a woman, paid from the age of 60, is about twice as much as that of the same pension for a man paid from age 65. When paid from the same age the difference in capital value is 10 per cent.

Mortality rates are still expected to improve and, if anything, the gap between men and women is likely to widen rather than narrow.[5] The life expectancy of a baby born in 1975 is estimated to be 71.9 years if male and 78.6 if female. This compares with an average life expectancy in 1975 of 69.1 years for males and 75.2 years for females.

A higher proportion of men and women are marrying than among the generation who are currently retired, and married men and women have lower mortality rates than single men and women. Marital status has a greater impact on the mortality rates for men than those for women (see Table 4.1).

Table 4.1: Standardised Mortality Rates at ages 15-84 by Sex and Marital Status, England and Wales, 1965-7

Marital Status	Male	Female
Single	110	104
Married	92	89
Widowed	128	109
Divorced	116	94

Source: Office of Population Censuses and Surveys, *Registrar General's Statistical Review of England and Wales for the year 1967*, Part III Commentary, p. 136.

In particular, widowhood has a more dramatic effect on men than on women. Thus survivors' pensions are of greater concern to women than to men. If equal treatment is defined to mean that the same level of contribution must earn the same level of weekly or monthly pension, and if the notion of survivors' pensions is retained, then in these circumstances women are likely to get more in total from their own contributions than men and more out of their husband's contributions as their survivors. But because they retire earlier and live longer they need more.

There has been a considerable debate about equalising retirement ages for men and women in the state scheme. The Trades Union Congress and the Labour Party support a common pension age of 60 years. However, they give priority to providing an adequate state contributory pension which does not require a means-tested supplement. The Occupational Pensions Board, which was set up under the 1973 Social Security Act to monitor and establish minimum standards for private occupational pension schemes, was asked to consider the question of equal status for men and women in occupational pension schemes in 1975. (The Social Security Pensions Act 1975 requires that men and women have equal access to membership of such schemes.) They reported in 1976 and concluded that 'equal status must mean equal pension ages. Any other arrangement can be based only on the assumed requirements of each sex, an approach which we consider to be incompatible with equal status.' They recognised that 'as long as the

State Scheme has different ages, we do not see how occupational schemes can be obliged to have the same ages for men and women'.[6] In 1975, one-third of the total number of members covered by occupational pension schemes were in schemes which had equal pension ages and they hoped that even without legislation this number would be increased by negotiation and voluntary agreement. However, they stressed that the problem of different pension ages must ultimately be tackled, and this means changes in the state scheme.

Successive governments, however, have made it clear that any alteration of the state pension ages is unlikely. As the Minister for Social Security said in 1976:

> a reduction in men's pensionable age is ruled out for the foreseeable future on grounds of cost . . . on the other hand, the government believes that raising the pensionable age for women would be unfair to women who have contributed over the years in the expectation of a pension at 60.[7]

In 1976 the Department of Health and Social Security estimated that the total cost to central and local government funds of an equal pension age of 60 would exceed £2,000 million a year, or about £100 a worker. (This compares with expenditure on retirement pensions of £4,800 million pounds in 1975/6). The labour supply would have been reduced by about 5 per cent and the reduction in potential output was estimated to be some 3-4 per cent of the gross national product. At the time unemployment was only half what it is today, six years later. Thus, assuming two-thirds of those retiring were replaced in work by unemployment beneficiaries, the financial costs could have been halved. However, the prevailing view seems to be that it is preferable for women to withdraw from the labour-market rather than for men to have to retire five years earlier. As a result, what *The Times* called 'the main stumbling block'[8] against full equal rights for men and women in the state and occupational pension schemes remains for the foreseeable future.

The second characteristic of the post-war national-insurance scheme, which will perpetuate the treatment of women as dependants on their husbands for some time to come, is the married woman's option. Until May 1978, all married women and widows had the right to rely on their husbands' contributions and forgo claims to short-term benefits (sickness, unemployment and maternity) as well as claims to pensions in their own right. Only when their husbands retire can they receive pensions as dependants. (Dependant's benefits equal 60 per cent of a single person's basic pension.) In the early 1970s, three-quarters of married women chose to opt out of the national-insurance scheme. This is not surprising as there was much to encourage them to do so. For example, married women who contributed fully in order to claim a retirement pension had to satisfy additional tests.[9] This inequality was removed under the 1975 legislation.

Under the Social Security Pensions Act 1975, only married women and widows already exercising their option to rely on their husbands' contributions could continue to do so, provided they did not leave the labour market for two or more years. The Government Actuary in 1975 estimated that only 15 per cent of those who would have exercised the contribution option would choose to be full contributors when the new scheme took effect.[10] He therefore concluded that:

It will be well beyond 30 years before the majority of married women and widowed retirement pensioners come to consist of persons who have paid full contributions throughout their periods of employment.[11]

The effect of Beveridge's view of marriage being a relationship which created economic dependency in the wife is therefore one which will remain in practice until well after the end of the century.

The gradual phasing out of the married woman's option has been accompanied by the introduction of credits toward the basic state pension for those who are out of the labour-market because of home responsibilities. Home responsibilities include the care of children until the age of 16 as well as the care of the sick or disabled. Married women who were not full contributors prior to leaving the labour-market are not credited. Being 'out of the labour-market' is defined as earning less than a quarter of the average male industrial earnings—£29.50 per week in 1982. Recently, home responsibility was extended to include the care of elderly relatives not living in the same household. This was important, because a national study in 1965 showed that one-fifth of women who were working part-time did so because they were caring for a sick or elderly person. In addition, it was shown that women living in the same household as the person for whom they were caring were more likely to be either working full-time or not at all; part-time employment was taken when the sick or elderly person lived elsewhere.

In order to qualify for the basic pension, men and women must either be full contributors or be credited with contributions for all of their working lives subject to a minimum of full contributions paid for twenty years. The additional earnings-related components of the state pension is based on the *best* twenty years' earnings, so those who are out of the labour-market for substantial periods (mainly women) have little choice of which periods of earnings to take. In addition, women's earnings on average are far lower than men's, so almost certainly women will earn a lower earnings-related component than men.

Under the Act the principle of earnings-related pensions in return for earnings-related benefits was firmly established. It is important to note, however, that contributions are not levied over the entire earnings range. This means that nearly all female workers and male manual workers pay a completely earnings-related contribution. However, about 25 per cent of male non-manual workers have earnings above the contribution ceiling: they therefore pay proportionately less than anyone else. Moreover, they are more likely to be members of an occupational pension scheme and those contributions attract tax relief, whereas contributions to the state scheme do not. (Under the scheme, those who belong to an occupational scheme which provides a pension at least as good as the state can partially contract out of the state scheme and pay a lower contribution.)

Survivors' pensions, too, will be based on the earnings-related component of *both* spouses. Moreover, a married woman can use her husband's contribution record to make up her basic pension to the level she would have got as his dependant. Only a widower who was retired or chronically sick or disabled when his wife died can use his former wife's contribution record. There are no age or health conditions for widows, for by definition a woman must have been dependent on her husband. This is the closest the British pension system has got to earnings sharing between spouses, and it does not apply to men and women whose marriages end in divorce. A divorced woman can only use her former husband's contribution record to establish her right to the basic pension and only provided she contributes in her own right as soon as the marriage ends and she does not remarry (unless she is divorced over the age of 60). Her claims are not affected by his remarriage. The same holds for divorced men. Widows also lose rights to pensions based on their former husbands' contribution records, if they cohabit or remarry.

Instead of taking account of and sharing variations in earnings and living standards between spouses, whatever the number of marriages, and then treating them as individuals, the British system as described above has preferred to recognise the work of caring for the young, the sick and the old by giving credits which maintain the care-taker's entitlement to the basic state pension. This is a more selective version of Beveridge's married woman's option, which in effect entitled every woman by virtue of being a wife to a pension (worth 60 per cent of the basic pension) on the basis of her husband's contributions record. Because of this all men paid a higher contribution than women. Now women pay contributions on the same basis as men. Broadly speaking, the introduction of the home-responsibilities credit is a subsidy to those (mainly, but not exclusively, women) who care for the young, the sick or the old on a nearly full-time basis. Women who combine their responsibilities in the home with a greater degree of participation in the labour-market, together with men and women without those responsibilities, will be subsidising them. In other words, the traditional division of unpaid labour in the home is being upheld rather than changed by the new scheme. One of the more radical features of the Social Security Pensions Act was, for the first time in the history of the British social-security system, the recognition of voluntary role-reversal. It was always intended that single men would have their pension rights protected while at home looking after children or dependent relatives, but it was not until the regulations were published in January 1978 that it was clear that married men would be included.

The tentative nature of this small recognition of husbands as carers (rather than recognition of wives as breadwinners) is underlined by the limited changes in the Social Security Act 1975. Under this legislation, for the first time a married woman who paid full contributions became entitled to unemployment and sickness benefits at the same rate as her single sister.[12] However, currently, unlike her husband she has no automatic rights to additional dependency benefits for her children and, unless her husband is incapable of paid employment, she gets no extra benefit for him either. As a result of the EEC directive requiring equal treatment for men and women in member countries' social-security schemes, the British system has had to be further modified. Dependants' benefits will disappear as they are being held down until the universal child benefit catches up with them. From January 1983, married women will have the right to apply for Family Income Supplement (a means-tested supplement for low wage-earners with children which currently specifies that only the husband in a married couple may apply) and, provided the couple agree that she has been and is the main breadwinner, a married woman may then apply for means-tested supplementary benefit.

Under the EEC directive further changes will eventually have to be made in two new non-contributory benefits introduced in legislation passed in 1975. One, the non-contributory invalidity pension is paid for those who are incapable of work and do not qualify for a contributory pension. Work is taken to be paid employment if the claimant is a man or single woman, but if she is a married or cohabiting woman then eligibility is based on her capacity to perform 'normal household duties'.[13] The other change is the invalid-care allowance which is paid to men and women who give up paid employment in order to care for a sick or elderly person, not necessarily a relative. However, married or cohabiting women are not eligible in any circumstances, although all the evidence shows that they provide substantial care for the sick and elderly and that their opportunities for paid employment are thereby reduced or removed altogether. These benefits, which were introduced in legislation passed in the year of the British Sex Discrimination Act, are perhaps two of the most blatant examples of the way in which married women are seen first and foremost as housewives and thus responsible for all the domestic work within the home.

Altogether none of these changes really recognise that the majority of families depend on the earnings of *both* husband and wife, even if the wife's contribution in most instances is smaller. (In 1980 it averaged 28 per cent of family income.) Families are still perceived as consisting of one breadwinner who only exceptionally is a woman, and one dependent spouse whose primary responsibilities lie in the home. These families are, in fact, a minority. The General Household Survey in 1979 found that only 20 per cent of economically active married men supported a dependent wife and children.[14] There is even less recognition of the needs of women who combine paid employment *and* care for their families, especially if their employment is part-time.

There are other processes which are undermining women's access to the social-insurance system. Although married women have won rights to benefit which are not affected by their marital status as directly as in the recent past, more women are being pushed beyond the reaches of the scheme altogether. In 1977, 22 per cent of female part-time employees were earning less than £15 a week, which at the time defined the boundary of non-employed for social-insurance purposes (that is, neither they nor their employers have to pay national-insurance contributions). By 1979 this had more than doubled.[15] National-insurance contributions now constitute 9 per cent of labour costs compared with 6 per cent in the mid-1970s so these workers are very attractive to employers. If their hours of work can also be limited to less than 16 hours a week, then these workers will also fall outside the employment-protection legislation, which means they can be used even more flexibly and cheaply as they then forgo rights to certain occupational benefits (which now comprise a further 9 per cent of labour costs). In other words, the boundaries of the formal labour-market are being more tightly drawn, a process associated now as in the past with high rates of male unemployment, and it is largely women, with responsibilities for caring, who are being pushed out. The lack of provision of income maintenance for those with part-time earnings stems from a failure to recognise that most women work part-time not from choice,[16] nor because their earnings are inessential, but because their employment opportunities are severely constrained by their family commitments.

Even those within the scheme are finding their rights to benefit in practice are limited not by the fact of marriage *per se* (as in the 1930s), but by their caring responsibilities. For example, part-time workers who earn enough to pay contributions may not qualify for unemployment benefit unless they can produce evidence that they have a 'reasonable chance' of getting part-time employment in the locality. In addition, as the responsibility for the registration of unemployment benefit is changing from job centres to unemployment-benefit offices, pilot studies are being conducted in twenty of the latter to test new administrative procedures for establishing 'availability for work'. Women are being asked detailed questions about their child-care arrangements, and failure to produce satisfactory answers may disqualify them from benefit. In other words, women's caring responsibilities are being used as a ground for *excluding* them from benefits.

Barbara Castle's attempts to make women full citizens of the social-insurance scheme, irrespective of their marital status, have had only limited success. Moreover, even full citizenship is being devalued as the earnings-related supplements to short-term benefits disappeared in January 1982, and the present administration is attempting, in the face of considerable opposition, to dismantle the sickness-benefit scheme and pass responsibility for short periods of sickness on to employers. (Perhaps there are analogies here with occupations which open up membership to women and subsequently decline in status and pay.) Certainly greater reliance on occupational benefits will disadvantage women until they have better pay and opportunities within the labour-market.

Taxation

The income-tax system has also been the subject of review during the past decade. The proposals for a radical restructuring of our tax and benefits systems in the form of a tax-credit scheme[17] fell by the wayside with the demise of the Heath administration. Apart from replacing child tax allowances and cash family allowances with a tax-free child benefit (the equivalent of a tax credit for children) the Labour government rejected the idea of tax credits. They did, however, set up a review of the personal income-tax system, not least because during the 1970s there were pressures from the Equal Opportunities Commission and other women's organisations in both major political parties to reappraise the assumptions concerning women, upon which our current tax system is based.[18] Meanwhile, a few token gestures were made in recognition of women who wished to be treated as individuals in their own right rather than as mere appendages of their husbands. For example, rebates of overpayment of tax on a married woman's earnings are now sent to her rather than to her husband, as formerly was the case, and the Board of Inland Revenue will correspond directly with her about her tax affairs if she wishes. However, some of the central pillars of the British tax system have remained, including the aggregation rule[19] under which a wife's income is deemed to be her husband's for tax purposes; the married man's tax allowance, which gives married men a personal tax allowance 40 per cent higher than a single person's allowance; and the assumptions about women's dependency on men. The Labour government was to have produced a Green Paper called 'Tax and the Family', which would have addressed these and related issues, but they left office before this was published. The current administration, however, produced a modified version of the Green Paper in 1980 called *The Taxation of Husband and Wife*. This has been the subject of comment and discussion[20] and the Board of Inland Revenue are currently considering reactions to it. However, the timetable for change is a leisurely one, because major changes will have to wait until the computerisation of the tax system is completed in four or five years' time. A government committed to making major reforms, such as changing the tax unit from the couple (meaning the husband) to the individual, could have done so *before* computerisation was embarked upon at the end of the 1970s, but resistance to changing the economic relationship between husband and wife is powerful in the Labour Party as well as in the Conservative Party, as the story of the introduction of child benefits shows.[21]

The Taxation of Husband and Wife, as the name suggests, had a narrower remit than that of the Labour government's Green Paper. This means that the opportunity to tidy up some of the small allowances which recognise groups with special needs, for whom there are now cash benefits, has been missed. I have argued elsewhere[22] that the conditions under which taxpayers become eligible for these allowances, particularly those concerning dependent relatives, elderly people requiring services of a daughter and housekeeper's allowances, for example, reveal the same assumptions about women's dependence on men and their primary responsibility for caring as are found in the social-security system. Without repeating the detail here, it is worth noting that these originated at a time when most taxpayers were middle class, that is the assumptions about the division of responsibilities within the family have not been, and are not, confined to the working class. However, the family circumstances of the middle classes were recognised much earlier in the tax system than in the social-security system.

The central issues of women's dependence on their husbands and the aggregation of the incomes of husband and wife are discussed in the Green Paper. However, the discussion is narrow and biased. It is acknowledged that the married allowance 'recognises the special legal and moral obligations on a husband to support a wife', but that 'in recent years the tendency has been for these obligations to become reciprocal'.[23] However, they accept first on fiscal grounds and subsequently on social grounds that 'where one spouse is dependent upon the other for financial support, there is a case for some recognition by the State'.[24] There is a very cursory attempt to distinguish between the reasons for that dependency. The paper therefore discusses equity in the tax system almost entirely in terms of relativities between married and single people, between one-earner and two-earner couples and men and women, taking little account of the existence of dependants, be they children or incapacitated relatives. There is little recognition that the care of children, the sick or the old is socially useful and necessary work, and that if, as a result of doing this work, an adult cannot support herself (or himself) through paid employment, the state has some obligation to provide maintenance. (There is, of course, the important and related question of the provision of collective services to share the work of caring with the family, but that will not be discussed here. It was not, of course, discussed in the Green Paper, except implicitly in the case of *lone* parents.) However, in the case where one spouse (nearly always the wife) is a full-time housewife solely because that is what she and, more important, her husband prefer, it is a private matter and of benefit only to the couple (and mostly the husband because it is he who gets the additional services). There are no grounds for arguing that the state should continue in the future to recognise that arrangement which, in any case, only a minority of couples (just over a million) with no dependants follow.[25]

The authors of the Green Paper clearly favour replacing the married man's tax allowance with a system which would allow non-earning spouses to transfer their tax allowances either fully or partially to their partners. This would protect the position of the childless single-earner couple and improve the position of the family with a married woman at home looking after children, compared with a two-earner couple. That this 'could well discourage married women from taking up work in the first place . . . [and] would be particularly true where she was contemplating part-time work'[26] is not presented as a major problem. It is no coincidence that such a proposal is favoured at a time of high male unemployment. They do, however, recognise that there would be substantial administrative costs, especially if reasons for there being only one earner were taken into account and the option made available only to those with specific home responsibilities.

The alternative approach of providing for the non-earning spouse through the social-security system is given short shrift. The discussion is much influenced by 'the Government's view [that] more than accounting conventions are involved here: the distinction between cash benefits (which increase public expenditure) and tax allowances (which do not) is an important one'.[27] (When in opposition both Sir Geoffrey Howe and Patrick Jenkin, who was Secretary of State for the Social Services at the time the Green Paper was being prepared, accepted that there was an equivalence between them.) The possibility of abolishing the married man's tax allowance and using the £3 billion additional tax revenue either to double child benefits and to extend the invalid-care allowance to married women, or to pay a special home-responsibilities payment is given a brief look and dismissed. But perhaps the rejection of this possibility arose not only from the weight of argument from the Treasury, but also because transforming a tax allowance into a benefit paid direct to the supported spouse would be transferring money from 'the wallet to the purse', as the media described the replacement of child tax allowances with the introduction of the cash child benefit. However, as the Green Paper states:

whereas with the child tax allowance it was not the claimant's own allowance which was at stake but only in effect an additional allowance for a dependant, with the addition of the married allowance *married men might be even more inclined to regard themselves as 'losers'* particularly if their circumstances were such that the family did not stand to benefit from the additional social security provision available. [My italics.] [28]

This, I suggest, is one of the reasons, if not *the* main reason, for the statement in the Green Paper that: 'in the Government's view, the arguments against provision for a dependent spouse through the social security system . . . are very weighty'.[29]

The view that this government is reluctant to alter the existing unequal economic relationship between husband and wife is supported by the Green Paper's very different approach to meeting the needs of one-parent families. In this case the equivalence of tax relief and cash benefits is acceptable and there is a willingness to put it into practice very quickly. The additional personal allowance for single parents (which originated as an offshoot of the housekeeper's allowance) means that their personal allowance is the same as the married allowance. (In 1980 this was worth £4.40 a week and cost the Exchequer £90 million in forgone revenue.) The Green Paper favours replacing this by increasing the already enhanced child benefit for one-parent families,[30] because 'it would concentrate help for lone parents in the single form of a cash benefit, low paid working lone parents whose earnings are below the tax threshold would gain financially and their incentive to work would be improved'.[31] All of these arguments could equally apply to married mothers too, but, as we have seen, they are rejected. The reason for supporting such a transfer is that it would be possible to provide financial support for lone parents much more selectively and therefore cheaply. The Board of Inland Revenue has not needed to become involved in administering cohabitation rules, and the eligibility criteria for the additional personal allowance for lone parents are very simple and are not concerned with cohabitation or financial support from the other parent. By transforming this tax relief into a greatly enhanced child benefit for lone parents, administered by the Department of Health and Social Security, cohabitation rules, etc., it could be applied to *all* lone parents seeking financial assistance from the state. The message seems clear: women with children should be dependent on their husbands or the men with whom they live. If they have no claims on a man, then they should be encouraged to seek paid employment.

Family Law

The original justification for the introduction of the married allowance in 1918 stemmed in part from a man's legal obligation to maintain his wife. As even the authors of the Green Paper acknowledge, family law has changed in this respect, especially since the Matrimonial Causes Act 1973. However, the principle of a lifelong obligation to maintain – accepted on marriage – is currently under review. In 1980, the Law Commission published a discussion paper[32] which reviewed 'the fundamental ideas which underlie the present law' and examined alternative principles which might form the basis of future law. In December 1981, it published its recommendations,[33] having considered the arguments and evidence put forward in response to the discussion paper.

Before discussing the proposals, it is worth looking very briefly at the background against which the financial consequence of divorce became an issue of controversy and concern. The Divorce Reform Act 1969, which was enacted in 1971, altered the basis of divorce and rejected the principle that a matrimonial offence should be the basis on which divorce was available. This was replaced by the principle that the only ground on which the court has power to dissolve a marriage is that the marriage has 'broken down irretrievably'. This has meant, as the Law Commission states in its discussion paper, that 'the concept of the indissoluble marriage no longer exists in English law: if either party wants a divorce, sooner or later he [sic] will be able to obtain one'.[34] Since 1971, the number of marriages ending in divorce has increased substantially. One in twenty couples married in 1975 had divorced within four years of marriage, compared with one in forty couples married in 1969. In 1980, there were 148,000 divorces, 70 per cent granted to the wife (as in previous years) and 60 per cent involving children under the age of 16 years. Many divorced people remarry, however, and of the 368,000 marriages which took place in 1980, 15 per cent were between partners both of whom had been married before and 18 per cent between partners one of whom had been married before.[35] It is not surprising, therefore, that questions about men's responsibilities for maintaining a wife and children of a first marriage after he or she had entered into a second became an issue, particularly as one of the duties of the courts was to exercise their powers so that 'the financial position of the parties should so far as possible be unaffected by their divorce'.[36]

In the discussion paper, the Law Commission explicitly confined itself to the law governing the obligations of husband to wife and each other. The possibilities and consequences of shifting away from private law for the enforcement of financial obligations against individuals towards a system under which claims to maintenance would be met by the state through the social-security system were not explored. The reasons for this were partly that the Finer Committee on One-Parent Families, which reported in 1974, had already done so, and partly because such a shift would have implications for public expenditure. The Law Commission did accept, however, that the reform of private law can have little impact on the alleviation of poverty and that hardship and deprivation were the most serious problems faced by the majority of single parents. (In 1981 there were 346,000 single parents receiving supplementary benefit, about 30 per cent of whom were divorced women.) The question addressed, therefore, was to what extent could or should individuals look to a former spouse for maintenance and to what extent could or should they (particularly wives) be self-sufficient?

The Law Commission's conclusions were that the objective of leaving the financial position of the parties unaffected by divorce should be abandoned. Provision of adequate financial support for children should have an overriding priority; more emphasis should be placed on the wife's earning potential; and 'any periodic financial provision ordered in favour of one spouse (usually the wife) for her own benefit — as distinct from the periodical payments made to enable her to care for the children — should be primarily directed to secure wherever possible a smooth transition from marriage to the status of independence'.[37]

On the face of it this sounds quite a radical departure from the principle that once married a woman is, and should be, a lifelong dependant of her husband. However, the context within which this principle would be put into practice may make 'independence' rather a sham. The Law Commission seems to have recognised this in the discussion paper when it quotes the Finer Committee who said:

Since the early days of industrialisation, women have constituted both a significant proportion of the country's labour force and a main source of cheap labour. An inescapable conclusion from the many recent studies of women's experiences in trying to reconcile

the claims of marriage, motherhood and work is the existence of a
traditional and firmly rooted double standard of occupational
morality. As a society we pay lip service to the ideal of equality for
women whilst practising discrimination in the very area where it
hurts most.[38]

However, what remains unacknowledged is the extent to which the
inequality that women experience in the labour-market stems as much
from the division of labour within and beyond marriage as from the
'double standard of occupational morality'. The Law Commission's
proposals would do little to alter this in practice. Far more women than
men continue to carry out their duties included in the marriage contract
long after the legal marriage has ceased to exist. In nearly 90 per cent
of divorces involving children custody is awarded to the mother, and
very few women cease caring for their children before they reach
adulthood. They will, therefore, continue to experience a conflict
between their family responsibilities and paid employment for a
considerable period after the marriage has ended. (Of course, if there
was a greater priority given to child-care provision and other collective
services, then the situation would be eased.) In contrast, marriage and
the aftermath of divorce rarely disadvantages men in the labour-market.
In most marriages the husband's work and career is still put first and,
in many ways, in the services she provides for her husband, a wife enhances
enhances his prospects in the labour-market. Given the low value our
society places on the work of caring, women are, in effect, de-skilled
by the experience of marriage. Men, then, gain in terms of their ability
to be financially self-sufficient as a result of marriage, women on the
whole lose. This is nowhere recognised in the discussion paper: if it were,
then basing a wife's financial claims on the principle of compensation
might have been considered, and more thought might have been given
before recommending that the courts' present powers to reallocate the
rights of former spouses under an occupational pension scheme be
reconsidered. Few married women can acquire as substantial an
occupational pension as men or their single sisters, not just because
their earnings are lower, but also because such events as periods of
maternity leave are rarely treated as generously as periods of sick
leave or training.[39]
  In addition, men more often and quickly break their side of the
contract, namely to provide maintenance for the children and their
former wife. The Finer Committee reporting in 1974 found that half
of the maintenance orders made in the magistrates' courts were in

arrears, half of them over £200 in arrears. In 1980, the House of Commons was told that only 6 per cent of one-parent families relied on maintenance as their sole source of support. This contrasts with over 50 per cent of lone mothers on supplementary benefit. In practice, then, the claims to maintenance which a woman has on the state are as important – and more reliable – than the claims many of them are able to make on their husbands.

Recent changes, however, in the supplementary-benefit system have had the effect of making women more dependent on maintenance rather than less. Maintenance payments made for the children, as well as for the lone parent, are included in the assessment of his, or more likely her, needs and income. (Contrast this with the income-tax system which, except for the period from 1969 to 1972, has never aggregated children's income with that of their parents.) Formerly maintenance payments for children affected the level of the dependency benefits included in the supplementary benefit paid to their parent, but it did not affect the parent's own entitlement. This, of course, may make some men even more reluctant to pay maintenance not only to their former wives but to their children (in the past defaulting on children's maintenance was less frequent than defaulting on a wife's maintenance), since they know that the maintenance allowance they pay will merely reduce or even extinguish her claims to state support. Certainly the Law Commission is right to ask for regular monitoring and evaluation of the impact of changes in family law on the operation of our income maintenance and tax systems and vice versa.

Conclusion

The overall picture of women's position in the three interlocking areas of state policy examined in this paper show that attempts made during the last decade to alter the assumptions about the division of responsibilities within the family have met with considerable resistance. In some areas, notably social insurance, women have acquired greater rights as individuals, but these are being undermined, not only by administrative practices, but also by changes in the structure and boundaries of the formal labour-market. Women's claims to maintenance from the state and from the labour-market are still substantially weaker than men's. Women are discriminated against because they have caring responsibilities in the family, rather than, as in the past, just because they are married. This, of course, affects most women. About 90 per cent of married couples have children. In addition, in 1980, 12 per cent of babies were born to unmarried women, and about half of all middle-aged housewives can expect at some time to be responsible for caring for a sick or elderly person. A recent study of people caring for the elderly and infirm found that on average they had been providing care for more than six and a half years.[40] Marital status is still an important determinant of eligibility for benefit, since married or cohabiting women who are prevented from being self-supporting because of their caring responsibilities do not have claims to maintenance on the state, but are expected to be maintained by their husbands (or the men with whom they live). In return for their maintenance, a woman must provide domestic services for her husband. The assumptions about the nature of the marriage contract upon which the recent changes in policy have been based have therefore altered very little indeed.

Women's work as wives, mothers and daughters is still as invisible and as much taken for granted by men and the policy-makers (and they are largely men)[41] as when Virginia Woolf was writing. However, increasing women's access to state benefits will not of itself necessarily meet women's needs and interests, unless they are able to participate more fully in the formulation of policy. As the Co-operative Women's Guild recognised over half a century ago, women and especially 'the independent working woman . . . must be given a voice in the shaping of the policy to be pursued and deciding the ideals to be instilled otherwise there might be danger of scientific, eugenic and official views of the work overruling individual and family rights'.[42] This would involve developing very different political structures, as well as challenging the economic and social institutions in our society which place so little value on women's work in the home and outside it.

Notes

1. V. Woolf, *Three Guineas* (1977), p. 63.
2. For example, the Equal Opportunities Commission has estimated that there are 1,200,800 people tied to their homes because of their responsibilities for a disabled relative and a further 1,600,000 involved in part-time care. See Equal Opportunities Commission, *Behind Closed Doors* (1981).
3. For example, see H. Land, 'Who Cares for the Family?' *Journal of Social Policy* (July 1978).
4. House of Commons, *Debates*, vol. 888 (1974), col. 1092.
5. There are indications that the continued improvement in mortality rates forecast for women may turn out to be too optimistic. It is argued that the stress

of combining family responsibilities with employment outside the home is showing up, for example, in the big increase in deaths due to cancer. Deaths from lung cancer increased by 30 per cent for women between 1968 and 1976, compared with only a 5 per cent increase for men. See World Health Organization, *Mortality Trends in Europe, World Health Statistics Report*, vol. 27, no. 1 (1974), p. 29.

6. Occupational Pensions Board, *Equal Status for Men and Women in Occupational Pension Schemes*, Cmnd 6599 (1976), p. 52.

7. 'Pension Age', Memorandum by the Department of Health and Social Security (1976), p. 18.

8. *The Times*, 19 September 1976.

9. For a fuller account of the unequal treatment of women see, H. Land, 'Women: Supporters or Supported?' in S. Allan and D. Barker (eds.), *Sexual Divisions in Society: Process and Change* (1976).

10. Department of Health and Social Security, *Report by the Government Actuary on the Financial Pensioners: The Social Security Pension Bill*, Cmnd 5928 (1975), p. 8.

11. Ibid., p. 18.

12. Prior to the enactment of the 1975 legislation they received unemployment and sickness benefit at two-thirds the rate for men and single women.

13. 'Normal household duties' include shopping, planning meals, cooking, cleaning, ironing, etc.

14. Office of Population Censuses and Surveys, *General Household Survey 1979* (1981), p. 77.

15. Ibid., p. 163.

16. For example, in 1978 only 18 per cent of women with no children had part-time employment, 67 per cent had full-time employment. The figures for women with two children were 39 per cent and 14 per cent. Office of Population Censuses and Surveys, *General Household Survey 1978* (1980), p. 98.

17. *Proposal for Tax Credit Scheme*, Cmnd 5116 (1972).

18. See, for example, Equal Opportunities Commission, *With All My Worldly Goods I Thee Endow . . . Except my Tax Credits* (1979).

19. Section 37 of the Income and Corporation Taxes Act 1970 states 'A woman's income chargeable to income tax shall (for any year) during which she is a married woman living with her husband be deemed for income tax purposes to be his income and not to be her income.'

20. See, for example: R. Lister, *Social Priorities in Taxation* (1981); and Equal Opportunities Commission, *Response to the Government's Green Paper* (1981).

21. For an account of the introduction of child benefits, see H. Land, 'The Child Benefit Fiasco' in K. Jones, S. Baldwin and M. Brown (eds.), *The Year Book of Social Policy, 1976* (1977).

22. See: H. Land, 'Sex Role Stereotyping in the Income Maintenance and Tax Systems' in J. Chetwynd and O. Hartnett, *The Sex-Role System* (1978).

23. *The Taxation of Husband and Wife*, Cmnd 8093 (1980), p. 24.

24. Ibid., p. 24.

25. In the vast majority of these couples the wife is over 40 years of age, so it would be possible to have transitional arrangements to avoid hardships, although many will be in the higher-income groups.

26. *Taxation of Husband and Wife*, Cmnd 8093, p. 27.

27. Ibid., p. 29.

28. Ibid., p. 31.

29. Ibid., p. 32.

30. Lone parents can claim a larger child benefit, worth £3.30 more than child benefit in 1982.

31. *Taxation of Husband and Wife*, Cmnd 8093, p. 42.

32. Law Commission, *The Financial Consequences of Divorce: The Basic Policy. A Discussion Paper*, Cmnd 8041 (1980).

33. Law Commission, *The Financial Consequences of Divorce*, HC 68 (1981).

34. Law Commission, *Financial Consequences of Divorce*, Cmnd 8041, p. 11.

35. Office of Population Censuses and Surveys, *Population Trends 26* (1981), p. 7.

36. Matrimonial Causes Act 1973, Section 25.

37. Law Commission, *Financial Consequences of Divorce*, Cmnd 8041, p. 11.

38. Ibid., p. 35.

39. See Occupational Pensions Board, *Equal Status for Men and Women in Occupational Pension Schemes*, Cmnd 6599 (1976).

40. Equal Opportunities Commission, *The Experience of Caring for Elderly and Handicapped Dependants* (1980).

41. In 1980, 46 per cent of civil servants were women. Out of 813 officers who were in the key policy-making positions at under-secretary level or above only 31 were women. In contrast women are 66 per cent of clerical officers and 86 per cent of data processors.

42. Co-operative Women's Guild, *Memorandum on the National Care of Maternity* (1917).

5 SEX EQUALITY AND SOCIAL SECURITY[1]

Brian Abel-Smith

Although much has been written about sex equality in terms of job
opportunities, pay, and roles in the home, and a certain amount about
income tax, the whole question of sex equality in social security has
been an under explored area, except perhaps in the context of pensionable age. This paper attempts to open up the area for wider discussion.
It does not attempt to cover every type of social-security provision, but
rather concentrates on those benefits which are drawn by the largest
number of persons in Britain. Provisions for the disabled are, for
example, excluded. After a brief discussion of definitions, there is a
short historical introduction explaining the process by which we
drifted into sex inequality in our social-security arrangements. The
rest of the paper discusses ways in which the present discrimination
between the sexes could be eliminated.

Definitions

The term 'social security' is interpreted here broadly. It is misleadingly
narrow to think simply in terms of national insurance, supplementary
benefits and other means-tested benefits. We need also to consider
occupational benefits. Second, we need to take account of relevant
personal allowances in the income tax—what have now come to be
recognised in public-expenditure White Papers as 'tax expenditures'.
Third, we have to consider relevant subsidies and provisions in kind,
which also contribute to income support, such as housing subsidies
and provisions for the care of children and others.

The term 'sex equality' is capable of different interpretations. Five
are defined below. The first is what might be called *actuarial sex
equality*. Under this definition, differences in treatment between the
sexes can be justified, if there are cost differences in providing benefits.
Thus, for example, if women live about six years longer than men, it is
not a breach of actuarial sex equality to give women lower pensions
from the same age as men, or alternatively to require women to pay a
higher contribution for the same level of benefit at the same age or, as a
third option, to have a later pension age for women than for men.

This interpretation of sex equality has long operated in occupational pension schemes. It was introduced into state pensions by the Boyd Carpenter graduated-pension scheme which has now been wound up (although the additions to pensions are still being paid). In its progressive report of 1976 the Occupational Pensions Board recommended that the test of equal status should be equal benefits not the actuarial cost of providing packages of benefits.[2]

This brings us to the second interpretation: what might be called *insurance-status sex equality*. Under this definition the two sexes have to be provided with the same rights to benefits. Objective differences in risk have to be averaged between the sexes, for example, differences in expectation of life, or the risks of sickness or unemployment. Differences in the level of benefits received on account of differences in periods of contribution or their amount are still justified.

A third interpretation is *citizenship sex equality*. Under this definition, citizenship gives rights to identical benefits. Whether the money is raised by taxes or what are called contributions, there is no relationship between what is or is not paid by the individual and what is received. Our national health service is based on this principle and so are child benefits.

A fourth interpretation might be called *positive sex equality*, on the analogy of positive discrimination. Under this definition the amount of contributions paid is allowed to determine the level of benefits obtained, but special credits or other provisions are built into the system to secure more equal benefits—by providing contribution credits for those who perform socially approved functions such as providing for the care of young children or of other social dependants, or to prevent the full rigour of unequal earnings being reflected in the benefits paid to either sex. Inevitably, the application of this criterion requires explicit social judgements about what is fair, judged in terms of the benefits paid out. But the important point is that precisely the same social judgements are applied to either sex. Positive discrimination can easily be applied in such a way that it involves sex discrimination, for example, by providing benefits for women but not for men as dependants. This was a marked feature of the Beveridge scheme, as pointed out later in this paper.

A fifth definition might be called *sex-role equality*. It too involves positive discrimination, but the primary aim is not to make *benefits* more equal but to enable *roles* to be more equal, although it may also have the former result. The purpose is to facilitate equal participation in paid work and allow both sexes to have a work 'career'. Measures to promote sex-role equality can be 'work biased', for example, free or subsidised care facilities for the children and other dependants of persons working outside the home. Or they can be 'work neutral': cash allowances which can be used to buy care from others (for example, minders or day nurseries) or to maintain the person providing the care for their own dependants.

Historical Development of Sex Inequality

Why and when did sex inequality in its varied forms come to be built into the social-security system we have today? It is a characteristic of any system of social security that a right to a benefit given by one government is extremely rarely taken away by a later one, although of course certain benefits can be left to rot by inflation, as has happened, for example, to the death grant. Thus over time a social-security system tends to become an increasingly complex inheritance of provisions, some based on outdated social assumptions, others implanted from rash manifesto commitments or conceded as ill-advised political sweeteners — an accumulation of the prejudices and bribes of past politicians, many of them in a hurry, whether to buy off opposition, win an election or simply a day's debate.

The 1908 old-age pension as finally passed was a model of sex equality, whatever the criticism that can be made of its tests of morality and of means. It provided five shillings for men and five shillings for women, whether single, married or widowed, and it provided this amount for both sexes at the same age of 70. What is interesting is that the Bill as originally presented to Parliament provided that two *persons* living together should get 7s 6d instead of 10s.[3] This formulation was abandoned during the progress of the legislation not so much because it would often involve sex discrimination, but because it was thought to involve anomalies, possibilities of evasion and administrative difficulties.

Unlike the 1908 old-age-pension scheme, provision for cash benefit in sickness was based in 1911 on contributory insurance. With national health insurance came notions of *actuarial sex equality*. Although the scheme provided flat-rate benefits, these were higher for men than for women. And from 1933 married women received a still lower level of benefit than single women because of their higher rate of claims.[4]

No extra benefits were added on to sickness benefit for wives and children until 1948. But additions for such dependants were introduced into unemployment insurance in 1921 as a cheap way of keeping more men off the poor law.[5] But these dependants' additions were also available to married women on the same terms.

Meanwhile, the means test applied to old-age pensions was coming under attack as a tax on thrift. But the old-age pension did not simply become a non-means-tested demogrant and thus establish the principle of *citizenship equality* at the base of our pension system. Instead, the contributory principle, as applied in 1925, introduced sex inequality to pensions. Men who had contributed to national health insurance became entitled to pensions at the age of 65 and by their contributions also conferred pensions on their wives if they were also 65. This meant that the married woman got no extra pension from working and thus contributing. No provision was made for a woman aged 65 to confer a pension on her husband.

But the principle of equal pensions paid at the same age survived until 1940. It was in this year that the decision to lower the pension age to 60 for women only was taken. This was a curious concession to fight off TUC and Labour Party pressure for an increase in the level of the pension.[6] It is true that the TUC was also worried at the same time about couples where the husband was older than the wife (the more usual case), who were not able to start drawing their pensions at the same time. The government met this subsidiary worry of the TUC by lowering the pension age of women as a sweetener for refusing to raise the level of the pension. The solution of allowing either younger partner in a marriage to draw pension subject to an earnings test when one partner reached 65 appears not to have been considered. This is strange in so far as Beveridge was to propose such a provision two years later, though only for men. The decision to lower the pension age was disastrous, because the cost of remedying it now by the politically easy way of lowering the pension age for men would be so great. It was also disastrous in so far as it set the pattern which occupational pensions have largely followed. It even seems to have established the perceived age for abdication.

The 1925 Act also introduced contributory pensions for widows, but not for widowers. Lloyd George had originally wanted to provide relatively generous pensions for widowed mothers and orphans, but not for childless widows, as the next step following the 1908 old-age-pensions legislation. But the opposition of the friendly societies made him abandon the idea. When, by 1925, the friendly societies had withdrawn their opposition, benefits of 10s a week for all widows were introduced in the hastily prepared 1925 Act without any tests of age, health, earnings or other conditions, despite the opposition of the trade unions, who feared that childless widows, if given pensions, might undercut wages. The decision was largely taken as an expensive way of providing for widowed mothers whose children had grown up. The option of a special high rate of pension for widowed mothers was rejected because it was thought that it would make it impossible to defend a lower rate of old-age pension – by then also 10s a week.[7] It would not have been possible to argue that widowed mothers needed more money than old-age pensioners.

Of course, it is easy to look back and criticise formative decisions taken in an inter-war period so dominated by high unemployment that it was commonly accepted that married women should stand aside to give such jobs as were available to men. It is, however, somewhat more justifiable to criticise Sir William (later Lord) Beveridge for failing to see the full implications of one of the key assumptions on which his report of 1942 was built: full employment. Despite what was happening during the Second World War, he did not expect the trend for married women to take paid work to continue in peacetime. He did not see the implications of a lower birth-rate and of more efficient reproduction (reduced miscarriage, still births and infant mortality). After the war he expected things to return to 'normal'. 'During marriage', he wrote, 'most women will not be gainfully employed. The small minority who undertake paid employment . . . after marriage require special treatment.'[8] He resisted the demands of the women's organisations that women be placed on the same footing as men, on the grounds that the vast majority of married women were dependent on their husbands. 'Social Insurance should be geared to the needs of the majority and not to the needs of an atypical minority.'[9]

Built into the Beveridge Report was what seems today to be incredibly crude chauvinism; for example, the assertion that 'On marriage a woman gains a legal right to maintenance . . . she undertakes at the same time to perform vital unpaid services'.[10] Did he mean housework or sex or both?

The 'special treatment' Beveridge meted out to married women was highly discriminatory. They were to lose on marriage whatever entitlement they had earned to the full rate of sickness and unemployment benefits, and only receive around 75 per cent of the sickness and unemployment benefit available to a man or single woman. They were also to be denied rights to dependency additions to sickness benefit for their husbands, although these were to be given to husbands for wives, unless the husband was 'incapable of self-support'. Their pensions by virtue of marriage were to be cut from 100 per cent of a man's or a single woman's to about 60 per cent. Their own contributions could thus only earn them 40 per cent of the pension rights received by men and single women because of the 60 per cent of their rights which came automatically from their husbands. And they were to be given an option not to contribute at all, which it would often be impossible for them to know how to exercise, because of all the uncertainties underlying the calculations (a woman had to contribute for half the years between marriage and pension age to get the extra pension). Most strange of all was Beveridge's tacit acceptance of the lower age of pension for women, introduced only two years earlier. It had been argued that this was justified because wives were normally younger than their husbands. His plan gave an increased pension to a man who was married however much younger his wife might be. He had, therefore, directly met the complaint about a common pension age of 65. This left no rationale for a pension age of 60 for single women and wives who had earned their own pensions. But in the process, Beveridge made married women into social-security dependants on a scale unequalled today by the vast majority of social-security schemes, in the world, even in the Arab world.

In the case of widows under pension age, Beveridge proposed an almost complete return to the principle Lloyd George had had in mind some thirty-five years earlier. Apart from a transition benefit of thirteen weeks, widows' benefits were to be entirely confined to widows with dependent children and even these were to be subjected to an earnings rule. Once those children grew up, the only provision was to be by public assistance. He did, however, want in principle to see a similar benefit for involuntarily deserted, divorced or separated wives,[11] but not for unmarried mothers. The problems of widowers and separated men are not even mentioned in his report.

Let us look more closely at Beveridge's social assumptions, what he called 'economic facts'[12] — which still underlie our social-security arrangements, although they are much less valid today than they were forty years ago. *First*, that men never have an interrupted work career, whereas married women always do. How else can we explain benefits for widows and not for widowers? *Second*, that a widow and never a widower will be out of paid work when there is a dependent child in the family whether the age of that child is 1, 3, 5, 10 or 16. How else do we explain the widowed mother's allowance without provision for any sort of widowed father's allowance? *Third*, that housework rather than paid work is the normal whole-time occupation of a legal wife.

How else do we explain the extra benefit for the dependent wife which is paid irrespective of whether there are or have been any children of the marriage? *Fourth*, that it is improper for men to do housework or care for children. How else do we explain the fact that no dependant allowance is paid for the husband of the unemployed or sick wife, unless he is disabled? And how else do we explain the fact that an allowance for a housekeeper or child-minder is only payable for a female?[13] Beveridge clearly did not envisage male 'gay' couples living together.

Beveridge's discriminatory treatment of women was implemented by the Labour government in the 1946 Act. They did, however, modify the abrupt change in the provision for widows. The old 10s widow's pension under the 1925 Act was kept going, but allowed to rot with inflation until 1964, when it was tripled and has been increased regularly since. Those becoming widowed at 50 or ceasing to care for dependent children at age 50 or over became entitled to a continuing benefit at the new higher rate. No provision was made for divorced, separated or deserted wives. And nothing was done for widowers. A vital change made in 1964 was to abolish the earnings rule as it applied to widows' benefits.

What the Beveridge scheme actually secured by its option for married women was the exclusion of the majority of them from their own right to social-security benefits. This majority had no rights to sickness and unemployment benefit and no possibility of achieving a pension equal to that of their husbands. This would have been less important, if the pension rate for a couple was such that mean-tested supplementation was unnecessary. But this has never been the case.

What is remarkable is that it took thirty years for this damage to be repaired in one major respect. From April 1978 married women have been required to contribute (with preserved rights for those who had already opted out). They not only earn full rights to the old Beveridge flat-rate benefits, but are also able to earn on top rights to the new earnings-related element of pension.

The solution found to the problem of persons, usually women, withdrawing from the labour force for family reasons has been to disregard years spent by *persons* caring for young children or dependent relatives, but they still need twenty years of contributions to get a full flat-rate pension. Moreover, the new earnings-related element of pensions is based on the best twenty years of earnings, which may be-before or after marriage. This is a remarkably progressive example of *positive sex equality*, as defined above.

Current Issues

Survivors over Pension Age

And what about the provision for survivors over pension age? It has long been the case that widows are the poorest group among the aged. The solution introduced by the 'better pensions' scheme – the 1975 Act – was to allow widows to take over their husband's basic pension rights, if they were more favourable, and add any earnings-related rights of their own up to the maximum of the scheme. This provision is also available for widowers, another excellent example of *positive sex equality*. But it is restricted, in so far as both parties must be over pension age for this addition to the survivor's pension to be made.

Dependant's Additions to Sickness and Unemployment Benefit

We have also recently allowed additions for dependants to be added on to sickness and unemployment benefit on the same terms, whichever party to the marriage is claiming the benefit. This was, however, to meet the requirements of the EEC directive on equal treatment in social security.[14] It does not mean that we can claim to have achieved *insurance-status sex equality*, let alone *sex-role equality*. What is currently required by the EEC directive is a modest first step. There are critical exclusions: unequal pension ages are still allowed; survivors' benefits are not covered by the directive; nor are entitlements to old-age or invalidity benefits by virtue of the derived entitlements of a wife; nor are additions to long-term invalidity or occupational-disease benefits for a dependent wife. Let us examine these issues in turn.

Unequal Pension Age

The lower pension age for women, hastily and almost casually granted in 1940, is a right which it is politically difficult to take away. The politically easy option of lowering the pension age for men to 60 should not be adopted, despite TUC support for it. Moreover, I personally do not favour the compromise of a common pension age at 63 – the idea floated by the Equal Opportunities Commission in its report of 1978.[15] First, money would be better spent in raising the level of pension and other benefits, particularly child benefit. Second, I do not believe that this is what most men want. Many people think they want early retirement until they are retired. Of course, there are exceptions in some particularly physically unpleasant and demanding occupations such as mining, for which special occupational provision either has been or can be made. I am all in favour of flexible pension ages and a gradual transition from work to retirement.. But this has still to take place in specified age-bands. If we want to share work opportunities more fairly, then there are in my view many better alternative ways of doing it, such as the 4½-day or 4-day working week, longer holidays, sabbaticals, etc. Eventually the differential in favour of women needs to be removed. And I do not think it politically impossible to achieve it, provided the change is agreed, or at least blessed, by the main political parties through, perhaps, a Select Committee of the House of Commons and provided the change takes place gradually – an extra year added to the pension age for women every three or five years until equality is finally attained at age 65 for both sexes.

Survivors with Dependent Children before Pension Age

Provision for survivors before pension age still discriminates against men; widowers do not enjoy the same rights as widows. Let us consider, first, provision for cases where there are dependent children. The widowed mother obtains a flat-rate benefit plus an element related to her deceased husband's earnings and possibly an occupational benefit as well. On top of all this, she can supplement her pension or pensions by earnings without loss of pension rights. The widowed mother may be a doctor back in full-time work before her husband died with children at school. Her husband may have been a low-paid parson. If she had died, no pension would have gone to him.

To extend the full provision for the widow to the widower would be unduly generous to many men, as it already is to some women. Most men left with the care of young children are at work and stay on at work.[16] But they do normally have to pay to have their children looked after. If it were possible to make a new start, at least the full earnings-related element of a parental-survivor benefit could be restricted to cases where the dead spouse was earning substantially more than the surviving spouse. Moreover, the levels of flat-rate benefit should be lower, perhaps 60 per cent of the full rate. Thus the level of benefit might be this lower flat-rate plus (say) half of the difference between the two levels of earnings up to the maximum of the scheme. Benefits for children would, of course, be paid in all cases. It is because the widowed mother's benefit is so generous when paid on top of earnings that it has not been extended to widowers.

Other One-parent Families

For the same reason, the widowed mother's benefit has not been extended to other one-parent families. It was to prevent one-parent families attaining a level of benefit-plus-earnings which would seem grossly unfair to young couples struggling to bring up a family on one low wage and inadequate family allowances that the Finer Committee favoured an income test on their proposed benefit.[17]

The income-tax provision for one-parent families is non-discriminatory. An additional allowance, equivalent to the difference between the single allowance and the married allowance, is available both to male single parents and to female single parents, irrespective of the cause of one-parent status. Like other tax allowances, it gives greater help to those with high incomes because it can be used against higher-rate tax. On the other hand, it is of no use to the one-parent family living on supplementary benefit because this source of income is not subject to tax. The introduction of a benefit for one-parent families could be paid for in part by the abolition of the additional personal allowance.[18]

I personally would argue that a basic benefit as of right of 60 per cent of the basic pension could be paid to all one-parent families, whether headed by men or women, without creating a sense of unfairness among one-wage, two-parent families or too much outcry from single women who have avoided getting into the position of having a child and view unfavourably those who have. To this could be added the earnings-related element mentioned earlier for survivors, male or female, based on the difference in earnings,[19] and the additions for each child. This would go some way towards the Finer Committee's objective of giving the single parent a practicable option to take paid work. It would, however, be extremely difficult to secure a transition from a benefit for widows calculated on the present basis to a benefit for one-parent families calculated on the less generous basis I am proposing. Politically, the widows' premium is likely to remain with us like the premium for injury caused at work.

Survivors without Dependent Children under Pension Age

What about survivors without the care of dependent children? In terms of social priority the indiscriminate provision of a full widow's benefit to women widowed at age 50 or over (and a reduced rate from age 40) is clearly the most wasteful provision in the whole of our social-security system. It comes irrespective of whether she ever had the care of young children or other dependants, irrespective of whether she married at age 49 or at age 18, irrespective of whether she has or has not been in full-time work through her years of marriage, and irrespective of whether she is earning more or less than her dead husband. A widow's benefit can, moreover, be blindly paid on top of full and substantial work income. This seems a more important issue than whether some families are better off on benefit than at work. Savings here could help to pay for improvements elsewhere in our social-security scheme which are badly needed. If the present over-50 provision for widows were applied unamended to widowers, there would rightly be an outcry from single people. If widowers were given what is, in effect, an allowance to pay for a housekeeper, why not other single people who go out to work?

The Women's Liberation Campaign for Legal and Financial Independence told the Occupational Pensions Board that widow's pensions were objectionable because they perpetuate the assumption that women are financially dependent on men.[20] I would not go as far as this. If it is right to compensate a wife for the loss of her husband's earnings, is it not right to compensate the husband for the loss of his wife's earnings, provided the surviving spouse really does suffer a loss? Where the wife earned substantially more than the husband (for example, where the wife is a doctor and the husband a parson), there can be no financial loss warranting compensation if the husband dies. If, on the other hand, the wife dies, there would at present be no compensation paid, despite the clear justification for paying it, with the one small exception of allowing him to use her earnings-related entitlement for his invalidity benefit, if this would be more favourable than to use his own. An unpopular solution would be to reintroduce the earnings rule at the present somewhat higher level, where it is applied to the retirement pension, and allow both sexes to apply for the benefit. But this would create a 'low-income trap', where extra earnings led to no extra income. An alternative is to base the benefit on the excess earnings (if any) of the deceased spouse in the case of new claimants as above.

By 1971 the widows of most men covered by occupational pension schemes were entitled to a pension. These were usually paid irrespective of the age of the widow and of whether she had any children, and there was rarely any test of financial dependency on the husband. In some cases there was discretion to award a pension to a cohabitee. Widowers' pensions were rarely provided and, where they were, there was usually a dependency test which was not applied to widows. This was partly because it is only recently that the Inland Revenue has allowed them to be provided as part of a scheme which could benefit from tax concessions.

As part of the contracting-out provisions to the new pension scheme, widows' pensions have to be provided to widows entitled to provision under the state scheme. The Occupational Pensions Board considered the question of widowers' pensions in their report of 1976 and concluded that, as resources permit, whatever provision made for widows' pensions in occupational pension schemes should apply equally to widowers.[21] They also concluded that when schemes provide cover for children this should be available on the same terms for men and women members, and that provision should be made wherever practicable without regard to the marital status of the member. Both these recommendations go further than the provision in the state scheme. It is to be regretted that the Board did not face up to this critical social issue and either recommend some sort of dependency test for both sexes or some such provision as I have outlined above.

Loss of Pension Rights on Divorce

Before leaving the question of survivors' benefits, I must mention a further problem – the loss of the prospective rights to a pension in cases of divorce. Under the state scheme a woman loses her rights to a widow's pension on divorce, but can use her husband's contribution record towards her retirement pension for the years of the marriage. Since 1978, a divorced man has also been able to use his spouse's record. If a woman is divorced at age 60 or over, her pension becomes the same as if she were a widow. A man divorced at age 65 or over gets the same pension as if he were still married.

Any rights to an occupational pension as a widow, not just before but also after pension age, are lost on divorce. If there were any rights to a widower's benefit, these would also be lost. Thus loss of prospective occupational pension rights in old age can be, and have been, a cogent reason for women to refuse to agree to a divorce. Where, as is often the case, the husband is not in a position to make a lump-sum payment to compensate for loss of pension rights, the courts can and have refused to allow a divorce. Thus we have some marriages held together not by the desire of either party to remain together, but by the understandable wish of the wife to retain the rights to a pension should her husband die before she does. Unlike the state scheme, an occupational pension scheme cannot be stretched to provide pensions for two wives, one of them divorced.

The solution recommended by the Occupational Pensions Board was for the courts to have the right to order that part of the widow's occupational pension should be paid to the divorced wife as part of the divorce settlement.[22] I personally would prefer the arrangement operating in the Netherlands, under which rights to widows' pensions are distributed among successive wives according to the duration of each marriage. This solution also seems right for the state scheme and should apply to survivor benefits for both parties to the marriage. Thus although marriages can be dissolved, rights to pension cover earned during them cannot. This is particularly important in an age of greater divorce and remarriage. I do not accept the Occupational Pensions Board's criticism of this proposal: that it could lead to trivial benefits for young childless widows.[23] This seems to me a criticism of schemes which provide such benefits. If the scheme is unwise in providing that a widow should receive a benefit for which there is little or no social justification, then it seems to me wrong for divorce to take away this right. This is another example of the unwillingness of the Board to face up to the question of in what circumstances survivors' benefits are justified.

Additions to Benefit for the Dependent Wife

If we are serious about sex equality, either we have to extend the spouse's addition to long-term benefits to married women on the same terms as to married men or abolish it, possibly by extinguishing it in an increase in benefit to the single. In the case of pensions there is a simple solution. The dependant's addition is paid to the wife as a 'by virtue' pension. In effect, it is a fall-back pension of 60 per cent of the basic rate. It could hardly be very expensive to extend a similar fall-back 'by virtue' pension to the husband who reaches pension age after his wife. Similarly, dependants' additions to pension could be made payable to both parties of the marriage, but a special provision would be needed to prevent partners to the marriage who had retired with a substantial occupational pension claiming for a spouse who was still at work. This would be particularly important for wives retiring at the age of 60 or earlier. Alternatively, both provisions could be phased out as the new pension scheme matures.[24] This is the better solution, as it is not possible to define a dependant in a way which does not involve anomalies. At present, apart from men claiming for their wives, men or women can claim for certain *female* dependent relatives, but not cohabitants of the same or opposite sex unless they are *women* caring for children.

Before we go on to consider the addition for a wife to other long-term benefits, we need to bring into account the parallel and much older provision for the dependent wife on the income tax. This comes in the form of the larger tax allowance available to a married man than is available to a single man or single woman. It is available whatever the age of the wife, whether she is working or not, and whether there are dependent children or not, and even whether she actually resides with him or not. In addition, a wife who earns is entitled to a wife's earned income relief, which is at the same rate as the personal allowance available to a single man or single woman. The total effect discriminates between the sexes. If the man works and the wife does not, the only tax allowance claimable is that of the married man. If, on the other hand, the wife works and the husband does not, not only can the man claim the married allowance against her income, but in addition he can claim his wife's income relief. So a couple's tax allowances are higher or lower than those of two single people, depending on who does the earning. If the husband and wife have equal earning capacity and one decides to stay at home to look after the children, it is financially advantageous for the man to act as housewife.

This question was discussed by the Equal Opportunities Commission and a number of alternative solutions were considered.[25] The option which attracted me most was to restrict the extra help now given to all married couples to those who were caring for social dependants on the same basis as the credits given in the new pension scheme. Thus extra help would be provided when a dependent child (or an adult receiving an attendance allowance) was living with the married couple. But the question which immediately arises is whether the allowance would not be better provided in the form of a cash benefit like a child benefit rather than as a tax relief. A non-taxable cash benefit could be claimed by whichever party to the marriage was caring for or providing for the dependant or dependants. It would be a flat rate unlike a tax allowance which can be set against higher-rate tax. Thus, in effect, it would become either an enhanced rate of child benefit or an enhanced rate of invalid-care allowance (extended to married women). Like the existing married allowance, it would be paid irrespective of whether the claimant was in paid work or not. It would be up to the claimant to decide whether to care for the dependant(s), to pay for someone else to do so at home or in a day nursery, etc. If the new care allowance was introduced on the same day as the addition for the dependent wife in long-term benefit was withdrawn, the remaining amount needing to be absorbed in a rise in benefit would be that much less. The same level of care allowance paid whether or not there was an earner would help, like child benefit, to reduce the extent to which benefits received when not at work could be greater than work income. The disadvantage, as with the switch from child tax allowances to child benefits, is that it would bring more poor families into tax.

Towards Sex-role Equality

Most important of all, this would be an important step towards what I have called *sex-role equality*. At first sight, progress in this direction appears to have been considerable. The economic activity rates for married women aged 25-34 rose from over 9 per cent in 1921 to over 38 per cent in 1971, and for those aged 20-24 from 12.5 per cent in 1921 to nearly 46 per cent in 1971.[26] On the other hand, maternity still generally appears to cause a break in work career. Although the position may be better now, in 1965 a survey showed that only about 6 per cent of married women returned to the same employer after a break in service.

Since then we have introduced the Employment Protection Act of 1974. Under this Act, a pregnant employee with two years' service has the right to maternity pay which, with maternity allowance, amounts to 90 per cent of full pay for six weeks. She has the right of giving notice to return to her job or a not less favourable job within twenty-nine weeks of the birth of her child. These provisions are nevertheless inadequate. First, the period of protected employment is too short. Second, the requirement of two years' service is too tough. Third, there is no provision for the father to take leave to look after his child, if at some stage that is the preferred arrangement. In Sweden a parental allowance is payable for whichever parent stays at home to look after a child for 210 days.[27]

In addition, we need a rate of child benefit which is a higher proportion of average earnings and a major extension of a variety of alternative arrangements for the care of young children. To go into the detail of all this would take me far from my main theme. Moreover, it is by no means clear how suitable arrangements for the care of young children can best be developed. What is certain, however, is that mothers with young children have been the most rapidly expanding section of the labour force. Mothers are voting with their feet, despite the present gross inadequacy of child-care arrangements and of cash provision for parents. How best to provide for *sex-role equality* will, I am convinced, force itself high on the political agenda during the next decade.

Conclusion

The social assumptions from which the main fabric of our social-security system was woven have been radically changed over the past forty years. So have Beveridge's narrowly perceived 'economic facts'. Our social-security system is in a state of incomplete adaptation as new social attitudes and behaviours are competing with older attitudes and behaviours. The problem is how to make the transition, and to do this without making our system so complex that it is neither comprehensible to its users nor to those whose task it is to administer it.

Notes

1. This paper is based upon a Sidney Ball Lecture delivered at Nuffield College, Oxford on 8 February 1980. The author wishes to acknowledge with gratitude comments on an earlier draft and assistance from Alan Deacon, David Donnison, Mike Reddin and Peter Townsend and others.
2. Occupational Pensions Board, *Equal Status for Men and Women in Occupational Pension Schemes*, Cmnd 6599 (1976), para. 6.29.
3. B. Abel-Smith, 'Social Security' in M. Ginsberg (ed.), *Law and Opinion in England in the Twentieth Century* (1959), p. 365.
4. H. Levy, *National Health Insurance* (1944), p. 66.
5. Such additions also reflected the extra provisions for wives and children which were part of the armed forces' pay and had been carried forward with the temporary 'dole' for discharged servicemen. See B.B. Gilbert, *British Social Policy, 1914-39* (1970), p. 85.
6. Sir John Walley, *Social Security: Another British Failure?* (1972), p. 69.
7. Ibid., p. 69.
8. Sir William Beveridge, *Social Insurance and Allied Services* (the Beveridge Report), Cmd 6404 (1942), para. 111.
9. Jose Harris, *William Beveridge* (1977), p. 404.
10. Beveridge, *Social Insurance*, Cmd 6404, para. 108.
11. He recognised that he had not resolved the administrative problem in securing this. See Department of Health and Social Security, *Report of the Committee on One-Parent Families*, Cmnd 5629 (1973), vol. II (1974), pp. 136-41.
12. Harris, *William Beveridge*, p. 404.
13. A similar assumption is made in our income-tax allowances. A housekeeper's allowance can only be claimed for a female, not a male housekeeper.
14. *Directive of the Progressive Implementation of the Principle of Equal Treatment for Men and Women in Matters of Social Security* (79/7/EEC).
15. Equal Opportunities Commission, *Equalising the Pension Age* (1978).
16. In 1971, about 56 per cent of widows with dependent children were economically active compared with 91 per cent of widowers with dependent children (Occupational Pensions Board, *Equal Status for Men and Women*, para. 10.5).
17. Department of Health and Social Security, *Report of Committee on One-Parent Families*, Cmnd 5629.
18. The additional personal allowance performs a second function as it is also available to a man whose wife is totally incapacitated where there is a dependent child. This allowance could also be turned into a cash benefit and paid to a disabled spouse. There would, however, be difficult decisions to be taken on what other benefits could be received in addition to it.

19. Periods of sickness or invalidity benefit preceding death would be excluded.

20. Occupational Pensions Board, *Equal Status for Men and Women*, para. 10.25.

21. Ibid., para. 111.

22. Ibid., para. 13.56.

23. Ibid., para. 13.48.

24. Equal Opportunities Commission, *Equalising the Pension Age*, p. 28.

25. Equal Opportunities Commission, *Income Tax and Sex Discrimination* (1977).

26. Occupational Pensions Board, *Equal Status for Men and Women*, para. 12.4.

27. Ibid., para. 11.2.

6 WOMEN AND HEALTH POLICY

Ann Oakley

Women are both major consumers and major producers in the health-care business. They have a double role as biological reproducers of the population and as producers of the labour force in the wider sense of constituting the social group responsible for overseeing the health and welfare of families. In both these capacities it has historically been women's function to utilise and provide health care. Today in Britain women form a majority of workers in the health-care industry and also outnumber men as users of the health services. In this chapter I shall look at the part women play in both sides of the health-care equation, and at how those aspects of social policy which determine patterns of health care affect the fate of women as a group. My argument will be that health policy reflects and helps to maintain gender divisions that characterise society as a whole. In this sense medicine is a form of social control: a way of putting women in their place – wherever that place is thought to be.

When Did You Last See Your Doctor? Women as Patients

More patients are women because there are more women in the population and women become patients for reasons to do with child-bearing, which men do not. Rates of admission to non-psychiatric hospitals are higher for women than men, but only marginally so when pregnancy and childbirth as reasons for admission are excluded.[1] Admissions by sex and diagnostic group for mental-illness hospitals and units in England in 1977 show that about 60 per cent of mental patients are women; the categories in which there is the greatest excess of women are those relating to depression, neurosis and psychosis.[2] General practitioners also see a preponderance of female patients. Table 6.1 is taken from the health section of the 1977 General Household Survey; 11 per cent of women and 8 per cent of men had consulted a general practitioner about health problems in the previous fourteen days.

One problem about such statistics is that they are only a very crude measure of the health or morbidity of the population. Health is an

Table 6.1: Persons Consulting a General Practitioner in the 14 Days before Interview about Health Problems, by Sex and Age, in Great Britain, 1977

Age	Males		Females	
	Percentage	Base = 100%	Percentage	Base = 100%
16-44	6	5,653	11	5,829
45-64	10	3,337	11	3,815
65-74	10	1,286	13	1,669
75 and over	13	453	14	1,001
Total	8	10,729	11	12,314

Source: Office of Population Censuses and Surveys, *General Household Survey* (1977), table 6.19, p. 89.

elusive concept; and what does it mean to be ill? One woman in an American survey said:

> I wish I knew what you mean by being sick. Sometimes I felt so bad I could curl up and die, but I had to go on because of the kids who have to be taken care of . . . How could I be sick? Some people can be sick anytime with anything, but most of us can't be sick, even when we need to be.[3]

Illness is socially defined. According to various epidemiological inquiries, a substantial amount of frank disease which 'ought' to convert people into patients does not do so, and between a quarter and a half of illness episodes are not, in fact, taken to doctors.[4] Conversely, providers of health care may disagree with self-styled patients as to whether they are 'really' ill or not. A third of all consultations in Ann Cartwright's recent study of general practice were deemed by doctors trivial, inappropriate or unnecessary.[5]

It is against this background—of the sociology of health and illness in general—that the particular position of women as users of health care must be set. Their position in society affects the kinds of health problems they are likely to get, the strategies they are likely to adopt when health problems occur, and the modes of treatment that are likely to be offered by the providers of health care to whom these problems are taken.

Biological sex differences are of some importance in this picture, not only in accounting for the exclusive use made by women of obstetric/gynaecological services, but in determining different risks and causes of mortality for males and females. Women appear to be less vulnerable than men to many common diseases of childhood and adulthood. For example, in middle age, men are 1.95 times more likely than women to die of heart disease, cancer, chest illness, kidney diseases and digestive disorders.[6] To the extent that occupation and life-style are linked to the risk of death, a narrowing of the social divisions between women and men might be expected to bring about some lessening of this differential. Lung cancer and ischaemic heart disease are two diseases for which this does seem currently to be happening: women are 'catching up' with men.[7]

As the *General Household Survey* and other data show, women are more prone than men to consult a doctor when they have a health problem. It has been suggested that this is because help-seeking is more concordant with the feminine than with the masculine role.[8] Investigation of people's sex-role stereotypes in health and illness does indicate that illness causes individuals to be viewed as having more feminine and fewer masculine characteristics than they do when well. However, the effect of illness on sex-typing is greater for men than women. Women's gender identities are apparently not so threatened by visits to the doctor as are men's.[9] Is this partly because doctors sex-type back? In a revealing study of general practitioners' attitudes to patients, Gerry Stimson asked which types of patients caused them most and least trouble. The least troublesome type of patient was defined as male, intelligent, employed and middle class with specific easily treatable organic illness. The most troublesome patient was female, 'inadequate', not employed, and working class with vague symptoms of psychiatric illness that were difficult to diagnose and treat.[10]

Such categorisation by gender has profound ramifications. One consequence is differential medical treatment. Presenting with similar symptoms, women are more susceptible than men to a 'diagnosis' of psychiatric, and particularly neurotic, disorder.[11] Women are prescribed more drugs than men, especially drugs of the psychotropic (mood-altering) variety. One study of five group practices showed that over a year 53.8 per cent of the men and 65.7 per cent of the women registered with these practices had received at least one drug. Psychotropic drugs were prescribed for 9.7 per cent of the men and 21.0 per cent of the women; psychotropic drug-prescribing was highest among middle-aged women (45-59 years), 33 per cent of whom were given such a drug.[12]

Encapsulated within medical ideologies of women are two principal themes: that of women's constant failure to withstand the ordinary strains of living; and their need to be 'readjusted' to a predominantly domestic situation. Both these are, of course, to some extent part and parcel of medical ideology as a whole. Doctors are trained to identify individual, not social, pathology. It is not their job to point out to someone in what ways her or his social circumstances are making them ill, nor to prescribe revolution. Neither is the pharmaceutical industry interested in revolution: only in expanding profits.[13] Yet a basically gender-divisive formula is in operation behind these common denominators of medical education and practice. When Broverman and colleagues asked clinicians to describe the characteristics of normal adult men, normal adult women and a 'healthy, mature, socially competent person', they found that healthy women were seen as submissive, unaggressive, excitable, emotional, easily hurt and incapable of objectivity compared with the standard for men.[14] Medical advertising for anti-depressants, tranquillisers, etc. focuses on the housewife as patient and beneficiary[15] (although in the United States in recent years the drug companies appear to have responded to allegations of bias by redressing the sex balance somewhat).[16]

It has become one of the functions of medicine in advanced industrial societies to call unhappiness disease and to locate its cause within the unhappy individual rather than the diseased social system. This is the medicalisation of which Illich speaks.[17] Because of the general difficulty and inherent contradictions of their social position, women are among the principal victims of this process. It is, of course, crucial that other social institutions and the state support the location of pathology in the individual. (Some instances of this in the case of women are discussed below.)

What Makes Women Ill? Social Causes of Ill Health in Women

The mental health of married women is considerably poorer than that of married men.[18] Conversely, unmarried women are at a relative advantage compared with unmarried men. It is difficult to avoid the conclusion reached by Jessie Bernard[19] and others, that the family and marriage as an institution suit men more than they suit women: that for men they come nearer to being 'the haven in a heartless world' of the dominant cultural mythology than they do for women, for whom they have a different meaning altogether.

The division of labour in marriage, which is buttressed by a whole range of state policies, still ensures that in most marriages most of the housework and child-rearing is done by women. There is no firm evidence that men are really shouldering this responsibility more than they did fifty or a hundred years ago, although there is evidence that in circumstances of marked segregation between the sexes the presence of a solitary all-female network (kin, neighbours, etc.) made this role a more autonomous and satisfactory one than it is today.[20] There is substantial evidence that the combination of housewife-wife-mother roles generates dissatisfaction and conflict, particularly when combined with the expectation, desire or reality of a paid work role as well.[21] Women may love their children (and their husbands) and derive great enjoyment from these relationships, but the fact is that such relationships do, for most women, involve hard labour and conflicting obligations. Housework compares with much industrial work in its monotony and fragmentation and with the psychological effects of unemployment in its lack of pay and social isolation.[22]

This reality of the female side of marriage is clouded by the mystification of marriage in our culture. Not only is marriage seen as equivalent to adulthood (95 per cent of men and 96 per cent of women currently achieve the marital state),[23] but the social pressure to marry, especially for women, is still extreme. What is portrayed in this pressure is not the harsh economics of a labour relationship in which she exchanges her sexual, domestic and childbearing services in return for his guaranteed upkeep,[24] but a quasi-mystical idea of sexual companionship and harmony for ever, a state in which children are seen to intrude not even as 'little troubles' but as great and untrammelled joys, and in which the personal relationship of husband and wife is one of unequalled intimacy and mutual pleasure. In fact men, in the form of male violence, pose one of the greatest of all health hazards to women, and it is the men women 'love' who are the most suspect: analysis of relationships between offenders and victims shows that a woman is most likely to be killed by someone she knows; 84 per cent of family violence or its threat is wife-assault;[25] a significant proportion of all wives are systematically beaten by their husbands.[26]

Aside from the question of whether or not they are beaten by their husbands, and irrespective of their labelling as depressed by the medical profession, it is the case that many married women do feel unhappy with, or at least in, the situation in which they find themselves, and much of this unhappiness goes uncounted in any statistics of health-care use. The classic study here was done by George Brown and Tirril Harris several years ago. Using a predominantly psychiatric definition of

depression, they found that 33 per cent of a random sample of women
in the community were suffering from definite psychiatric symptoms.
However, almost half of these had not been thus diagnosed or treated.
The women at highest risk of developing depression were working-class
women with young children; these women had the highest rates of
severe life events and chronic difficulties, and were least likely to see a
doctor about their depression.

Housework and motherhood as occupations are detrimental to
women's health, at least when performed under the conditions that
obtain in many industrialised communities today. It is difficult to be
exact about other links that may exist between women's occupations
and their health, because of the tendency not to collect data on women's
occupations and to rely instead on those of their husbands or fathers.
(The official statistical disdain for such information can be viewed as
a matter of overall 'policy' whereby the material basis for women's ill
health is rendered invisible.) The possibility of occupational health
hazards is most often raised in relation to pregnancy. It is known that
some occupations, for example that of anaesthetist,[27] carry an increased
risk of fetal loss. But until government and other statistics-producing
agencies systematically collect data on women's occupations, we are
not likely to know more about the health effects of different types of
employment for women.

These social causes of women's ill health cannot, of course, be
regarded as a matter of policy in the strict sense. However, they are a
consequence of the lack of any positive policy aimed at ameliorating
the condition of women in these areas of life. Looking at the protective
effect of employment on mothers' mental health, for instance, it is
immediately obvious that state provision of out-of-home child care
would enable more mothers to go out to work and to do without the
traditional medical remedy of a pharmacological adjustment to their
situation. Only 1 per cent of the public money spent on health,
education and social services in Britain in 1976 was used to provide the
type of child care needed by employed mothers; the government
provides full or part-time day care for only 13 per cent of under-5s
with employed mothers, and whenever any assessment of the unmet
demand for out-of-home childcare is made it is very substantial
indeed.[28] In the same way the absence of any policy to combat some
of the negative influences of marriage on women's health signifies
official support for its gender-differentiating effects. Examples would
be the asymmetrical burden of housework (an area defined as too
'personal' to fall within the scope of sex-discrimination legislation) and

the informal sanctioning by the police, other judicial bodies and the medical profession of the male 'right' to violence within marriage.

A Womb of One's Own: Reproduction and Health

Women's capacity to bear children is one very important and unique way in which they are affected by health policy. The resources available to them for preventing or promoting pregnancy and for managing pregnancy and childbirth are critical determinants not only of these reproductive experiences but of all others as well. Reproduction is one of the four structures identified by Mitchell[29] as forming the 'unity' of women's condition; it is one of the areas in which women may be either liberated or oppressed, either able to choose their own fate or forced to have it defined by others; but the point is that the freedom (or otherwise) which women have to determine their reproductive careers influences their exercise of all other freedoms.

Abortion

The 1967 Abortion Act in Britain defined the termination of pregnancy as a non-criminal offence when carried out before 28 weeks and with the certification of two medical practitioners to the effect that *either* the pregnancy is likely to end in the birth of an abnormal child *or* it is a danger to the mother's health. Figure 6.1 shows the impact of this legislation on deaths from illegal abortions in Britain. Illegal abortion is still — worldwide — a crucial strategy used by women for the prevention of unwanted births; for every five births there is probably one illegally induced abortion,[30] and in only a handful of countries is abortion freely available as the accepted right of pregnant women. Even where appropriate legislation exists, there is no guarantee that doctors will interpret it to mean that the pregnant woman's wishes should be respected. In Britain national health service abortions are matched by a roughly equal number in the private sector; different interpretations of the Act by different doctors mean that there is great regional variation in the proportion of abortions carried out in NHS hospitals — from 90 per cent in Newcastle to 23 per cent in Birmingham.[31] Moreover, NHS abortions tend to be done at a later stage in pregnancy than private ones, and one of the safest techniques for controlling reproduction, menstrual aspiration, has met with enormous resistance among doctors and those who formulate health policy, because of its dubious legal status as an abortion procedure (it

Figure 6.1: Death-rate per Million Maternities from Illegal Abortions, 1952-75

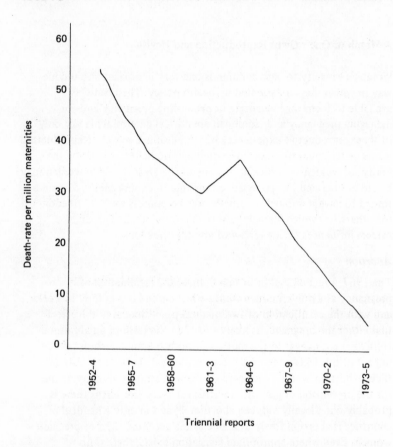

Source: Department of Health and Social Security, *Report on Confidential Enquiries into Maternal Deaths in 1973-5* (1979), p. 49.

is done before pregnancy can be reliably confirmed, which is its very advantage to women).

Surveys of medical attitudes have uncovered entrenched sexist opinions. General practitioners in Ann Cartwright's survey of *Parents and Family Planning Services* were asked if they thought a woman with several children should be able to get an abortion if she became pregnant and did not want another baby: only 22 per cent answered an unqualified 'yes' to this question, and 36 per cent gave an unqualified 'no'.[32] The doctor's personal moral values may be given the title of 'clinical freedom': it is this licence to control women's lives that was (and is) hotly defended by the professional medical bodies in the debate about just who is entitled to abortion on just what terms.[33]

The terms on which abortion and other means of fertility control are available to women reflect pro- or anti-natalist policies of governments in the widest sense. Such policies can theoretically have three aims: to increase the personal freedom of women, to improve national health and to control overall population trends. In practice the last two have dominated the picture in most countries. For example, James Mohr has shown that the evolution of a public abortion policy in nineteenth-century America had two main impetuses: the professional aggrandisement of doctors, and a governmental concern for the falling birth-rate and rise in the number of 'better class' women resorting to abortion as a means of family limitation.[34] It is important to note that the free availability of abortion may not indicate a policy of promoting women's liberation; in socialist countries such as the USSR the dominant ideology is often one of the woman's 'natural' obligation to motherhood, and the ebb and flow of abortion policies represents the state's attempt to match projected economic and population factors.[35]

Contraception

In the same way that the development of abortion practice and policy is the outcome of many influences (very few of which have anything to do with women's own desires in the matter), so the contraceptive techniques that are available to women (and men) reflect many different considerations: the character and aims of the contraceptive research industry, the motives and morals of those who control the distribution of contraceptive skills and resources, the official promulgations of government health departments about the role of contraception in fertility control and its priority *vis-à-vis* other health and social measures for ensuring national welfare. Summing up the current position in Britain, Helen Roberts has said:

> contraception remains an area where all heterosexual women are disadvantaged by limited choice. Either they can 'choose' systemic methods like the contraceptive pill ... which may be relatively 'safe' as contraceptives but which have been shown to have dangers in terms of general health, or they can choose an 'invasive' contraceptive such as the intra-uterine device which can also endanger their health.

Figure 6.2: Percentage of Currently Married Women using Contraceptives, by Method

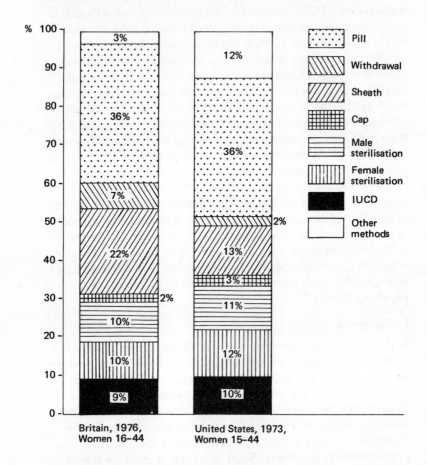

Sources: K. Dunnell, *Family Formation* (1979), p. 42; National Center for Health Statistics, USA, *Contraceptive Utilization United States* (United States Department of Health, Education and Welfare, Publication no. (PHS) 79).

Barrier methods are frequently unacceptable to women for other reasons.[36]

Figure 6.2 shows the relative popularity of the main contraceptive methods among British married women in 1976 and American married women in 1973. (Only data on married women are available because of the still-powerful cultural bias against non-marital sexuality.) The pill, used by 36 per cent of women in both countries, is often hailed as 'the' liberator of women. But its history since its approval for general use in Britain and the United States in 1961 constitutes a very mixed recommendation. The 1974 official report on *Oral Contraceptives and Health* by the Royal College of General Practitioners in Britain showed a mortality 39 per cent higher in users and ex-users of the pill than in non-users, and 17 per cent more illness in pill-users, including a raised incidence of chickenpox, urinary infection, depression (up 30 per cent in pill-users), high blood pressure, deep vein thrombosis and 'cerebrovascular accidents' (stroke).[37] Any official policy of pill-promotion carries these hazards for women. In addition, it carries the implication that the control of fertility, as defined by a male-dominated birth-control industry, requires millions of women to be permanently under the influence of artificial hormones with all the known and unknown effects that this implies. The 'hormonal adjustment' of women is not limited to their being rendered temporarily sterile by ingestion of the contraceptive pill, but represents a major medical strategy for controlling women's bodies (as, for example, in the practice of administering artificial oestrogens to post-menopausal women in order to make them more 'youthful').[38] It implies a primarily mechanical view of women's bodies, as machines to be maintained rather than repositories of whole people, which is in fact the dominant ideology of women as reproducers in most quarters of the industrialised world today.

Of the other contraceptive methods shown in Figure 6.2, sterilisation is subject to the same rules of unequal availability as abortion, and women who are sterilised do face a small risk of death or unpleasant complications of the operation; the cap and the sheath are entirely safe procedures, but require a teaching of skills for which many medical practitioners are not qualified;[39] and the intra-uterine contraceptive device (IUCD) has, like the pill, been found to possess a number of devastating side-effects. These include heavier menstruation, pelvic inflammatory disease, perforation of the womb, ectopic pregnancy, septic abortion, and limb-reduction deformities in fetuses gestated alongside an IUCD.[40] The most revealing uses of devices such as the IUCD, the pill and its injectable alternative, Depo-provera, are in lower socio-economic group women and in Third World countries. Despite considerable evidence as to its substantial hazards, Depo-provera, for example, is aggressively promoted by commercial and medical interests, to the extent that it is used by half of all African women using birth control, and is given without consent to poor black women in countries such as Britain.[41] Such cases demonstrate clearly the male hegemony of the birth-control industry today. They point to important questions about who controls contraceptive technology and which developments are likely to be in women's best interests. It is certainly the case that, as Jalna Hanmer has persuasively shown, research on artificial reproduction and on such possibilities as the predetermination of fetal sex, can be either in women's interests or against them, and there is currently little sign that the former is likely to be the case.[42]

It has been customary to calculate the greatest risk faced by women because of reproduction in terms of maternal mortality, calculated as the number of mothers who die for every 1,000 live babies born. However, the situation is really one in which the mortality associated with the prevention of pregnancy and birth must also be taken into account as important consequences of health policy for women. Valerie Beral has suggested that the most appropriate calculation would be of 'reproductive mortality' and would include not only deaths due to pregnancy and childbirth, but those following spontaneous or induced abortion and those which represent adverse effects of contraception or sterilisation. Using this approach Beral has shown that although *maternal* mortality has decreased significantly since 1950, among women aged 35-44 *reproductive* mortality is now significantly higher than it used to be (due mainly to pill-associated deaths).[43]

Pregnancy and Childbirth

The same caveats that apply to abortion and contraception technologies in a male-dominated society and medical culture also apply to the management of childbirth itself. A large number of surveys of women's attitudes to the maternity services done in the last twenty years show that many are dissatisfied with their maternity care and that for many childbirth is a creative, purposive and responsible act *despite*, and not *because* of, the social and medical context in which it occurs.[44] The most common complaints are both pragmatic (long waiting times, hard chairs, and lack of privacy in antenatal clinics and high travel costs) and profound (depersonalisation, non-communication with care-providers, medical interventions amounting to assault, lack of choice about where, how and with whose help the birth will take place). The picture adds up to one in which, despite the centrality of motherhood to the dominant cultural psychology of women, mothers do in fact have very little control over the act which makes mothers out of them.

In a sample of London women having their first babies in 1975-6, 58 per cent were allowed no choice by their GPs as to where they would have their babies; 61 per cent were given no choice as to where their antenatal care would be done.[45] These are not unrepresentative figures.[46] In Britain in 1979 the hospital-confinement rate was 98.6 per cent; hospital clinics are also now highly involved in giving antenatal care – 64 per cent of women whose births were included in the 1970 British Births Survey had some or all of their antenatal care in a hospital setting.[47] What these figures mean is that the alternatives of community or domiciliary-based care have been largely phased out. The 'choice' for many women is between one hospital or another: hence Sheila Kitzinger's *Good Birth Guide*,[48] giving hospitals different ratings and consumers the information on which to 'select' a preferred pattern of care.

The issue of home versus hospital deliveries is only one of many issues in maternity care that health-care consumers and women's groups currently feel rather strongly about. It is, however, a good illustration of general developments in maternity policy in Britain and other countries over the past half century or so. The proportion of births in institutions in Britain has shown a steady rise from the late 1920s onwards; the figure was 15 per cent in 1927; 35 per cent in 1937; 65 per cent in 1957; 70 per cent in 1965; 81 per cent in 1968.[49] What accounts for this development? Perhaps the most extraordinary fact about it is that the official government reports that have, over the years, made recommendations as to the proportion of births that 'ought' to occur in hospital have uniformly not produced 'scientific' evidence as to the merits of their case. Thus the Peel Report of 1970 which came out in favour of a 100 per cent hospital-confinement rate, declared:

> We consider that the greater safety of hospital confinement for mother and child justifies the objective of providing sufficient hospital facilities for every woman who desires or needs to have a hospital confinement. Even without specific policy direction the institutional confinement rate has risen . . . and shows every sign of continuing to rise, so that discussion of the advantages and disadvantages of home or hospital confinement is in one sense academic.[50]

The argument that something is already happening hardly seems a good reason to encourage it to happen more frequently.

The second most striking fact about the emergence of the 'policy' of hospital confinement in Britain is that it has not been based on the wishes of those who use the services. Although the Peel Committee refers to women's 'desires and needs' for a hospital confinement, these have never in fact been directly taken into account by policy-makers. (At times, for example in the great maternal mortality debate of the 1930s,[51] women's own views on the matter have influenced the tide of events and forced a certain dim imprint on the consciousness of policy-makers, but that is a different matter from their being systematically consulted.) This raises the whole thorny question of the medical profession's 'clinical freedom' to determine modes of health care. Defence of this principle, together with the claim to possession of superior 'scientific' knowledge about those medical strategies most likely to ensure the survival and health of mothers and babies, are the chief weapons in the arguments of obstetricians and policy-makers against the opinion of 'consumer' groups that mothers ought to be able to at least share in the determination of their own fate. One of the most recent examples of this is the Short Committee's report on *Perinatal and Neonatal Mortality*. In chapter 2, 'Place of Birth', the committee observes that 'The mothers themselves have strong views on this question.' They go on to note that 'In contrast to the mothers' views were those of the professionals.' After considering some statistics and some opinions as to the relationship between mortality and place of delivery, the committee decides that the evidence confirms their 'feeling' that only 'very carefully selected mothers' should be advised to have their babies in a GP unit or small maternity unit: the rest should be confined in large hospital units with '24-hour expert supervision and technological aids'. Finally, they lament 'the unresolvable dilemma that the understandable preferences of mothers in regard to place of delivery may not be compatible with the requirements for the maximum lowering of perinatal and neonatal mortality'.[52]

As one liberal-minded obstetrician noted some time ago, once the debate is cast in terms of an international league table of mortality rates, the response amongst policy-makers is akin to the desperate flourishes of those who manage unsuccessful football teams: 'managers are sacked and large sums of money are likely to be spent to buy in expensive talent'.[53] The solution in the perinatal mortality debate is seen in terms of more money, more technology and more medical expertise. Such a solution flows smoothly from the professional ideology of medicine and the state in a medicalised and increasingly technological society. It does, however, ignore four essential considerations. First, the utility of obstetric technology in lowering mortality for mothers and babies in general has not been proved.[54] Second, several important determinants of perinatal mortality, including the proportion of babies born at low birthweights or congenitally malformed, cannot be overridden by intensive technological care at the time of birth. These factors are, in a very profound sense, a reflection of the health of society and specifically the outcome of the long-term health and position of women as a group.[55] Third, women having babies are usually not ill and the grounds for making them 'patients' in the first place are shaky, to put it mildly. Fourth, there is growing evidence that stress, or its absence, influences the success or otherwise of pregnancy and birth, and that many common obstetric procedures (such as long waits at antenatal clinics, blood and amniotic-fluid tests for congenital malformations, induction of labour, and episiotomies for delivery) are sources of stress for many women.[56] Although nobody would argue that the very best in modern techno- logical expertise should not be available to women with problematic pregnancies and births, the point many women are now making is that the application of this 'expertise' to women who do not have problems is itself problem-creating.

In the sphere of reproduction women are increasingly becoming victims of iatrogenesis – doctor-produced illness. Given that a pregnant woman is normally not ill, how is it that women have allowed themselves to be put in this position? A persuasive portrayal of what constitutes normal feminine psychology and normal motherhood pervades much communication between the providers and users of maternity care. For example:

Doctor How many babies have you got?
Patient This is the third pregnancy.
Doctor Doing your duty, aren't you?

Doctor Have you felt movements yet?
Patient Yes.
Doctor When?
Patient They started on March 18th.
Doctor That's a good girl, a very good girl, that's what we like to see, someone who knows the date.[57]

Surveying such patterns of communication between doctors and maternity patients, and looking also at the antenatal advice literature available to British women today, five basic characterisations of normal motherhood can be identified.[58] These are that normal mothers are: people especially in need of medical care and protection; childish; altruistic; married; and constantly prone to anxiety and depression. Although there are certain contradictions between these themes (signalling the experts' recognition that normal motherhood really is problematic), they amount to the message that when women have babies what they are involved in is an exercise in the denial of the self. Putting one's body, child and future into the hands of medical experts is acknowledging that other people know best. The expectation of altruism – that mothers will put their children first – denies the legitimacy of any needs the mother herself has. The link with wifehood pretends that women's emotional satisfaction can be guaranteed within the triad husband-wife-child. Childishness and being depressed – the other two themes – do accede the right for women to express their own requirements. But the childish behaviour attributed to pregnant women ('Every woman enjoys shopping for the pram';[59] 'it is common for a girl who is highly delighted with her pregnancy . . . to burst into tears without the slightest provocation',[60] etc.) is a caricature of femininity. The depression is seen by the experts as normal in pregnancy and afterwards it is attributed principally to hormonal malfunction. It is not attributed to malfunctions in the social and medical system in which women have babies, despite the very large amount of evidence that depression in mothers is a label for a whole range of ordinary unpleasant states (exhaustion, pain, etc.) which have specific causative medical and social factors.[61]

Finally, I want to note an important cultural paradox remarked on by mothers themselves. Despite the fact that motherhood is still held out to women as their most important role, the most probable source of personal fulfilment and satisfaction, it is a disadvantaged social status. One sign of this is the low status and provision of out-of-home child care. Another is the level at which governments pay maternity grants. Table 6.2 shows the level at which maternity grants were set by the governments of thirteen countries in 1977.

The position of mothers is indistinguishable from the position of women in general, and there is no better demonstration of this than the case argued by Margaret and Arthur Wynn in *Prevention of Handicap and the Health of Women*. They show intimate associations between the ill health and low living standards of women and perinatal mortality: 'By neglecting women's special needs the health services

Table 6.2: The Level of Maternity Grants in Britain and Some Other Countries, 1977

Country	Maternity grant (in sterling)
Austria	283
East Germany	279
Luxembourg	278
France	218
Czechoslovakia	106
Iceland	94
Norway	93
Hungary	72
West Germany	64
Portugal	29
United Kingdom	25
Australia	20
Cyprus	7.80

Source: I. Kendall, *Mothers and Babies First?* (1979), p. 14.

give a second rate standard of health care to women';[62] of course, because women are second-class citizens.

Old Wives' Tales? Women as Practitioners of Health Care

It is true to say that: 'In a statistical sense women have always been the main healers in English society. They have delivered babies, rendered first aid, prescribed and dispensed remedies and cared for the sick, infirm and dying, both as a neighbourly service and as paid work.'[63] In fact this is an authentic picture of women's role in health care in most societies throughout most of history. Midwifery has almost everywhere been a female function. In addition, it has usually been allianced with the role of 'wise woman', that of the female healer who provided the only form of health care available to the poor and who, in the process, developed a large armoury of empirical methods for treating common ailments. As recent work has shown, the step from 'wise woman' to 'witch' is a short one. The exclusion of women from an autonomous role in health care has been a long process involving the misogyny of church, state and the medical profession in promulgating a derogatory picture of women. In this picture women, because of their natural weakness, are the sources of all evil and a danger to the health of society.[64]

The exclusion of women from health care was an integral part of the process of medical professionalisation; thus, they have had to fight to be allowed back in. What is the position of women as providers of health care in industrialised societies today? The first thing to note is that they are certainly not in a minority, statistically speaking. Figure 6.3 is taken from Vicente Navarro's analysis, 'Women in Health Care'; it shows the gender distribution of jobs in the US health labour force in 1970. The proportion of women is small in the 'upper-middle-class' segment of the health labour force, increasing to form a major proportion in the working-class segment. In fact, as Navarro notes, 'The occupational, class and sex structure of the United States health labour force is similar to the competitive sector of the economy . . . Upper-middle-class men compose the great majority of medical professionals, whereas lower-middle and working-class women form the greatest proportion of all middle-level, clerical and service workers.[65]

The situation is much the same in Britain. Overall, about 75 per cent of workers in the national health service are women. However, they are not equally represented at all levels of the hierarchy. About 10 per cent of hospital medical staff are women. This proportion varies from 23 per cent at senior-house-officer level to 10 per cent at consultant level,[66] and the same relationship between gender and status holds for local authority medical staff (54.3 per cent female overall, but only 5.5 per cent at Medical Officer of Health level), and for general practice to a lesser extent (13.8 per cent female overall, 2.5 per cent female at 'unrestricted-principal' level).[67] It is the association between women's health-care work and the traditionally feminine role of family-oriented 'caring' and related domestic tasks which explains why so many low-status ancillary workers in the NHS are women. But this connection also structures the division of labour by gender at higher-status levels. Table 6.3 shows the twelve most 'feminine' and the twelve most 'masculine' specialities among NHS hospital consultants in England and Wales in 1977. Specialities relating to children and mental disorder are those that attract the highest proportions of women; they also put people to sleep (anaesthetics), chart the behaviour of microbes (microbiology), concern themselves with people's skins (dermatology) and take pictures of people (radiology). It is not coincidental that these areas lack status within the medical profession, whereas the surgical specialities, a masculine sphere, command more respect.

Studies of medical careers have shown that women are much more liable to take breaks from practice because of the unequal division of

Figure 6.3: Persons employed in the Health Labor Force in 1970 according to Sex

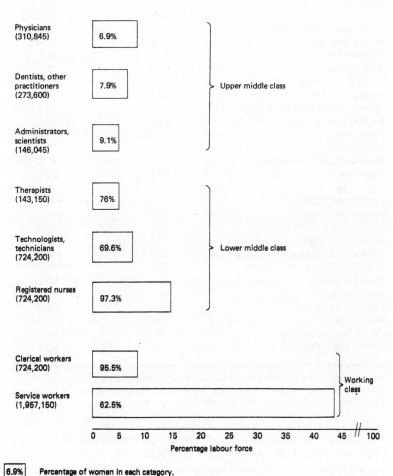

6.9% Percentage of women in each category.

Source: K. Navarro, 'Women in Health Care', *New England Journal of Medicine* (20 January 1975), p. 40.

Table 6.3: Twelve most 'Feminine' and twelve most 'Masculine'
Specialities among NHS Hospital Consultants, England and Wales, 1977

Speciality	Women (percentage)	Men (percentage)
Child and adolescent psychiatry	32.7	67.3
Mental handicap	19.6	80.4
Neuropathology	17.2	82.8
Anaesthetics	17.2	82.8
Immuno-pathology	17.2	82.8
Paediatric surgery	16.7	83.3
Clinical neurological physiology	16.2	83.8
Medical microbiology	14.8	85.2
Paediatrics	14.4	85.6
Dermatology	12.6	87.4
Gynaecology and obstetrics	12.2	87.8
Radiology	10.9	89.1
Forensic psychiatry	0.0	100
General pathology	0.0	100
Urology	0.0	100
Gastroenterology	0.0	100
Clinical pharmacology and therapeutics	0.0	100
Infectious diseases	0.0	100
General surgery	0.9	99.1
Neurosurgery	1.2	98.8
Plastic surgery	1.3	98.7
Nephrology	2.4	97.6
Cardio-thoracic surgery	2.6	97.4
Clinical physiology	3.9	96.1

Source: Department of Health and Social Security, Statistics and Research Division, *Hospital Medical Staff, England and Wales, National Tables, 30 September 1977* (February 1978), Table 7a; crown copyright.

family responsibilities.[68] This demonstrates the rule that policies affecting women in the public sphere cannot afford to ignore the private domain. Only minor moves in the direction of acknowledging this have so far been made by health policy-planners. Thus the retainer scheme for women doctors provides £130 per annum for registration and medical defence fees and one journal subscription for women unable to undertake a full-time commitment to medicine. In return they are expected to attend at least five educational sessions a year and work up to one day a week. This and other minor modifications to the normal medical career structure have met with considerable opposition in some quarters, one manifestation of which is the uneven regional implementation of such schemes. However, to see the problem of women doctors as women's problem is to ignore several other salient facts aside from the domestic inequality of medical women. Among these is the insignificant attrition of medical womanpower due to reproduction compared with the loss of medical manpower consequent on emigration, death, alcoholism, suicide and removal from the Medical Register,[69] and the exploitation in the NHS (and other health-care systems) of women doctors to solve the persistently recurring problems of structural imbalance between the supply of, and demand for, medical staff in different specialities and at different status-levels.[70]

The main division of labour by gender in health care is between medicine, a male monopoly, and nursing, a female sphere. The relegation of women to the nursing function was a process that occurred simultaneously with the professionalisation of medicine, and with the demotion of women's role as managers of childbirth from that of autonomous expert to that of obstetric nurse. One reason for the rise of nursing as a profession was the introduction of institutions for the care of the sick away from home. It is important to recognise that much nursing in industrialised countries today is still done in the home by women as an unpaid 'labour of love' for their families – the old, the young, the acutely or chronically sick and the disabled. Thus, although the male doctor-female nurse division is a fairly new one, it represents a crucial and pervasive axis of gender differentiation in society at large. Not surprisingly, the doctor-nurse relationship can be said to mirror 'the stereotype of the bourgeois family, where father dominates and performs the role of decision-maker and protector whilst mother's role is passive, consisting of servicing activities and carrying out the wishes of father'.[71] In terms of the hierarchy of the doctor-patient relationship, the nurse acts to maintain distance between the two, conveying information about the patient to the doctor and interpreting the doctor's wishes and decisions to the patient (not unlike the way mothers in the traditional patriarchal family mediate between fathers and children).

What happens in the future to traditionally female health-care occupations is capable of a dual interpretation. Because nursing and midwifery, for example, have been in the past all-female pursuits, the practice of these occupations has to some extent inevitably been the repository of female values. The values that inform female socialisation, personality and social roles in our present gender-divided culture are very different from those that obtain for men. The core-cluster concern participating in the development of, and contributes to the welfare of, others, not oneself: putting others first and being sensitive to their needs. The paradox of these values is that their intense social useful-ness has made them the possession of a minority group. They are at one and the same time women's strengths and their weaknesses; they are enormously valuable qualities to have, but they in no way confer power.[72] Sensitivity to the patient's needs is often remarked on by patients and practitioners alike as an attractive and unique property in midwifery and nursing; but reclaiming lost ground by vigorously asserting new rights to what is now delineated as medical territory may carry the unintended corollary of a shift towards masculine values.

Conclusions: Women and the National Health

In this chapter I have looked at some aspects of women's roles as users and providers of health care. Inevitably, my coverage of this field has been incomplete, and it has also at times not been entirely clear as to how these characteristics of women's health-care behaviour have related to the question of health-care 'policy' as such. It is one thing to quote from the report of a government committee on the future of health-care policy in Britain, and quite another to discuss long-term developments in the relations between 'society' and its health-care system and in the relations between men and women as though these were a matter of policy in the strict sense. Obviously, they are not. But the term 'policy' can have a broad, as well as a limited meaning, and it is in this spirit that I have appealed to the idea of policy in this chapter – as comprising 'the principles that govern action towards given ends.'[73] What this means is that, like social policy in general, health-care policy cannot be taken to refer to some closed system that is altogether separate from the forces that mould social life as a whole. So far as the special role of women in health care is concerned, a sexist society shapes a sexist health-care system – in all possible ways. For this reason, and because women have special reasons for using health care, a critique of medicine has been a very important element in the broader feminist critique of capitalist society.[74]

The situation obtaining in Britain at the moment with respect to health care is one of a double crisis. There is not enough cash to spread health care sufficiently thickly in places where it is 'really' needed, and there is not enough confidence in the capacity of medicine 'really' to solve all those problems its practitioners have over the years claimed to be able to solve. In this situation the role of women as users and providers of health care is brought out particularly clearly. Because of their central role in the family since the establishment of the industrial system of production, there has always been a tendency to see women as the guardians of the national health; hence, for example, the attention motherhood is given when wars deplete the population and draw attention to the biological fitness of its individuals; hence the attribution to women in a whole mass of psychological theories of the long-term responsibility for causing or preventing ill health in the next generation. Such a doctrine becomes especially attractive in an era in which the *social* causes of ill health are emphasised and in which funds are lacking with which to treat them. Hence a series of government reports, consultative documents and White Papers have over the last few years in Britain put forward a philosophy of preventive health, in which women are the key figures, the key promotors of health and preventors of ill health. (Given that the cash and confidence crisis applies to Western health care generally, this new philosophy is to be found in other countries, too.)

Hilary Graham, in her discussion of this development in health-care policy, observes that:

The key terms in the new vocabulary of prevention are those of health education and personal responsibility on the one hand; and life-style and risk-taking on the other. Specifically, the path to good health is seen to lie in health education and the appropriation of a personal responsibility for health which, together, will result in the adoption of healthier life-styles and the avoidance of risk-taking behaviour.

She goes on to say that 'Although the rhetoric of prevention extends across the spectrum of health and social policy, it is in the field of maternal and child health that it has been most fully articulated'; and she points out that the new philosophy of adult or child health 'emerges as something closely akin to the traditional notion of maternal sacrifice which permeated the nineteenth and early twentieth century writings on the family'.[75] In other words, if women devote themselves to protecting everyone's health, money will be saved because 'unnecessary' illnesses, such as those induced by smoking and poor nutrition, will not happen, and medicine will be left with more money to spend on the residue of 'real' illnesses. Significantly, women's revamped responsibility as guardians of the nation's health includes taking their responsibilities as patients and the mothers (or daughters, or wives) of patients more seriously. Community care for various categories of sick or otherwise disabled people is a humane concept, but its realisation often means an extra burden for women.[76] There are equal, if different, problems for women in the urging of policy-makers that failure to take advantage of necessary medical care is also a female fault. Such failure is most often mentioned these days in the field of antenatal care, where a variety of mechanistic solutions (including cash incentives) have been proposed to overcome women's reluctance to attend clinics, and where it is said that the main obstacle to further reduction in the British perinatal mortality rate does, in fact, lie.[77] However, since it has been known for a long time that antenatal clinics are dissatisfying places for women to be, given that no causal relationship between lack of antenatal care and perinatal mortality has ever been established for the bulk of childbearing women,[78] and in the light of what is known about the social and economic difficulties of mothers today, the clarion call for more antenatal attenders is a subtle version of the old formula: blaming the victim.

If the new philosophy of preventive health fails to question the sexual division of labour, and if it fails to connect external social and economic constraints with the logic of the individual's health-care behaviour, it is not original in adopting such a narrow, conservative stance on health and social relations. But women as a group are not able to contain and solve the problems of the nation's health, any more than they are able, on their own, to solve the problems and contradictions of their particular position in society.

Notes

1. OPCS, *Hospital In-Patient Inquiry* (1976).

2. Department of Health and Social Security, *Health and Personal Social Service Statistics for England and Wales* (1977).

3. E. Koos, *The Health of Regionsville; what the people felt and did about it* (1954).

4. D. Tuckett, 'Becoming a Patient' in D. Tuckett (ed.), *An Introduction to Medical Sociology* (1976), pp. 161-4.

5. A. Cartwright, *General Practice Revisited* (1981).

6. Editorial, *New England Journal of Medicine* (20 October 1977), p. 863.

7. See the discussion in A. Oakley, *Subject Women* (1981), pp. 47-8.

8. S.L. Bem, 'The measurement of psychological androgyny', *Journal of Consulting and Clinical Psychology*, vol. 42 (1974), pp. 155-62.

9. M.T. Westbrook and R.A. Mitchell, 'Changes in Sex-Role Stereotypes from Health to Illness', *Social Science and Medicine*, vol. 13A (1979), pp. 297-302.

10. G.V. Stimson 'General Practitioners, "Trouble" and Types of Patients' in M. Stacey (ed.), *The Sociology of the NHS* (Sociological Review Monograph 22, 1976).

11. M. Shepherd, B. Cooper, A.C. Brown and G.W. Kalton, *Psychiatric Illness in General Practice* (1966).

12. D.C.G. Skegg, R. Doll and J. Perry, 'Use of Medicines in General Practice', *British Medical Journal* (18 June 1977), pp. 1561-3.

13. See the discussion of the role of the drug industry in the Brighton Women and Science Group, *Alice Through the Microscope* (1980).

14. I. Broverman, D. Broverman, F. Clarkson, P. Rosenkrantz and S. Vogel, 'Sex-role Stereotypes and Clinical Judgements of Mental Health', *Journal of Consulting and Clinical Psychology*, vol. 34 (1970), pp. 1-7.

15. S. Chapman, 'Advertising and Psychotropic Drugs: the place of myth in ideological reproduction', *Social Science and Medicine*, vol. 13a (1979), pp. 751-64.

16. E.L. Thompson, 'Sexual Bias in Drug Advertisements', *Social Science and Medicine*, vol. 13A (1979), pp. 187-91.

17. I. Illich, *Medical Nemesis* (1975).

18. W.R. Grove, 'The Relationship between Sex Roles, Mental Illness and Marital Status', *Social Forces* (1972), pp. 34-44; W.R. Grove and J.F. Tudor, 'Adult Sex Roles and Mental Illness', *American Journal of Sociology*, vol. 78 (1973), pp. 812-35.

19. J. Bernard, *The Future of Marriage* (1973).

20. C. Smith-Rosenberg, 'The Female World of Love and Ritual: Relations Between women in Nineteenth Century America', *Signs: Journal of Women in Culture and Society* (1975), pp. 1-30.

21. S. Ginsberg, 'Women, Work and Conflict' in N. Fonda and P. Moss (eds.), *Mothers in Employment* (1976).

22. See A. Oakley, *The Sociology of Housework* (1974).

23. J. Ryder and H. Silver, *Modern English Society: History and Structure 1850-1970* (1970).

24. See the analysis in D. Leonard, *Sex and Generation* (1980).

25. J. Hanmer, 'Violence and the Social Control of Women' in G. Littlejohn, B. Smart, J. Wakeford and N. Yurah-Davies (eds.), *Power and the State* (1978), p. 221.

26. S.K. Steinmetz and M.A. Straus (eds.), *Violence in the American Family* (1974).

27. E.N. Cohen, J.W. Belville and B.W. Brown, 'Anesthesia, Pregnancy, and Miscarriage: a Study of Operating Room Nurses and Anesthetists', *Anesthesiology*, vol. 35 (1971), p. 343.

28. Central Policy Review Staff, *Services for Young Children with Working Mothers* (1978).

29. J. Mitchell, 'Women: the Longest Revolution', *New Left Review*, no. 40 (1966).

30. P. Diggory and J. McEwan, *Planning or Prevention: The New Face of 'Family Planning'* (1976).

31. F.G.R. Fowkes, J.C.Catford, and R.F.L. Logan, 'Abortion and the NHS: the first decades', *British Medical Journal* (27 January 1979), pp. 217-19.

32. A. Cartwright, *Parents and Family Planning Services* (1970), p. 72.

33. See S. Macintyre, 'The Medical Profession and the 1967 Abortion Act in Britain', *Social Science and Medicine*, vol. 7 (1973), pp. 121-34.

34. J.C. Mohr, *Abortion in America* (1978).

35. A. Heitlinger, *Women and State Socialism: Sex Inequality in the Soviet Union and Czechoslovakia* (1979).

36. H. Roberts, 'Male Hegemony in Family Planning' in H. Roberts (ed.), *Women, Health and Reproduction* (1981).

37. Royal College of General Practitioners, *Oral Contraceptives and Health* (1974).

38. W. Cooper, *No Change* (1976).

39. I. Allen, *Report on Family Planning, Sterilisation and Abortion Services in two AHA's* (Policy Studies Institute for the Department of Health and Social Security, 1979).

40. H. Barrie, 'Congenital Malformations associated with Intrauterine Devices', *British Medical Journal* (28 February 1976), pp. 488-90; J. Guilleband, J. Bonnar, J. Morehead and A. Matthews, 'Menstrual Blood-loss with Intrauterine Devices', *Lancet* (21 February 1976), pp. 387-90; M.P. Vessey, R. Doll, B. Johnson, and R. Peto, 'Outcome of Pregnancy in Women using an Intrauterine Device', *Lancet* (23 March 1974), pp. 495-8; P. Williams, B. Johnson and M. Vessey, 'Septic Abortion in Women using Intrauterine Devices', *British Medical Journal* (November 1975), pp. 263-4.

41. J. Rakusen, 'Depo-provera: the Extent of the Problem: A Case Study in the Politics of Birth Control', in H. Roberts (ed.), *Women, Health and Reproduction* (1981).

42. J. Hanmer, 'Sex Predetermination, Artificial Insemination and the Maintenance of Male-dominated Culture' in H. Roberts (ed.), *Women, Health and Reproduction* (1981).

43. V. Beral, 'Reproductive Mortality', *British Medical Journal* (15 September 1979), pp. 632-4.

44. See, for example, S. Arms, *Immaculate Deception* (1977); D. Breen, *The Birth of the First Child* (1975); A. Cartwright, *The Dignity of Labour* (1979); A. Oakley, *Becoming a Mother* (1979); A. Oakley, *Women Confined* (1980); N.S. Shaw, *Forced Labour* (1974).

45. Oakley, *Becoming a Mother*.

46. See the references in note 51.

47. G. Chamberlain, E. Philipp, B. Howlett and K. Masters, *British Births 1970* (1978).

48. S. Kitzinger, *The Good Birth Guide* (1979).

49. S. Kitzinger and J.A. Davies, *The Place of Birth* (1978).

50. Standing Maternity and Midwifery Advisory Committee, *Domiciliary Midwifery and Maternity Bed Needs* (the Peel Report) (1970).

51. See A. Oakley, 'The Origins and Development of Antenatal Care in Britain' in M. Enkin and I. Chalmers (eds.), *Effectiveness and Satisfaction in Antenatal Care* (forthcoming).

52. Social Services Committee, *Perinatal and Neonatal Mortality* (the Short Report), (1980), pp. 23, 27.

53. M. Kerr, 'Problems and Perspectives in Reproductive Medicine', University of Edinburgh Inaugural Lecture, 25 November 1978.

54. See, for example, I. Chalmers, 'Implications of the Current Debate on Obstetric Practice' in S. Kitzinger and J.A. Davies (eds.), *The Place of Birth* (1978).

55. M. Wynn and A. Wynn, *Prevention of Handicap and the Health of Women* (1979).

56. See A. Oakley, I. Chalmers and A. Macfarlane, 'Social Class, Stress and Reproduction' (forthcoming).

57. Oakley, *Women Confined*, pp. 39, 40-1.

58. A. Oakley, 'Normal Motherhood: an exercise in self-control?' in B. Hutter and G. Williams (eds.), *Controlling Women* (forthcoming).

59. British Medical Association, Family Doctor Publication, *You and Your Baby Part I: From Pregnancy to Birth* (1977), p. 42.

60. G. Bourne, *Pregnancy* (1975), p. 3.

61. See Oakley, *Women Confined*.

62. Wynn and Wynn, *Prevention of Handicap*, p. 155. (this is a quotation from 'A Health Service that Provides for Women's Needs', Save the Elizabeth Garrett Anderson Hospital Campaign, 1978).

63. M.C. Verluysen, 'Old Wives' Tales – Women Healers in English History' in C. Davies (ed.), *Rewriting Nursery History* (1980), p. 175.

64. See B. Ehrenreich and D. English, *Witches, Midwives and Nurses: A History of Women Healers* (1973); A. Oakley, 'Wisewoman and Medicine Man: changes in the management of childbirth' in J. Mitchell and A. Oakley (eds.), *The Rights and Wrongs of Women* (1976).

65. V. Navarro, 'Women in Health Care', *New England Journal of Medicine* (20 February 1975), p. 398.

66. Department of Health and Social Security, *Health and Personal Social Services Statistics of England and Wales* (1977).

67. Department of Health and Social Security, *Health and Personal Social Services Statistics* (1973); and also *Health and Personal Social Services Statistics* (1976).

68. M.E. Elston, 'Medicine: Half our Future Doctors' in R. Silverstone and A. Ward (eds.), *Careers of Professional Women* (1980).

69. A point made by B.R. Bewley and T.H. Bewley, 'Hospital Doctors' Career Structure and Mis-use of Medical Womanpower', *Lancet* (9 August 1975), pp. 270-2.

70. This is the argument put by M.E. Elston, 'Women in the Medical Profession: Whose Problem?' in M. Stacey, M. Reid, C. Heath and R. Dingwall (eds.), *Health and the Division of Labour* (1977).

71. J. Leeson and J. Gray, *Women and Medicine* (1978), p. 63.

72. J.B. Miller, in *Toward a New Psychology of Women* (1976), analyses women's personalities and social position in these terms.

73. R.M. Titmuss, *Social Policy: An Introduction* (1974), p. 23.

74. See, for example, E. Frankfort, *Vaginal Politics* (1972); B. Seaman, *Free and Female* (1972); C. Dreifus (ed.), *Seizing Our Bodies: the Politics of Women's Health* (1978).

75. H. Graham, 'Prevention and Health: Every Mother's Business, A Comment on Child Health Policies in the 1970s' in C.C. Harris (ed.), *The Sociology of the Family: New Directions for Britain* (Sociological Review Monograph no. 28, 1979), p. 169.

76. A. Flew, 'Looking After Granny: the reality of community care', *New Society* (9 October 1980).

77. See A. Oakley and A. Macfarlane, 'A Poor Birthright', *New Society* (24 July 1980), pp. 172-3.

78. See M.H. Hall, P.K. Chng, and I. MacGillivray, 'Is Routine Antenatal Care Worthwhile?', *Lancet* (12 July 1980), pp. 78-80.

Introduction

Most commentators on women's employment in Britain would agree
that women remain unequal in the labour-market despite the 'equal-
opportunities' legislation of the 1970s. There is, however, little
agreement as to *why* this is the case.

One aim of this chapter is to look at the different explanations for
the continuation of sexual inequality in the labour-market. These
range from the explanations offered by many orthodox economists,
who assume that 'the innate abilities' of women differ from those of
men, to those of feminists, who see sex inequalities in the labour-market
as manifestations of wider conflicts between the interests of men and
women. There has been very little dialogue in Britain between the two
schools; the neo-classical literature is hardly ever considered by people
outside the economics profession, and orthodox economists appear to
take little notice of the work of sociologists, Marxists or feminists.

This chapter attempts to bridge this divide so as to provide the
basis for a better understanding of what has been happening to women
in the labour force. In order to place the theories and legislation in
context, the next section (pp. 131-6) looks at the changing demographic
composition of the female labour force and of the occupational and
industrial composition of the labour force.[2] In the third section, the
Equal Pay Act is discussed (pp. 136-43) and this is followed by an
analysis of pay differentials between men and women (pp. 143-51).
This focuses on the neo-classical economists' account. The following
section (pp. 151-4) looks in more detail at the Sex Discrimination Act,
maternity provisions and protective legislation, and the penultimate
section (pp. 154-62) looks at occupational differentiation. Here the
focus is more on 'structural theorists', both radical and feminist. The
conclusion briefly discusses proposals for additional legislation.

The review of the literature in the chapter is necessarily selective.
It concentrates on the explanation of sex differences in employment
in the 1970s to the neglect of any detailed consideration of differences
between women or of the deterioration in the relative position of

women in the labour-force that has come with the slump in the
British economy during the 1980s.

What Has Changed?

Women have always worked. The idea that the last twenty or thirty
years have led to an increase in the number of working women rests on
a particular definition of work: one that excludes household work
from consideration. Not only is unpaid housework not assessed as
economic activity, but also baby-minding, home-working and work in
family businesses often escape the *official statistics* of women workers.[3]

Despite their deficiencies, the official statistics do show important
changes in women's work roles this century. As many as a quarter of
married women were economically active in the 1850s, according to
the definitions of the time. This fell to about 10 per cent for most of
the period before the Second World War, shot up in wartime to about
50 per cent, fell back in the late 1940s and then rose steadily between
1951 and 1978, when some 62 per cent of married women were classed
as economically active (see Table 7.1). In contrast, the proportions of
men and single women who were in paid work fell after 1961, as young
people stayed on longer in education and older people retired earlier.
This means that, above the age of 34, married women are as likely to
be in employment as single women. The typical woman worker has
become the older married woman with children, often working part-
time. Moreover, although the majority of the workforce is still male,
that majority is no longer substantial (Table 7.2). As a consequence of
these changes, the ability of women to earn money in the labour-market
has become an issue of prime importance to the welfare of households.[4]

The rise in the number of working women is not primarily due to
women delaying or refusing childbearing, for women with children
over the age of 10 are now more likely to work—albeit part-time—than
childless women (Table 7.3). It is only when children are below school-
age that mothers are likely to be full-time housewives, and even then,
many of these mothers would work if there was adequate childcare.

The 'typical' household has become one of two earners rather than
one, and yet women are still the housewives, responsible for all the
domestic chores and child-care work, even if men 'help out' more now
than once they did.[5] This 'double burden' is central to understanding
women's position in the economy. Women's paid employment is
structured around their domestic responsibilities and fitted into the

Table 7.1: Economic Activity Rates in Great Britain, 1901-80[a]

Year	Men	Unmarried[b] women	Married[b] women	Mothers with dependent children	Married women
	(15-64)	(15-59)	(15-59)	(15-59)	(45-54)
1901	96	n.d	10	n.d	16
1911	96	n.d	10	n.d	11
1921	94	n.d	10	n.d	9
1931	96	n.d	11	n.d	8
1951	96	76	26	n.d	24
1961	95	76	35	24	36
1971	92	72	49	41	51
1978	92	68	62	52	69
1980	90	72	62	54	67

Notes: a. Economic activity is the proportion of the total population within an age-group who are employed or looking for work.

b. Divorced women are included with married women in 1901-11. The 1978 figures are for people aged between 16 and retirement age.
Sources: *Census of England and Wales, 1901-71*; and Office of Population Censuses and Surveys, *General Household Survey* (1978).

Table 7.2: Composition of the Labour Force (Employed and Unemployed), 1901-80

Proportion of the labour force who are	1901	1951	1961	1971	1978	1980
Men	70	66	65	62	59	59
Women	30	34	35	38	40	40
Married women	4	14	18	25	28	27
Women aged 35-59	7	10	14	21	21	22
Part-time women workers	n.d.	4	9	16	17	16
Mothers of dependent children	n.d.	n.d	7	12	15	16

Sources: *Census of England and Wales, 1901-51*; and Office of Population Censuses and Surveys, *General Household Survey* (1978).

Table 7.3: Activity Rates of Mothers of Dependent Children, 1961-80

Year	Children aged 0-4 years	Children aged 11-16 years
1961	12	35
1971	20	70
1974	27	71
1978	27	72[a]
1980	30	71[a]

Note: a. Aged 10+.
Sources: *Census of England and Wales, 1961*, and *1971*; and Office of Population Censuses and Surveys, *General Household Survey* (1974, 1978, 1980).

time left after household tasks have been dealt with.[6] Nowhere is this more clearly seen than in the fact that the rise in women's paid employment has taken the form of a rise in part-time work.

Since 1951, the size of the full-time female labour force has remained steady at 5.6 million. The expansion of the total female labour force from 7.4 million to 9.1 million by 1977 was thus due to an expansion of almost 2 million part-time jobs. In 1956, only 12 per cent of women worked part-time; by 1977 this figure had risen to 40 per cent.[7] And although there is no intrinsic reason why part-time work should be poorly paid hour for hour or be low-status work, the increasing concentration of women workers into part-time work is important in explaining the continued underprivileged status of women in the labour-market.

A second, related reason why women workers remain underprivileged is the small range of jobs they work in, a range that has barely expanded with the increased size of the female workforce.[8] Table 7.4 shows that in 1971, 84 per cent of women were in occupations dominated by women, twice as many as would be expected if women were to be spread in the same way as all workers across all occupations in the economy, and no fewer than were found in such occupations in 1951. Chart 7.1 shows the pattern of concentration between occupations in 1979. The majority of women work in the service sector in jobs which have not been done by men.

Catherine Hakim has also shown how the expansion of women's employment has brought little improvement in the status of women workers (Table 7.5). The expansion of women's employment has been in junior and intermediate non-manual work and in semi- and unskilled manual work, with the result that women have remained segregated in

Table 7.4: Occupational Segregation, 1901-71

Year	Proportion of women in disproportionately female occupations (a)	Proportion of women 'expected' in those occupations (b)	Index of overrepresentation of women in those occupations (a/b)
1901	88	33	2.67
1911	87	36	2.42
1921	88	38	2.32
1931	87	37	2.35
1951	86	39	2.21
1961	84	40	2.10
1971	84	42	2.00

Source: See note 8.

Table 7.5: Under and Overrepresentation of Women in Major Occupational Groups, 1911-71

Occupational group	Degree of under or overrepresentation in each group in relation to the female proportion of the total labour force. Proportional representation = 1					
	1911	1921	1931	1951	1961	1971
Employers and managers	0.64	0.69	0.66	0.65	0.63	0.68
White-collar workers:	1.01	1.27	1.20	1.37	1.37	1.31
(a) Managers and administrators	0.67	0.58	0.44	0.49	0.48	0.59
(b) Higher professionals	0.20	0.17	0.25	0.27	0.30	0.27
(c) Lower professionals and technicians	2.13	2.01	1.97	1.74	1.57	1.43
(d) Foremen and inspectors	0.14	0.22	0.29	0.44	0.32	0.36
(e) Clerks	0.72	1.51	1.54	1.95	2.01	2.00
(f) Salesmen and shop assistants	1.19	1.48	1.25	1.68	1.69	1.64
All manual workers	1.03	0.95	0.97	0.85	0.80	0.81
(a) Skilled	0.81	0.71	0.71	0.51	0.43	0.37
(b) Semi-skilled	1.36	1.37	1.44	1.24	1.21	1.27
(c) Unskilled	0.52	0.57	0.50	0.66	0.69	1.01

Source: See note 8.

low-status, non-manual or manual work. Indeed, with the decline in industries employing skilled women workers, their status has declined in some respects. Women are not simply concentrated in a small number of occupations, they are concentrated to a large extent in occupations

Chart 7.1: Occupations of Women Workers
Percentage of women in each major female occupation
Percentage of part-time women of all women in each major female
occupation

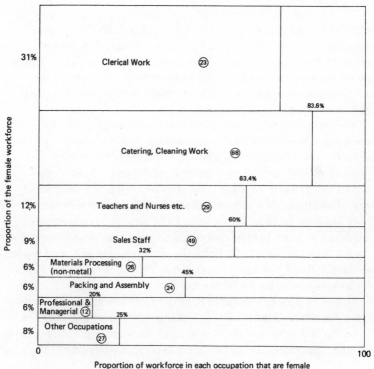

Proportion of the female workforce

31% | Clerical Work ㉓ | 83.6%
Catering, Cleaning Work ㊲ | 63.4%
12% | Teachers and Nurses etc. ㉙ | 60%
9% | Sales Staff ㊾ | 32%
6% | Materials Processing (non-metal) ㉖ | 45%
6% | Packing and Assembly ㉔ | 20%
6% | Professional & Managerial ⑫ | 25%
8% | Other Occupations ㉗

0 — 100

Proportion of workforce in each occupation that are female

◯ Proportion of females in each occupation that are part-time

Source: *New Earnings Survey* (1979 and 1980).

which pay both men and women poorly. Moreover, in the period
between 1973 and 1980, this concentration increased. In 1973,
according to the *New Earnings Survey*, some 60 per cent of employees
in the six lowest-paying occupations were women, when women held
only 37 per cent of all jobs; by 1980 this proportion had risen to 64
per cent. Indeed, there is good reason to believe that the second figure
is an underestimate, because of changes in the recording of part-time

women workers which had taken place in the interim. Part-time women workers are even more concentrated in these low-paying occupations. In 1973, 14 per cent of all workers covered by the *New Earnings Survey* were part-time women, but in the low-paying occupations one-quarter were part-timers.[9]

The expansion of women's paid employment took place in a sector of the labour-market which was poorly unionised. The least unionised sectors of all are hotels and catering (8 per cent) and distribution (15 per cent), both areas of high concentration of women workers.[10] Since pay in any sector is closely related to the level of unionisation, the concentration of women in poorly unionised workplaces will in itself lead to lower pay for women.

The changes outlined here – the expansion of employment for women in relatively low-paid, non-unionised, low-status work – go some way towards explaining the lack of change in the relation between women's earnings and men's from the early 1950s to the mid-1970s. As Table 7.6 shows, women's pay fell, as a proportion of men's from the early 1950s until the mid-1960s, and then remained fairly stable in the early 1970s. Until 1977 there was a convergence of full-time men's and women's average hourly pay, but this improvement has not been maintained. By 1980, the average hourly pay of all women workers (full and part-time) was no better than in 1975, before the full implementation of the Equal Pay Act.[11]

This pattern raises some important questions which we will discuss in the rest of this chapter. How is it that in 1980, five years after the Equal Pay Act came into force, women's hourly earnings had improved by little more than a few percentage points relative to men's? [12]

The Equal Pay Act

To consider this question in more detail, we will examine the social and economic assumptions of the equal-opportunities legislation.[13] The Equal Pay Act assumes that equality of opportunity – the equal treatment of persons of equal merit – is all that is required. It rests on the premises that the market mechanism is basically just and that the achievement of equality of opportunity requires only marginal adjustments of labour-market processes, not full-scale restructuring.

Despite a Royal Commission on Equal Pay in 1949 and an International Labour Office convention in 1951, which required member states to adopt equal pay, it was not until 1970 that the

Table 7.6: Women's Earnings as a Proportion of Full-time Men's Earnings, 1913-80

	1913-14	1922-4	1935-6	1955-6	1960	1966	1970	1975	1977	1980
A Full-time women workers' average *weekly* earnings[a]	53	57	56	50	54	nd	48	61	65	63
B Full-time workers' average *hourly* earnings						59	60	69	74	71
C *Part-time* women's average *hourly* earnings[a]						56	56	63	60	58
D *All women's average hourly* earnings[a]						58	59	67	70	67

Note: a.   The women's earnings are given as a proportion of full-time men's earnings.
Sources: A   G. Routh, *Occupation and Pay in Great Britain, 1906-79* (1980), p. 123.
B, C and D   *New Earnings Survey.*

British government sought to use its power to make discrimination in pay on account of sex illegal. Professional women in the public sector were the first to win equal pay, but by the late 1960s manual women workers were also demanding equality in this regard. In 1968, 400 women machinists went on strike at Fords in Dagenham in a dispute over the grading of their work. After a three-week strike, they gained not equal pay, but 92 per cent of male skilled rates. More significantly still, a National Joint Action Committee on Equal Pay was formed, which organised a massive equal-pay demonstration in May 1969. This kind of action eventually forced both the trade unions and Barbara Castle, then Minister for Employment, to make equal pay a serious political issue. Furthermore, the EEC's Treaty of Rome made equal pay for the same work a condition of membership, so that those groups in Britain who supported British membership of the EEC, such as the Confederation of British Industry (CBI), came to recognise by the late 1960s that some legislation was inevitable.

Meaning of Equal Pay

However, although the principle of equal pay was conceded, there was no consensus about what the term meant. Few people took it to mean that women's overall average weekly or hourly earnings should be raised to equal those of men, although in common parlance this is often what is understood by equal pay. The legislation made a firm distinction between:

(a)   differences in earnings due to differences in 'worth' or productivity; that is, in effect, differences in hours worked, training, work experience, education, etc.;

(b)   differences in earnings for workers of equal 'worth', that is wage discrimination.

The first issue was placed outside the ambit of the Equal Pay Act. Differences in pay due to differences in value or worth are taken to be fair and, indeed, necessary for the efficient operation of the economy. Moreover, it was argued with considerable force that wage increases beyond those necessary to overcome wage discrimination would not benefit women, but simply price them off the labour-market. As we shall see, the Sex Discrimination Act of 1975 and the maternity provisions of the Employment Protection Act (1975) did touch on some of the processes that led to a lower value being attached to to women's work. However, the Equal Pay Act itself was specifically designed to perpetuate those differences in pay between men and women which could be related to differences in the value of work done.

In practice the relative value of work, or worth, of a worker is not easily known or readily agreed. Indeed, most employers would argue that even before the Act they were paying women according to their worth. Thus there was fierce argument about the way in which differences in pay for workers of equal 'worth' should be eliminated. Employers' organisations argued that equal pay should be granted only for the *same* work (as in the EEC definition), since only when men and women were doing the same work alongside one another could one begin to assume their work was of equal worth. On the other hand, women's organisations and trade unions argued for the International Labour Office definition—equal pay for work of equal value—recognising that job segregation meant that the vast majority of women did not do the same work as men and therefore would not benefit from the EEC formulation. In the event the Equal Pay Act went further than the 'same-work' criterion for equal pay, but still limited itself to those instances where wage discrimination could reasonably clearly be demonstrated.

The Equal Pay Act is concerned only with differences in pay (and terms of employment, such as holidays and overtime rates) within any given establishment such that, if a woman is doing the same or broadly similar work as a man, or work that has been rated of equivalent value in a job-evaluation scheme, she is entitled to the same rate of pay as the man. Where women are covered in the same collective agreement as men, the Act makes a special women's rate or grade of pay illegal. If a union (or employer) believes a collective agreement to be discriminatory, they (but not an individual) may refer the agreement to the Central Arbitration Court.

Defining the Same or Broadly Similar Work

If a woman believes that she is doing the same or broadly similar work to a man (or work that has been rated of equal value in a job-evaluation scheme) and that she is being discriminated against in wage rates, overtime rates, holiday pay or any such contractual term, she or her union, can take a case to the industrial tribunal and beyond that, if necessary to an Employment Appeals Tribunal, right through to the European Court. The problems women have in taking cases before an industrial tribunal have been well described by Gregory.[14] The number of cases taken has fallen dramatically from 709 in 1976 to just 26 in 1980 and the success rate is now down to 17 per cent. Only four cases were successful in 1980.

Work is taken to be the same or broadly similar where the woman successfully demonstrates to the industrial tribunal that the differences between her work and a man's 'are of no practical importance'. Case histories of tribunal decisions are replete with instances of sexist bias, and this certainly serves to deter any but the most determined of women from applying for equal pay.

From the point of view of women, a major limitation of the section of the Act dealing with broadly similar work is that it only applies where a woman can point to a comparable man working for the same employer. As we have seen from the discussion of Hakim's study of occupational segregation, most women work in occupations where there are few, if any men. Even in relatively integrated occupations the chances of a woman working alongside a 'comparable man' are not high because, as a recent study by Industrial Facts and Forecasts shows,[15] many firms employ only one sex or the other in any given occupation. Thus, it is not surprising that this section of the Act—though hotly contested—appears rarely to have been used as a means of gaining equal pay. In their study of the implementation of equal pay in 25 firms covering 37 groups of workers, Snell *et al.* found only two cases of women doing the same or broadly similar work to men (and in one case a woman clerk was moved to prevent her claiming equal pay when the Act came in).[16]

Defining Work of Equal Value

Where men do work in the same establishment but in dissimilar jobs, the job-evaluation section of the Equal Pay Act appears to offer possibilities to women seeking fairer pay. Indeed, Snell *et al.* found that in two-thirds of the 37 groups of workers studied, job evaluation was used as the means of implementing equal pay.

However, wage discrimination may still persist in firms employing both men and women, despite the job-evaluation clause. There are three main reasons why this is so. First, employers are not obliged to carry out job evaluations, so wage structures which systematically downgrade women's work relative to its value remain legal as long as no man works alongside a woman. Second, job evaluation in Britain is carried out on a firm by firm basis. This means that it may have no direct impact on the differential in pay between men and women caused by the greater concentration of women in low-paying firms and low-paying industries. Third, the objectivity of job evaluation as a method of determining fair differentials in pay must be seriously doubted.[17] Only if women are in a position to challenge the often unconscious predispositions of male work-study engineers, employers and trade unionists, will job evaluation overcome the traditional undervaluation of women's work.

In practice, the limitations of job evaluations are implicitly acknowledged in that most job-evaluation exercises attempt to cover only a narrow spectrum of jobs with quite similar attributes. This being so, the gross undervaluation of female skills in the female ghettos of secretarial work, nursing, and intricate-assembly jobs are unlikely to be affected.

Material Difference

But even where a tribunal has accepted that a woman is doing the same work or work of equal value to a man, there is no guarantee of equal pay. The Act allows pay to vary between men and women in the same or 'equal' work for reasons of 'material difference' (other than sex) between individuals as, for example, when men have greater seniority, or work more overtime. The Act does stipulate that overtime *rates* and annual increments have to be the same for men and women; however, differences in overtime or seniority *payments* arise where men work more overtime or where men have worked for more years in a firm. Such additions to pay do not have to relate to any measurable difference in the value of the work done, and so can generate a large amount of indirect wage discrimination: the greater men's access to overtime, seniority and merit rewards relative to women's, the greater the possible discrepancy between actual pay and equal pay (for work of equal value).

Amongst non-manual workers, indirect wage discrimination more often occurs with seniority payments (annual increments) and through the grading system. Teachers, who have had equal pay in terms of the Act since 1961, are a good case in point. In April 1980, women teachers on Burnham school scales earned on average £14 (12 per cent) a week less than men. By and large, this was because they are concentrated in the lower grades and at lower points within these. Department of Education and Science figures show that 38 per cent of women primary teachers were on the bottom grade, compared with 13 per cent of men. A detailed study of teachers' pay[18] shows that this low grading and pay cannot be attributed to lesser experience or to lower qualifications, indeed female graduates in primary schools earned less than male non-graduates in primary schools.

In general, where there is a material difference, differential payment between men and women doing the same work is judged 'fair'. It is assumed that additional payments for overtime, shift-working, seniority

or additional responsibilities *do* relate to the enhanced value or
productivity of the work, the underlying assumption being that of the
rationality of the market mechanism: employers would only make
additional payments for more productive work.

However, there are circumstances when no such justification for
additional payment is attempted and the case for additional pay for
men rests on the preservation of a pre-existing differential. This has
come to be known as 'red circling'. At Trico in 1976, an industrial
tribunal ruled that men were entitled to higher pay than women doing
the same work because in the past the men had worked on night shifts
and, although the night shift had been discontinued, their pay
included the 'red-circled' night-shift bonus. In the event the women
won equal pay (and got the night-shift bonus) after a strike lasting
five months, but in law such a bonus can constitute a 'material
difference' and hence a bar to equal pay.

The Trico case underlines the point that relative pay reflects levels
of organisation as much as, or more than, relative productivity.

Central Arbitration Court and Discriminatory Collective Agreements

This point assumes even greater importance when one considers the
collective-agreement clause of the Equal Pay Act.

This clause has potentially broad implications in that any
discriminatory aspect of a collective agreement can be referred to the
Central Arbitration Court, which has wide discretion. However, only a
union or an employer or the Secretary of State can make such a referral,
and whether or not they do so will depend on the pressure exerted by
women. In practice the clause has ensured that collective agreements
no longer contain grades labelled as women's grades. Such women's
grades are now illegal. However, in practice women may still find
themselves concentrated in the lowest unisex grade, where only a few
token men work.[19] In this case, however skilled they are they may
only be paid as much as the lowest-paid man. For example, the
implementation of the Equal Pay Act in the Yorkshire wool textile
industry meant that all the pre-existing women's rates (which included
a skilled woman's rate) were amalgamated with the lowest male rate.
Since skilled women had previously been paid less than the lowest-paid
men, this amalgamation did improve their pay. Nevertheless, at the end
of the implementation period, skilled women still only earned 81 per
cent of the skilled male rate[20] and can hardly be said to have gained
equal pay for work of equal value. Indeed, looking at the use of this
collective-agreements clause in the implementation of equal pay, Snell

et al. judged that in seven out of twelve cases women were underpaid relative to the value of their work after the implementation of the Act, because they were only paid the lowest male rate.

In summary there are two major limitations to the Equal Pay Act. First, it deals only with certain instances of wage discrimination and hardly touches the differential in wages between men and women which arises because women workers are concentrated in low-paying firms. Second, it makes unwarranted assumptions about the balance of power between men and women; the onus is on the individual woman to establish her case for equal pay, either to the industrial tribunal or to her union. In both cases these are male-dominated institutions which do not necessarily give high priority to women's rights and may indeed be part of the problem rather than the solution.[21] Not only are the formal rights given by the Equal Pay Act deficient, but also the institutional processes employed by the Act make it difficult, if not impossible, for many women to claim these formal rights.

Explaining Wage Discrimination

Contrasting Models of the Labour-Market

We have looked at the Equal Pay Act in some detail to illustrate how limited its *direct* outlawing of wage discrimination is. Neo-classical economists, however, tend to argue that the direct elimination of wage discrimination in certain areas of work will filter through the whole labour-market in time. For them and for others who share their assumptions, the Equal Pay Act provides the necessary stimulus: so long as *some* women get equal pay as a result of the Act, the labour-market will ensure that, in time, all will.

The neo-classical model familiar in elementary economics textbooks is that of an economy where resources are perfectly divisible and mobile, where knowledge is perfect (and costless), and where there is perfect competition between producers, workers, landlords, etc. The individual profit-maximising entrepreneur will, if he (*sic*) is rational, only employ people where the value of what they produce is equal to the wages paid; if he employs more he will make a loss, if he employs fewer he will not maximise profits. In a perfectly competitive economy, all entrepreneurs must act rationally to stay in business. As a result, wages will be equated to marginal productivity throughout such an economy. If some workers are more efficient than others, competition between employers raises their wages. More profitable industries will pay better in the short term, but over time workers will tend to move to such jobs, depressing relative wages. In the end, wages throughout the economy will tend to be brought into line with the workers' productivity. Differences in pay between men and women not due to differences in productivity (that is, unequal pay in our definition) will only be a temporary marginal occurrence.

If women provided the same labour more cheaply than men, then rational employers would tend to employ them in preference to men. In the end men could only stave off unemployment by offering themselves at the same wages as women. Thus lower women's wage rates — for work of similar quality — are inherently unstable. The dynamic process of the 'free' market reduces both male and female wages to the lowest level acceptable by either, and the raw dynamic of capitalism is seen as capable of overcoming sex differences in pay.

This view is disputed by those economists and sociologists who take a more 'institutional' view of how the labour-market works. Labour-market processes are themselves seen as operating systematically to downgrade women or black workers. In this view, the Equal Pay Act, and indeed any legislative approach, can only skim the surface of the problem because the labour-market as a whole is structured to discriminate. Neo-classical and institutional theorists differ in the way they conceptualise discrimination and in the stress they place on the fact that women work at different jobs in different firms from men.[22] For the neo-classical school, discrimination is a fairly straightforward concept, defined as differences in pay not accounted for by differences in productivity, and is something that can be measured. To institutional economists, the neo-classical idea, that discrimination is simply a residual after differences in productivity have been allowed for, makes the unwarranted assumption that pay normally reflects productivity in our society. Neo-classical economists do not see the occupational or industrial segregation of women as an issue; they argue that the market will ensure that wages are related to productivity, across firms, industries and occupations. Institutional economists see the differentiation between jobs and between firms as creating a segmentation of the labour-market into non-competing groups. Such segmentation means that there is no mechanism for bringing wages into line with productivity. Discrimination is then interpreted as a pervasive feature of the market and not as a marginal aberration.

This section will concentrate on the views of neo-classical economists because their analysis focuses on questions of pay; the section entitled 'Explaining the pattern of women's employment' takes up the arguments of the institutional theorists regarding labour-market segmentation.

Neo-classical Models: Discrimination as Market Imperfection

Neo-classical economists have tried to reconcile the reality of discrimination with the neo-classical model. Their basic model assumes that capitalists and workers have full knowledge of alternatives and are able to respond to better returns and higher wages; and that the economy is competitive. Discrimination is thus inconsistent with these conditions. However, if any of these conditions is not met, it follows that discrimination can occur. Neo-classical economists explain the existence of discrimination variously by relaxing different assumptions of the basic model. Gary Becker, for example, argues that if employers choose not to maximise profits but instead to indulge their personal 'tastes' for discrimination, then they could be willing to pay men (who produce the same as women) more, just so as to employ men.[23] In this case they will only employ women at a discount; a prejudiced employer is 'bought off' by women being prepared to work at lower wages than men.

Alternatively, male workers may be prejudiced. In this instance Becker suggests that male workers would only be prepared to work alongside women, if they were paid a premium for their 'discomfort'. In Becker's model, employers lose profits from discriminatory practice because they fail to employ workers at the cheapest price. Unequal pay of this kind is then unstable in a competitive environment. In time, employers who discriminate against women (or blacks), or who employ men who discriminate, will be undercut by other less discriminatory firms.

But Becker cannot explain why discrimination persists within competitive industries. His model is also at odds with empirical studies which show that men who work alongside women tend to earn *less* than other men in similar jobs.[24] Theoretically it explains discrimination by a taste for prejudice, but this simply begs the question as to why such tastes exist. Thus the model is inadequate on empirical and theoretical grounds. There is, nevertheless, a certain congruence between this model and the thinking behind the Equal Pay Act. In both, discrimination is seen as an irrational aberration rooted in outmoded ideas and of benefit neither to employers (who lose profits if they discriminate), nor to workers. It is thus perceived as a field where the state can legitimately intervene in the long-term interests of all; any resistance by employers to equal pay will be shortlived.

In practice, employers in Britain continue to resist equal pay. This fact is more effectively explained by so-called 'statistical models' of discrimination than by Becker's model. In these employers are seen as rational and profit-maximising when they discriminate. Discrimination arises because employers do not know the true value of women workers relative to men, and hence value them less. Their lack of knowledge is not simple prejudice. Since, in the real world, information costs money, lack of knowledge (and hence discriminatory behaviour) can be interpreted as rational. But as Aiger and Cain point out, discrimination is still unstable in this model. Once one firm recognises the value to it of equal pay, all others in competition would have to follow suit. It is, then, difficult to reconcile this modification of the neo-classical model with the persistence of discrimination.[25]

The *persistence* of wage discrimination against women can only really be explained in a neo-classical framework by dropping the assumption of perfect competition. Madden,[26] following the earlier work of Joan Robinson, demonstrates how employers can profit from wage discrimination in certain circumstances. If women are prepared to work for less than men and if the employer has no competitors in the labour-market (that is, he is a monopsonist), then it is possible for him to introduce lower-paid women to an existing male workforce at a profit; for, short of union organisation, the women have little alternative but to accept. Men, on the other hand, through unionisation and greater mobility, are seen to have greater power to resist low wages.

It is still difficult to see that a situation of this kind – with men and women, working together on the same job – is stable. If women are equally productive, then the monopsonist would employ women rather than men, so long as they were available. In time the labour force would tend to become all-female (and others would become all-male), such that unequal pay, as defined by the Act, would no longer exist. In contrast to the male prejudice and statistical discrimination models, the 'monopsonist' model does provide some explanation for the persistence of unequal pay across the economy. Because women are less mobile, they are more subject to (monopsonistic) employer power. Hence, it will be profitable to pay them less, irrespective of their value. Unequal pay will be rife, but because the tendency will be to separate male and female workers, there may not be many instances where men and women work together at the same job.

The monopsony model is used within a neo-classical framework to explain isolated divergences from a generally competitive market which causes (isolated) examples of unequal pay; however, the generalisation of this concept of power relations to the economy as a whole breaks decisively with the neo-classical view. Instead of wages reflecting the relative value of work done, they are seen to reflect the relative *power* of different groups of workers *vis-à-vis* employers. Women's lower wages are thus traced to their inferior power, which may not be reflected in discrimination of the kind outlawed by the Equal Pay Act.

However, in general, neo-classical models conceptualise the labour-market as a process by which wage relativities are related to productivity differentials. Discrimination at the level of the firm is possible, but unstable and hence readily amenable to legislation. From this point of view the Equal Pay Act can be expected to overcome what residual discrimination exists.

Measuring Wage Discrimination as a Residual

Economists have tried to test whether (and how far) discrimination has been overcome. Using the human capital variant of neo-classical economics,[27] that is the assumption that differences in productivity between workers are due to differences in personal qualities such as education, training and work experience,[28] a model is built to 'predict' what women would be paid if there was no discrimination. This 'prediction' is then compared to actual earnings and the remainder (the residual) is, in theory, a measure of discrimination.[29]

In practice, however, different attempts to measure the scale of discrimination have come up with very different results, depending on how the predictions of what women's earnings would be in the absence of discrimination were made.

These differences arise because there is no agreement about which human capital attributes contribute to productivity, and how these should be measured. Siebert and Sloane, for example, argue that many studies tend to overestimate discrimination, because some factors relevant to productivity may not be included. They suggest that many of the 'unexplained' differences in pay between men and women may be due to differences in motivation rather than discrimination, and that this is illustrated by the fact that single women's pay is closer to men's than that of married women.[30] In a similar vein Polachek suggests that women may gain less in earnings for each extra year of work experience without there being any discrimination, because each extra woman-year of experience may enhance individual productivity less than each extra man-year of experience. That is, there are qualitative differences in experience dependent on sex.[31] In the end the argument is circular: individual productivity is not directly measured, nor can it be in a complex integrated economy such as we have, so it is always open to

economists to argue that *any* unexplained difference in earnings
between men and women is due to a hidden, unmeasured productivity
differential, rather than to discrimination. But these arguments are
not necessarily convincing to people who do not assume women to be
inferior.

Nevertheless, some interesting points do arise from studies applying
this kind of approach to the British experience. There have been two
types of study: those looking at pay differences between men and
women in the same firm, doing much the same type of work, and those
looking at wage differentials across the economy.[32] The results show,
first, that some firms discriminate in wages and promotion far more
than others, but more importantly, that wage and promotion discrimination *within* firms is only a small proportion of the total discrimination.
When Greenhalgh compared the wages of single women and married
men, *none* of the gap appeared to be explained by differences in
personal attributes. Single women had as much experience in the
labour-market on average as men (25 years), they had more formal
educational qualifications, and had just as often been in their current
jobs over a year. They were also more likely to live in Greater London,
where wage rates are generally higher, and yet they earned only 73
per cent as much as married men.

The reason for this differential must then lie, not in personal
characteristics, but in the type of occupations and industries employing
women, and in the fact that within occupations women are found in
firms and industries paying lower wages. People with very similar
experience and education get very different pay according to their
place of work. In particular, workers doing similar jobs in smaller firms
tend to be less well-paid.[33] Moreover, the industries which tend to pay
workers badly relative to their individual attributes tend to be
industries where women are a high proportion of the workforce. Layard,
Piachaud and Stewart's study for the Royal Commission on the
Distribution of Income and Wealth[34] showed significant differences in
hourly earnings between industries, even after length of education,
father's occupation, colour, health and work experience were allowed
for. Apart from agriculture, the lowest-paying industries—experience
for experience, education for education—were distribution, miscellaneous
services and leather, all of which have a predominantly female labour
force.

The empirical studies suggest that the persistent differences
between the pay of men and women cannot be adequately explained
by differences in human capital attributes, and that the distribution of

men and women across different firms and different jobs is an important factor in and of itself. This is not sufficient to disprove the neo-classical model of the labour-market, since economists with a neo-classical orientation can (and do) argue that the concentration of women and firms is to be explained by the preference of women for these types of jobs.[35] Just as Becker's prejudiced employer trades his profits for the satisfaction of discriminating, so women are seen to trade higher pay for other satisfactions. The net benefits of work for individuals of equal potential are, then, argued to be the same, whatever the sex of the individual. However, this argument becomes tautological when pursued. *Any* unexplained differences in pay could be said to be due to unmeasurable 'other' satisfactions women derive from their jobs rather than to discrimination. However, the conditions of much women's work[36] are so poor as to make this neo-classical view unconvincing.

Wage Differentials and the Concentration of Women's Employment

What needs to be explained is why those sectors (and types of firm) which employ women tend to be low paying. We have already seen that this cannot be explained adequately by the characteristics of women themselves, and we have rejected an explanation which is based on 'compensating' non-monetary advantages. The 'crowding' model elaborated by F.Y. Edgeworth, the economist, and discussed by Millicent Garrett Fawcett, the suffrage leader, as early as 1918[37] goes some way in furthering our understanding of the relationship between the proportion of women in an industry, or in an occupation, and the general level of pay in that sector. If, instead of the free flow of labour between sectors envisaged in the textbook neo-classical model, there are constraints on the entry of women into some sectors of the economy, either through outright bans or through social conventions, then the potential supply of labour to the 'closed' sectors will be lower and the available supply to the open 'crowded' sectors greater. If the constraints on mobility are maintained, wages will tend to be higher in the closed sector, irrespective of productivity and profitability, and lower in the open sector. If it is women who are crowded out of certain sectors of the labour-market, then wages in sectors dominated by women will tend to be lower (for men and women) than elsewhere for people with similar attributes. And, of course, wages in the closed sector will tend to be higher, for both men and those women who do manage to enter. It is for this reason that male earnings between industries vary, reflecting the proportion of women in these industries.[38]

Taking the definition of low pay as £60 or less a week (in 1979), a Low Pay Unit/Equal Opportunities Commission study showed the disproportionate concentration of low-paid workers in industries employing women (see Table 7.7). Routh provides evidence which

Table 7.7: Low-paid Workers by Industry, 1979

Industry	Percentage of workforce female	Percentage of workforce earning less than £60 week			
		Manual men	Non-manual men	Manual women	Non-manual women
All industry	39	9.6	6.1	66.6	48.4
Clothing and footwear	75	19.4	11.9	77.1	67.6
Distributive trades	53	22.2	14.6	80.4	78.8
Professional services	68	27.7	(6.0)	83.3	(33.8)
Miscellaneous	55	26.7	14.3	79.7	52.9
Agriculture	16	39.1	14.8	—	—

Source: *New Earnings Survey* (1979).

shows how this is a long-term cumulative process. As women entered clerical work and teaching, so men's pay in these occupations fell relative to that of other men. For example, in 1913/14, when 69 per cent of clerical workers were men, male clerks' earnings were 22 per cent above average. In 1976, 70 per cent of clerical workers were female and male clerks earned 4 per cent below average.[39]

There are indeed low-paid male occupations and industries where few women work; for example, agriculture. This is explained by the fact that many factors, such as ability to organise unions, affect pay. There are also industries employing large numbers of women where male wages are relatively high because, in one way or another, male wages have been protected from female competition. It should be clear, then, that the occupational and industrial distribution of women across the economy is only one factor, but an important one, in determining women's lower pay relative to ability; it does not account for the whole difference.[40] American studies of pay levels between *firms* suggest that in any one occupation in any one industry women tend to be congregated in the lower-paying firms.[41] In Britain women are known to work in smaller firms, where they are less well unionised and where they are dependent either on the national base-level pay agreement, or on wages councils, or on the employers' goodwill.[42]

These factors will lead to unequal pay and will not be corrected by the Act.

This was clear from early in the debate on the Equal Pay Act. The response from the labour movement was to call for further legislation aimed at preventing discrimination in access to well-paid jobs, and at reducing the handicap which childbearing imposes on women pursuing careers.

Anti-Sex-Discrimination Legislation

The Sex Discrimination Act and Employment Protection Act (conferring certain rights to maternity leave and reinstatement) were both passed in 1975 and were seen as filling the remaining legislative loopholes which barred the way to equal employment opportunities for women.

Concept of Discrimination

By 1973, both major political parties were agreed that an Equal Pay Act without a sex-discrimination law would be counter-productive: there was a danger that equal pay would lead to the exclusion of women from better-paid jobs, leading to an increase in sex segregation. However, just as the Equal Pay Act aimed to provide women in comparable jobs to men with equal pay, not equal earnings, so the Sex Discrimination Act aimed to promote the equal treatment of women, without touching the basic division of labour between the sexes in the allocation of household duties.

The Sex Discrimination Act covers two types of discrimination. Direct discrimination is where a woman (or man) is treated less favourably than a man (or woman) is treated or would have been treated. Indirect discrimination is where a condition or requirement is imposed on a group that does not appear to have anything to do with sex, but where more of one sex can comply with it than the other. Height restrictions are the example most often quoted. But Belinda Price won a case against the Civil Service Commission in 1977, which showed how widely the concept of indirect discrimination could be interpreted. Ms Price complained that an upper age-limit of 28 for recruitment to the Executive Officer grade indirectly discriminated against women because a large number of women took time off from work during their twenties to bear and rear children.

This case illustrates how a career structure which had been taken for granted for a long time as necessary, could be illegal under the Sex Discrimination Act. In the Price case, no direct discrimination was involved, since women did work as Executive Officers; indirect discrimination occurred because women were shown to be more often excluded by the age bar. This judgement and another favourable ruling in the Mustoe case, where a woman had been dismissed because she had children, represented important advances for women, but were based on damaging sexist assumptions. If a man were to be unfairly treated because he had responsibility for his children's care, he could not bring a charge of indirect sex discrimination, since only women are assumed to carry such responsibilities. A similar assumption underlies the maternity rights granted by the 1975 Employment Protection Act, by which mothers, but not fathers, have the right to paid leave after the birth of a child.

The Sex Discrimination Act covers a wide range of issues: appointment promotion, dismissal, redundancy, access to training, to education (in mixed schools), to credit and other services. But discrimination is still permitted in social security, pension rights and taxation, areas in which, as many feminists have shown, government policy works to reinforce the traditional sexual division of labour and power in the home.[43] In so far as these sexual divisions are a prime cause of the low pay and status of women in the labour-market, the state can be seen to be pulling in two directions at once. On the one hand, social-security regulations support a family structure of male breadwinner and female secondary worker and/or dependant, but, on the other hand, anti-discrimination legislation appears to question that structure.

The Sex Discrimination Act also ignores any reference to the issue of protective legislation, other than to require the Equal Opportunities Commission (established by the Act) to report on it. Protective legislation excludes women from certain jobs, and stops them working at night and for long hours in manufacturing industries, unless an exemption order has been granted. How far these laws are an important factor in causing sex segregation and unequal pay is subject to dispute.[44] Given the ease with which exemption orders are obtained, it is unlikely that the protective legislation in itself is a major bar to the employment of women in better-paid jobs. What it does, however, is to reinforce the idea that women are more marginal, problem workers.

The Sex Discrimination Act is in any case hedged with qualifications. In particular, when attempting to claim discrimination in hiring or promotion practices, women face an additional hurdle in the form of the 'genuine occupation qualification' clause. That is, if requirements of 'decency', 'privacy' or 'authentic male characteristics' can be argued to necessitate the employment of a man, no discrimination against women is deemed to have occurred. In one case the dismissal of a woman shop assistant was justified under this clause because the job required her to take the inside trouser-leg measurements of men.

Nevertheless the sex-discrimination and maternity-rights legislation does represent an advance over the equal-pay legislation in that it recognises, albeit in an extremely limited way, that equality between men and women cannot be achieved by assuming that men and women start equal and simply need to be assured of equal opportunity. The Sex Discrimination Act allows for some positive discrimination in training in favour of women in order to redress the long-term effects of discrimination. However, these provisions are extremely limited and discretionary. There is no obligation to set up positive-action programmes and while men are available for training there is no incentive to provide special facilities for women.

Similar comments apply to the maternity rights given in 1976 by the Employment Protection Act (1975). The Act gave women a statutory right to maternity pay and the right to return to their jobs within 29 weeks of childbirth, subject to certain conditions. In theory, such legislation should have helped women wishing to have children to retain their jobs and hence their career positions. In practice, however, the rights are so narrowly defined that only a minority of mothers qualify. This, together with the limited facilities available for child care, has meant that no more than one woman in ten who leaves work to have a baby has returned. Only some 5 per cent of manual workers who took maternity leave and stated their desire to return to work were able to do so.[45]

For many women, then, both the Sex Discrimination Act and the statutory maternity rights merely provide formal rights of which they cannot take advantage. Catherine Hakim shows that the degree of sex segregation in the labour force diminished between 1975 and 1977, only to rise again to the 1973 level by 1979. Only the proportion of women in professional occupations improved between 1973 and 1979; women in managerial or skilled manual occupations made little headway.[46] Figures on entry to training show a similarly dismal picture. In 1970, less than 1 per cent of students on day-release courses in engineering were girls; by 1977, an extra 1,000 girls a year were getting day-release in engineering, a rise of 0.3 per cent.[47]

Although the Sex Discrimination Act provides that there should be no discrimination on grounds of sex in redundancy, this provision has had little effect in protecting women against job loss. Wherever employment has declined since 1974, the decline in the number of women's jobs has been greater, especially in the manufacturing industry and in the distributive trades.[48] The provisions of the Sex Discrimination Act have not proved strong enough to counter the general belief that jobs are more important for men, and women remain particularly vulnerable to job loss in times of recession. The recent ruling, that redundancy procedures which select part-time workers first discriminate against women, may help stem the use of part-time workers as a disposable workforce;[49] but women would still tend to be more vulnerable on a last-in first-out basis.

The Act relies on an individual taking a case against her employer or her potential employer (or persuading her union to do so), and demonstrating that the actions taken by the employer are discriminatory. This tends to assume a fairly even balance of power between employer and employee. The situation is made more problematic by the fact that, although the onus is put on the woman to prove that discrimination has occurred, she does not have the right of access to all the relevant documentation to establish her case.[50] In the event, less than a tenth of applications made under the Act are upheld. In 1980, only fifteen cases were successful.

Despite the advance represented by the indirect-discrimination clause, the Sex Discrimination Act is still based on a very limited view of the inequality that women experience. The Act can only deal with discrimination which a woman herself recognises and feels sufficiently roused to do something about. But much discrimination operates by consent. On the whole, women accept the limited alternatives open to them. They do not attempt to get training or to enter management, for a whole range of reasons, not least because submission and acceptance are considered desirable attributes of femininity.

Explaining the Pattern of Women's Employment

Sex-discrimination legislation has had only very limited effect because, it seems, women do not aspire to men's jobs and do not attempt to compete in the labour-market with men on their terms. Some commentators have argued that this signifies an absence of discrimination: the concentration of women in women's work reflects choices freely made by them. And yet these apparent choices should raise a further question: how is it that women arrive at decisions which render them second-class workers?

Different types of answers to this question are provided by three different groups of people. The first group consists of those neo-classicists who take the household divisions of labour largely for granted and locate women's 'choices' of employment within that framework. Human capital theorists are the most important members of this group.

Among the second group are those who see the differentiation of male and female work stemming from the capitalist labour process itself, either for technical reasons (internal dual labour-market models), or for reasons of social control by capital (radical dual labour-market models). Institutional theorists argue that women fill certain jobs because their domestic roles differentiate them from male labour. Again, domestic roles are, largely, taken as given.

The third group includes those who believe that a conflict between the interests of men and women exists at the heart of both the division of labour in the labour-market and in the home, such that the operation of the labour-market is an aspect of, and a contributory factor to, more general domination by men in society. Unlike the human capital and many of the segregated labour-market models, such feminist models do not point to women simply as a category of labour to be compared with other categories in its achieved position. Rather, they view the *relations* between men and women as structuring the labour-market processes, in much the same way as Marxists reject the view of classes as merely differentiated positions in a given labour-market and attempt to analyse them in relation to one another.[51]

Human Capital Models

The human capital models of job differentiation are as individualistic as their models of wage determination. They take individual human capital investment — time spent in education and training — as the key factor explaining both pay and job 'choice'. Women are said to choose jobs where the penalties for a break in career for childbearing, or the penalty for working part-time, are less than elsewhere. In particular, women are seen to choose jobs which require less 'investment' in education or training than typical male jobs. Given that women expect to spend fewer years in employment, the 'returns' on any investment in education would be lower and therefore less justified.[52]

Harriet Zellner attempts to explain the types of jobs women take on this basis.[53] She argues that jobs differ in the rewards offered for greater 'participation', that is, for long service or for longer hours. Some jobs (like *a* in Figure 7.1) pay much the same per hour, however many hours are worked or however long one has been in the job. Other jobs (like *b*) pay relatively badly at the start, but as experience accumulates, pay increases or, alternatively, they pay relatively low base hourly rates but good overtime premiums. Polachek and Zellner argue that if women know their participation is going to be low, then they will opt for type *a* jobs, even if the average pay in such jobs is lower ($b_2 > a_2$) because at the participation rates they expect, wage rates are higher than in type *b* jobs ($a_1 > b_1$).

Figure 7.1: Relationship between Wages and Work Experience for Different Types of Work

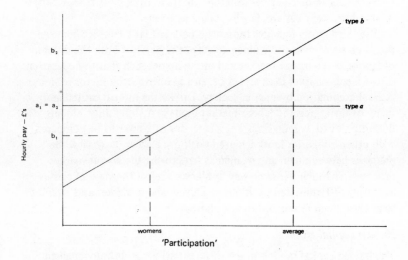

Source: After H. Zellner, 'Determinants of Occupational Segregation' in C. Lloyd (ed.), *Sex Discrimination and the Division of Labour* (1975).

This explanation for occupational segregation is based on the following assumptions.
(a)   Jobs do differ significantly in 'returns' to participation (the argument for this is considered below).
(b)   Training and educational decisions are based on the individual's own expectations rather than on externally imposed hurdles.[54]
(c)   Women will necessarily participate less in the labour-market.

If these assumptions are valid, there will be a tendency towards sex segregation. By the same token, segregation could be overcome by action to invalidate the assumptions. For example, if the costs of education and training are met by the state and generous grants are provided, then women would cease to be handicapped by their own expectations. Moreover, if pre-school child care were to be organised on a collective basis, or men were to take an equal share in housework, then according to this model, segregation would disappear as women adjusted their expectations and began to choose type *b* jobs more readily. But by taking the domestic division of labour for granted, the model illustrates only one-half of the process whereby women's choices are constrained. It does not consider *how* the domestic division of labour is itself reinforced by the processes of occupational segregation and the fact of unequal pay for women.[55] And yet the same theorists under a slightly different guise do show how the domestic division of labour between men and women need not be a necessary given.[56] They argue, indeed, that *because* women earn less (that is because of occupational segregation and discrimination), it is rational for women rather than men to stay at home to look after children. Thus, on the assumption of heterosexual coupling and no collective child-care provision, the human capital approach is suggestive of a vicious circle (Chart 7.2) trapping women within certain roles both in the labour-market and the home. But the human capital approach looks at each part of the vicious circle in isolation, rather than looking at the cumulative process, and it is feminists, rather than human capital theorists, who have attempted to develop an overall understanding of this set of relations.

Human capital theories of low pay and job choice are based on individualistic assumptions. They suggest that, if a woman chooses to, she can get training or pursue a career. Other theories take a more structural view. Although not denying that some individuals can 'break out', they are concerned with the systematic processes which trap women as a group in the vicious circle.

Internal Dual Labour-Market Models

Dual labour-market theorists look at segregation from the demand side — the demand for different types of workers, or for a differentiated labour force—rather than the supply side, and emphasise the fact that people come to the labour-market with different characteristics. Indeed, they tend to argue that differentiation of occupations causes, or at least reinforces, the division of the workforce into different types of workers,

Chart 7.2: The Vicious Circle

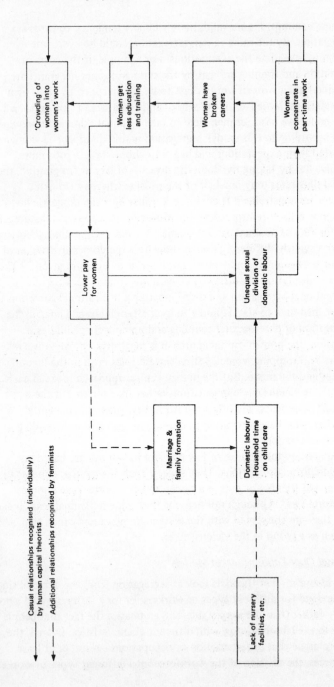

→ Casual relationships recognised (individually)
    by human capital theorists

⇢ Additional relationships recognised by feminists

adding an extra twist to the vicious circle.

Internal labour-market theorists make the same distinction between types of jobs as do Zellner and Polachek. They are, however, concerned to explain why certain jobs have career ladders while others do not; in other words, why differentiation between what they term a primary and a secondary labour-market exists. The basic argument put forward by Doeringer and Piore[57] is that skills and knowledge specific to one company (job-specific skills) are important in contemporary production processes and have grown in importance relative to transferable (occupationally based) skills. For this reason, they argue that firms have an incentive to try and retain long-serving workers, and hence tend to develop career ladders (jobs of type *b*), not just for managerial and technical workers, but also for manual workers. This is done through grading structures and annual increments. As a result, people who gain entry to these types of jobs are assured a stable career with rising wages and hence will become long-term workers with extended work experience. Employers will then find it worthwhile to train them further, so that their initial advantage will be enhanced.

At the same time, according to the dual model, there are other production processes where employers get no advantage from keeping the same worker over many years and hence offer no incentives for long service. Such work will often be unskilled, but could also include jobs with highly transferable skills (that is, skills of value to many firms). As a result, people who are forced into secondary labour-market jobs will have no incentive to stay long. In consequence, they will not improve their skills as readily and will come to be seen as unstable workers. This confirms them in their position as a secondary labour force. Thus, one group of workers is progressively advantaged from their initial point of entry into the labour-market, whereas the second group have their 'negative' characteristics progressively reinforced. The labour-market itself is thus argued to have multiplied the differentiation of the workforce. Unionisation is greater amongst more stable workforces, and hence the gap in pay and conditions between the sectors will be increased still further.

This model does provide some insight into the experience of women in the British labour-market.[58] In particular, part-time women can be seen to have their marginality reinforced by their confinement to a secondary labour-market, where, if anything, their *lack* of attachment is valued.[59] Moreover, the unionisation pattern amongst women owes something to this process. Women's lower levels of unionisation have more to do with the type of jobs they do than with any intrinsic antipathy to unions or inability to organise.[60]

However, a model which differentiates the labour-market principally on the basis of tenure in an individual firm leaves too much unexplained. As Grim and Stern[61] point out, many of the jobs women traditionally enter do have career ladders, for example, teaching and nursing. In general, women may leave the labour-market more often than men but, age for age, full-time women tend to stay just as long with individual employers. Short service cannot, then, be held to be the central differentiating factor, especially since men in 'primary' jobs often progress by moving *between* companies rather than by remaining with one firm for their whole careers.

Radical Dual Labour-Market Models

More radical dual labour-market theorists question the central assumption of the internal labour-market model: that job-specific skills explain the development of career hierarchies and grading structures, and hence the corollary (shared by the human capital model) that women's disadvantage in the labour-market stems from a shorter expected career-span and higher turnover between firms. Rather, they point to the process of de-skilling (elaborated by Braverman),[62] which, other things being equal, would tend to lead to a breakdown of gradings and skill differentials. Remaining differentials are then interpreted as outcomes of a struggle for power and control, and not as reflections of productivity differentials.

In the American literature the emphasis is placed on employers creating artificial systems of stratification between workers on a divide-and-rule basis.[63] White working-class men, especially skilled unionised manual workers, gain privileges over other workers through this process of stratification. Women remain low-waged workers either at the bottom of the pile in highly stratified monopolies or, in other versions of the model, remain confined (with blacks) to the peripheral, competitive, marginal industries and firms.[64] In most versions of this model, men are the passive beneficiaries of capitalist strategy, rather than active perpetrators of women's oppression. But beyond a recognition that divisions along lines of sex and race are useful for capitalists to build on, there is no mechanism to explain why women should, as a group, find themselves at the bottom of a labour-market hierarchy.

Feminist Models

Rubery[65] argues that the radical labour-segmentation models developed in America underestimate the strength of the organised working class.

She argues that in Britain, at least, job segmentation is not so much a reflection of trade union weakness as of trade union power. Feminists, then, tend to point to the role of men organising through trade unions in two ways: first, by creating hierachies of skill, and defining skills in ways which have devalued women's work;[66] and, second, by excluding women from certain areas of skilled work, either directly or by precipitating legislation.

Feminists do, however, differ amongst themselves as to how far exclusion and devaluation of women's work reflects the power of male trade unionists over women or the weakness of trade unions *vis-à-vis* capital. Jane Humphries views the strategy of attempting to exclude married women from the labour force, adopted by the organised working class in the nineteenth century, as a means of protecting the conditions of working-class families from the raw dynamic of capitalism.[67] In that dynamic, wages are reduced to subsistence-level earnings, or below, as more and more people are driven to seek wage-labour. That reduction itself throws more and more family members (old, young and women) on to the labour-market, so exacerbating exploitation and reducing wages still further, down to the subsistence costs of each individual. In these circumstances, the working class reacted by attempting to restrict labour supply, in the belief that this would allow the wages of the remaining workers to rise sufficiently to cover the costs of keeping the non-workers as dependants. Humphries argues that in the nineteenth century, when substitute child care was poorly developed and dangerous, it made sense for the workers to concentrate on trying to raise the *male* wage to a level sufficient to maintain a family by restricting the employment of women. Humphries's argument is, then, historically based. She sees the development of the dependent-family form, with the male wage becoming the family wage, arising in particular historical circumstances. Given these, the action was not sexist, although the attempt to maintain the male wage as the family wage through the exclusion of women from certain labour-market sectors in the twentieth century is less justified.

Hartman, on the other hand, sees the same developments coming much more directly from men's desire to maintain their privileges over women.[68] She classes trade unions as organisations of male power, which developed as much to exclude women from favoured areas of work as to defend the working class generally. Such exclusion of women, whether through protective legislation or direct action, would raise men's wages *vis-à-vis* women's and hence maintain their position of power within the family. Thus the domestic division of labour is not seen as a given, but as a direct outcome of the organisation of trade union struggle, which attempts to defend men's wages as family wages and includes in its strategy action to exclude women from certain areas of the labour-market.

In the feminist account, then, the vicious circle outlined above does not simply operate at the level of individual decision-making; the process of mutual reinforcement of the domestic division of labour and the segregation of paid labour is more deeply, historically, rooted, in both the institutions of the trade union movement and of the state.

Conclusion

The equal-opportunities legislation of the 1970s sought to ensure that *like* individuals are treated equally in the labour-market, irrespective of their sex. In many ways, as we have seen, it failed even in this modest aim of preventing outright discrimination. But there is a yet more fundamental criticism. At a time when an increasing proportion of the labour force were mothers, legislation which aimed solely at treating people according to merit would never provide equality for a majority of working women. For the continuing assumption that mothers are primarily responsible for the day-to-day care of children (and husbands) means that the majority of women workers enter the labour force on different terms from men. The equal-opportunities legislation all but ignores the effects of this prior domestic division of labour; only the maternity-leave provisions make any attempt to counterbalance it.

As we have seen, both groups of non-feminist theorists tend to take the domestic responsibilities of women as given. Neo-classical economists attempt to show that the lesser pay and status of women workers derive directly from it, assuming that the domestic division of labour is either a fact of nature or, in more sophisticated accounts, a rational choice on the part of households. For them, discrimination in the labour-market is a historical aberration of marginal significance in explaining women's pay or the work women do. The equal-opportunities legislation was conceived within such a framework of ideas; the market mechanism was seen as basically fair, requiring only limited intervention to overcome isolated imperfections.

Where the non-feminist institutional accounts differ from this view is in seeing market processes themselves extending the initial differentiation of male and female workers. Although the domestic division of labour may tend to predispose women to certain types of employment, the institutional processes of the labour-market multiply the effects of this occupational and industrial segregation. In such an account, occupational and industrial segregation becomes a key to understanding the lesser pay and status of women workers. Legislation which fails to tackle such segregation or its effects, as the British equal-opportunities legislation manifestly fails to do, is of limited benefit to women. It is for such reasons that groups like the National Council for Civil Liberties and Rights of Women have begun to demand positive discrimination on the lines of affirmative action in the USA. As a more immediate means of overcoming the effects of sex segregation in the labour-market, the Low Pay Unit has continued to advocate minimum-wage legislation to raise women's average wages relative to men's.

In contrast to the neo-classical and institutional accounts, the emerging feminist analysis of the labour-market points to a division of interests between men and women. The labour-market is seen as structured in the interests of men — both reflecting and reinforcing the domestic division of labour. In this view, women's unequal pay and status can only begin to be tackled by a determined effort to break down that division, both through the provision of suitable child-care facilities and through the reversal of legislation which perpetuates the dominant household form of male breadwinner and female dependant. Groups such as the Child Poverty Action Group and the Women's Liberation Campaign for Financial and Legal Independence have suggested changes in social security and tax law to bring about such changes, as well as increases in child benefits.

Feminist analysis suggests additionally that existing institutions are necessarily limited in the degree to which they can foster change to the benefit of women. For the legal system, trade unions and Parliament are all seen as male institutions operating in the interests of men. Moreover, in an era of economic recession, any gains made by women are more likely to be seen as being at the cost of men, so that the prospects for an extension of legislation are dim.

What the feminist model, with its emphasis on the gains made by men through organisation, does suggest, however, is that the organisation of women for women is crucial to any reversal of existing labour-market inequalities. Although further legislation of the kind proposed by the National Council for Civil Liberties would certainly help, the experience of the Equal Pay and Sex Discrimination Acts suggests that equality in the labour-market will not be brought by statute, but only through the actions of women themselves.

Notes

1. The help of Ann Sedley of the National Council for Civil Liberties was invaluable in the preparation of this chapter. She provided a full account of cases brought under the equal-opportunities legislation and explained current proposals for change. I would also like to thank Jane Lewis, who worked through major sections of this chapter with me.

2. Occupational composition refers to the distribution of the workforce across different types of work, for example, clerical, sales, etc. The industrial composition refers to the distribution of workers across different types of product or service: in each industry there are a range of occupations.

3. For a discussion of the inadequacies of official statistics with regard to women workers, see Audrey Hunt, 'Some Gaps and Problems arising from Government Statistics on Women and Work', *Equal Opportunities Commission Research Bulletin*, no. 4 (1980); and Ann Oakley and Robin Oakley, 'Sexism in Official Statistics' in J. Irvine, I. Miles and J. Evans, *Demystifying Social Statistics* (1979).

4. Figures from the *Family Expenditure Survey* (1979) show that women's earnings were the major income source for 10 per cent of households in 1979 and contributed between a third and a half of wage income for a further 40 per cent of households. When women are not employed, two-parent households are three times as likely to be in poverty.

5. Although there is evidence to suggest that men do more housework when women are in paid work, the distribution of household tasks between family members is still unequal and highly sex-bound. See P. Dickens, N. Bullock, M. Shapcott and P. Steadman, 'Time Budgets and Models of Urban Activity Patterns', *Social Trends* (1974); and Central Policy Review Staff, *People and their Families* (1980).

6. For a more sustained discussion of this point see A. Pollert, *Girls, Wives, Factory Lives* (1981); and Hilary Land, 'The Family Life Cycle and Women's Pay Opportunities', unpublished paper, EOC/SSRC (1981).

7. See Olive Robinson and John Wallace, 'Relative Pay and Part Time Employment in Great Britain', *Oxford Bulletin of Economics and Statistics*, vol. 43 (May 1981). For a more detailed discussion of the situation of part-time women workers, see also J. Hurstfield, *The Part-Time Trap* (1978); and V. Beechey and T. Perkins, *Part Time Women's Work* (forthcoming).

8. C. Hakim, *Occupational Segregation*, Department of Employment Working Paper (1979). A shorter version is available in Department of Employment *Gazette* (November 1978) and an updated one in the *Gazette* (December 1981). Hakim defines a set of disproportionately female occupations (those where the proportion of workers who are women exceeds the proportion of women in the whole labour force at that date) and then calculates how many women are in such occupations as a proportion of all women in the labour force. This is given as column (*a*) in Table 7.4. She then compares this figure to the proportion of women expected in these occupations on the basis of the size of the occupations at that date (col. *b*) to give a ratio (col. *c*) as an index of overrepresentation. In the *Gazette* of December 1981, she refines this by calculating an index of segregation based on the underrepresentation of women in disproportionately male occupations as well as the overrepresentation index.

9. Unpublished information from the *National Training Survey* (1975) (Manpower Services Commission), which covered all workers, even low-paid part-time women, suggests that low-paid occupations became increasingly women's occupations during the period 1965-75 and that part-time women workers not

only had a disproportionate share of these jobs, but an *increasingly* disproportion-ate share. Unfortunately, the figures were not available for publication at the time of writing (1982).

10. The figures on unionisation are taken from *Social Trends* (1981). S. Nickell, 'Trade Unions and the Position of Women', *British Journal of Industrial Relations* (July 1977), shows how the union 'mark up' is important for women as well as men.

11. Difference in men's and women's weekly earnings are greater than differences in hourly earnings because men work longer hours. The traditional comparison of full-time workers pay (Table 7.6, B), which is used by both the TUC and the Equal Opportunities Commission in their annual reports, fails to take account of the increasing proportion of part-time workers in the female labour force and the lower hourly earnings of part-time women. Line D in Table 7.6 makes such allowances.

12. Indeed, there is some dispute as to how far the equal-pay legislation did in fact contribute to this rise. In the period in question (1970-7) incomes policies were in force which may have had some effect on increasing women's relative pay; moreover, there was a considerable rise in unionisation and militancy amongst low-paid women workers at the time; see P. Sloane (ed.), *Women and Low Pay* (1980); and A. Weir and M. McIntosh, 'Towards a Wages Strategy for Women', *Feminist Review*, no. 10 (1982).

13. See also Shelley Adams, *Sex Discrimination* (1981); Jean Cousins, *The Equality Report* (1976); Ann Sedley, *Part Time Workers Need Full Time Rights* (1980); Labour Research Department, *Women's Rights at Work* (1979); and the *Annual Reports* of the Equal Opportunities Commission.

14. Jeanne Gregory, 'Some Cases that never reached the Tribunal', *Feminist Review*, no. 10 (1982), shows that the majority of women in her sample gave up their case before getting as far as the tribunal because of unsympathetic treatment by conciliation officers, trade unions and others.

15. Industrial Facts and Forecasts, *Women and Work* (1981), quoted in A. McIntosh, 'Women at Work', Department of Employment *Gazette* (November 1980).

16. M. Snell, P. Glucklich and M. Povall, *Equal Pay and Opportunities*, Department of Employment Research Paper No. 20 (1981).

17. See, for example, Pollert, *Girls, Wives, Factory Lives*, who cites the effects of the job-evaluation scheme at Churchmans tobacco plant in Bristol, where much of the women's work was skilled. However, the scheme left ten times as many women as men on the bottom grade; in the top four grades there were ten women and over 2,000 men. See Cynthia Cockburn, 'The Material of Male Power', *Feminist Review*, no. 8 (1981) for a discussion of this issue.

18. P. Turnbull and A. Williams, 'Sex Differentials in Teachers' Pay', *Journal of the Royal Statistical Society*, pt. II, series A, vol. 137 (1974).

19. See Pollert, *Girls, Wives, Factory Lives*; National Council for Civil Liberties, *The Shift Work Swindle* (1979); and J. Hunt, *Organising Women Workers*, Workers' Educational Association pamphlet (1975), for a discussion as to how this occurs.

20. Snell *et al.*, *Equal Pay and Opportunities*.

21. See Counter Information Service, *Women Under Attack* (1976); and Jeanne Gregory, 'Cases that never reached the Tribunal', for a discussion of the problems with trade union officials and the Advisory, Conciliation and Arbitration Service (ACAS) personnel encountered by women seeking equal pay. Only about 3 per cent of trade union officials are women (J. Hunt, 'A Woman's Place is in her Union' in J. West (ed.), *Work, Women and the Labour Market* (1982)) and only 23 per cent of industrial tribunal members are women – A. Coote and T. Gill, *Women's Rights*, 3rd edn (1981).

22. For further discussion of the difference between the two approaches, see A. Amsden (ed.), *The Economics of Women's Work* (1980); and M. Granovetter, 'Towards a Sociological Theory of Income Differences' in L. Berg (ed.), *Sociological Perspectives on Labour Markets* (1981).

23. Gary Becker, *The Economics of Discrimination*, 2nd edn (1971). Becker's model is discussed further in B. Chiplin and P. Sloane, *Sex Discrimination and the Labour Market* (1976); C. Lloyd and B. Niemi, *The Economics of Sex Differentials* (1979); and by Steve Lord, 'Neo-Classical Theories of Discrimination' in F. Green and P. Nore, *Issues in Political Economy* (1977). As with most neo-classical models, Becker's was originally developed to explain racial discrimination.

24. Chiplin and Sloane, *Sex Discrimination and the Labour Market*, find that wage differentials between men and women bear no relationship to the degree of concentration in an industry, firms in competitive industries appear to be as likely to discriminate as those in monopoly sector. Francine Blau, *Equal Pay in the Office* (1977), provides detailed evidence that in a number of occupations the fewer the number of women employed by a firm the higher the men's pay.

25. E.S. Phelps, 'The Statistical Theory of Racism and Sexism', *American Economic Review*, vol. 62 (1972) and reprinted in Amsden (ed.), *Economics of Women's Work* (1980); K. Arrow, 'The Theory of Discrimination' in O. Ashenfelter and A. Rees (eds.), *Discrimination in Labour Markets* (1973); L. Thurow, *Generating Inequality* (1975); and D. Aiger and G. Cain, 'Statistical Theories of Discrimination in Labour Markets', *Industrial and Labour Relations Review*, vol. 30 (1977).

26. J.F. Madden, *The Economics of Sex Discrimination* (1973), discusses the earlier work of the British economists, including Joan Robinson. See also J.F. Madden, 'A Spatial Theory of Sex Discrimination', *Journal of Regional Science*, vol. 17 (1977), which develops the theories of relative immobility further.

27. The human capital model is discussed in more detail later in the chapter (pp. 155-7). Individuals are said to choose a strategy for investment in their own education, training, etc. which depends upon their subjective valuation of the costs and returns. Such choices lead to a spectrum of skills (human capital levels) in the workforce. People then distribute themselves between jobs according to their human capital 'attainment'. Hence differences in pay between jobs (and employers) are seen to reflect only the differences in human capital amongst the workforce. As Granovetter, in 'Towards a Sociological Theory of Income Differences', makes clear, this is a development of the standard neo-classical account. For an elaboration of the human capital model, see J. Mincer, *Schooling, Experience and Earnings* (1974); and G. Becker, *Human Capital* (1964).

28. In practice most studies have used a proxy for this and have not adequately taken account of the fact that women tend to have discontinuous experience. J. Mincer and S. Polachek find that the career-break in itself tends to reduce wages. They argue that this is because human capital 'depreciates' through lack of use; see 'Family Investments in Human Capital: Earnings of Women' in Amsden (ed.), *Economics of Women's Work*. But M. Corcoran, 'Workplace, Labour Force Withdrawals and Women's Earnings' in C. Lloyd, E. Andrews and C. Gilroy (eds.), *Women in the Labour Market* (1979) questions the emphasis they place on discontinuity in women's career pattern.

29. See Lloyd and Niemi, *Economics of Sex Differentials*; Chiplin and Sloane, *Sex Discrimination and the Labour Market*; and P. Sloane, *The Earnings Gap between Men and Women in Britain*, EOC/SSRC (1981), for a more detailed discussion of the procedure and its problems.

30. W. Siebert and P. Sloane, 'The Measurement of Sex and Marital Status Discrimination at the Workplace', *Economica*, vol. 48 (1981).

31. S. Polachek, 'Differences in Expected Post-School Investment as a Determinant of Market Wage Differentials', *International Economic Review*, vol. 16 (1975). An alternative explanation of a similar kind is to argue that lower pay is due to higher turnover and hence higher hiring and firing costs, see Sloane, *The Earnings Gap between Men and Women.*

32. Siebert and Sloane, 'Measurement of Sex and Marital Status Discrimination at the Workplace'; Chiplin and Sloane, *Sex Discrimination and the Labour Market*; Christine Greenhalgh, 'Male-Female Wage Differentials in Great Britain: Is Marriage an Equal Opportunity?' *Economic Journal*, vol. 90 (1980).

33. H. Wachtel and C. Betsey, *Employment at Low Wages, Review of Economics and Statistics* (1972), showed that wages varied across industries in the USA, once personal characteristics had been allowed for. R. Bibb and W. Form, 'The Effects of Industrial, Occupational and Sex Stratification on Wages in Blue Collar Markets', *Social Forces*, vol. 554 (1977) conclude that 'Human capital investments are less crucial in the income biographies of blue collar women than industrial and occupational stratification', and show that the size of firms typically employing women is important in explaining pay differences between men and women. See also Blau, *Equal Pay in the Office.*

34. R. Layard, D. Piachaud and M. Stewart, *The Causes of Poverty*. See also C. Pscharopoulos and R. McNabb, 'Further Evidence of the Dual Labour Market in Britain', *Journal of Human Resources*, vol. 4 (1981).

35. Chiplin has advanced this type of argument with some vigour. See B. Chiplin, 'Sexual Discrimination: are there any lessons from criminal behaviour?' *Applied Economics* (1976).

36. R. Cavendish, *Women on the Line* (1982); Pollert, *Girls, Wives, Factory Lives*; K. Purcell, 'Militancy and Acquiescence in Women Workers' in S. Burman (ed.), *Fit Work for Women*, (1979); and M. Herzog, *From Hand to Mouth* (1980).

37. See Madden, *Economics of Sex Discrimination*, for a discussion of this.

38. See W. Hood and R. Rees, *Inter-Industry Wage Levels in Manufacturing* (1974); and P. Antonello and P. Gaglini, 'Wages, Salaries and Female Employment', *European Economic Review* (May 1977).

39. G. Routh, *Occupation and Pay in Great Britain, 1906-79* (1980).

40. Chiplin and Sloane, in *Sex Discrimination and the Labour Market*, tend to argue that sex differences in pay *within* industries are of far greater importance and that the redistribution of women's to men's jobs would not alter wages significantly. However, they consider only the one-off, rather than the dynamic effects, of desegregation on wages. Moreover, because women are employed at lower grades and in less well-paying firms, Chiplin and Sloane's industry-level analysis fails to allow for the major effects of job segregation and crowding on pay.

41. Blau, *Equal Pay in the Office*; and J.E. Buckley, 'Pay Differentials between Men and Women in the Same Job', *Monthly Labour Review*, vol. 94 (1971).

42. Nickell, 'Trade Unions and the Position of Women'; and E. McLennan, *Minimum Wages for Women* (1980).

43. Mary McIntosh, 'The State and the Oppression of Women' in A. Kuhn and A. Wolpe (eds.), *Feminism and Materialism* (1978).

44. Equal Opportunities Commission, *Health and Safety Legislation: Should we distinguish between Men and Women*^ (1979); and National Council for Civil Liberties, *Shift Work Swindle*. On the protective-legislation controversy, see also: Angela Coyle, 'The Protection Racket', *Feminist Review*, no. 4 (1980).

45. W.W. Daniel, *Maternity Rights* (Policy Studies Institute, 1981).

46. C. Hakim, 'Job Segregation Trends in the 1970's', Department of

Employment *Gazette* (December 1981). Hakim gives the following figures:

	1973	1977	1979
Percentage of women in disproportionately female occupations	84	84	86
Percentage of index of overrepresentation in these occupations	2.00	1.86	1.45
Index of underrepresentation (1 = proportional representation) in:			
Professional supporting management	0.38	0.41	0.54
Professional in science, etc.	0.13	0.15	0.23
Managerial	0.51	0.49	0.54
Processing, making and repairing, metal and electrical	0.16	0.16	0.13

47. See Department of Education and Science, *Statistics of Further Education* (1978). Figures from the Engineering Industry Training Board show that the proportion of trainees who are women rose, yet the *numbers* of women employed as skilled workers and technicians fell over the period 1967-77. P. Brayshaw and C. Laidlaw, *Women in Engineering* (1979).

48. I. Bruegel, 'Women as a Reserve Army of Labour', *Feminist Review*, no. 3 (1979).

49. *Powell and Clark* v. *Elley (IMI) Kinnok* (1980), see: A. Sedley, 'Part time Workers Win a Major Victory', *Rights* (January 1982).

50. *Nasse* v. *SRC* (1979), see: S. Robarts, A. Coote and E. Ball, *Positive Action for Women* (1981).

51. See the Conference of Socialist Economists Sex and Class Group, 'Sex and Class', *Capital and Class*, vol. 16 (1982).

52. Mincer and Polachek, 'Family Investments in Human Capital'; and S. Polachek, 'Occupational Self Selection: A Human Capital Approach to Sex Differences in Occupational Structure', *Review of Economics and Statistics*, vol. LXIII (February 1981).

53. H. Zellner, 'Determinants of Occupational Segregation' in C. Lloyd (ed.), *Sex, Discrimination and the Division of Labour*, (1975).

54. The assumption is that the costs of education and training are individually rather than socially borne. Were they to be socially borne, then the problem would more likely be discrimination regarding access than 'faulty' individual decision-making.

55. Amsden, 'Introduction' in A. Amsden (ed.), *Economics of Women's Work* (1980).

56. See, for example, G. Becker, *A Treatise on the Family* (1982).

57. P. Doeringer and M. Piore, *Internal Labour Markets and Manpower Analysis* (1971).

58. See, in particular, R.D. Baron and G.M. Norris, 'Sexual Divisions and the Dual Labour Market' in D. Leonard Barker and S. Allen (eds.), *Dependency and Exploitation in Work and Marriage*, (1976); but also V. Beechey, 'Women and Production' in A. Kuhn and A. Wolpe (eds.), *Feminism and Materialism* (1978).

59. Hurstfield, *Part-Time Trap*; Beechey and Perkins, *Part Time Women's Work*; and A. Hunt, *Management Attitudes to Women Workers* (1975), gives some information on the way employers see part-time work.

60. Econometric studies of unionisation suggest that once other factors have been taken into account, such as size of firm, whether the union is recognised, and type of company, the proportion of women in a workplace has a limited effect on unionisation. See G.S. Bain and F. Elsheik, 'Inter-establishment Analysis of Unionisation', *British Journal of Industrial Relations*, vol. 16 (1980); and

R. Richardson and S. Catlin, 'Trade Union Density and Collective Agreement Patterns', *British Journal of Industrial Relations*, vol. 17 (1979). Purcell, 'Militancy and Acquiescence in Women Workers', makes the same point less technically.

61. J.W. Grim and R.N. Stern, 'Sex Roles and Internal Labour Market Structures: the "Female Semi-Professions"', *Social Problems* (1974).

62. H. Braverman, *Labour and Monopoly Capitalism* (1974).

63. See, in particular, papers in R. Edwards, M. Riech and D. Gordon (eds.), *Labour Market Segmentation* (1975).

64. B. Bluestone, 'The Characteristics of Marginal Industries' in D. Gordon (ed.), *Problems in Political Economy*, (1971); and Bibb and Form, 'The Effects of Industrial, Occupational and Sex Stratification on Wages in Blue Collar Markets'.

65. Jill Rubery, 'Structured Labour Markets, Worker Organisation and Low Pay' in A. Amsden (ed.), *Economics of Women's Work* (1980).

66. See, in particular, A. Phillips and B. Taylor, 'Sex and Skill: Notes towards a Feminist Economics', *Feminist Review*, no. 6 (1980); and Cockburn, 'The Material of Male Power'.

67. Jane Humphries, 'Class Struggle and the Persistence of the Working Class Family' in A. Amsden (ed.), *Economics of Women's Work* (1980).

68. Heidi Hartman, 'Capitalism, Patriarchy and Job Segregation by Sex' in M. Blaxall and B. Reagan (eds.), *Women and the Workplace*, (1976).

8 EQUAL OPPORTUNITY POLICIES: SOME IMPLICATIONS FOR WOMEN OF CONTRASTS BETWEEN ENFORCEMENT BODIES IN BRITAIN AND THE USA

Elizabeth Meehan

Introduction

With the exception of the idea of affirmative action, laws in Britain and America embody similar principles in respect to equality for working women. Enforcement responsibilities are placed on institutions that are, on the face of it, also similar. But, in terms of political discourse and action, women's rights have been taken more seriously in the United States than in Britain; that is, at least, until the advent of President Reagan's administration. Paradoxically, at the material level of pay, Britain appears to be in advance of the United States.

The aim of this chapter is to explore some differences in approaches to the implementation of similar policy intentions in the two countries. The next section provides a brief account of reasons for treating the subject comparatively and discusses the contradictory indicators of female equality. For reasons suggested in this section, the chapter then focuses on the ways in which the main enforcement institutions in each country carry out their statutory obligations. The concluding section considers the presence or absence of 'policy networks' incorporating institutions and interest groups. It is argued that the relative incompleteness of a policy network in Britain may place British women in a more vulnerable position than Americans in securing tangible benefits from legal norms or in maintaining them when 'backlashes' are produced by economic recession.

Reasons for Comparison: the 'Diffusion of Innovations'

The American Equal Pay Act was passed in 1963 and the Civil Rights Act in 1964. (Title VII of the latter bans sex discrimination in employment.) The equivalent British laws are the Equal Pay Act (1970) and the Sex Discrimination Act (1975).[1] Affirmative action in the United States results from Executive Orders promulgated in 1965 and 1967.

These require government contractors to promote the employment of women and minorities. The British provision in the Sex Discrimination Act for positive discrimination in training is a minimal equivalent. There is no compulsory system of scrutiny in Britain to ensure that firms in contract with the government are complying with equality laws.

Although the passage of the Equal Pay Act in Britain revealed no conscious emulation of the American, the most important concept of the Sex Discrimination Act — indirect discrimination — has no domestic precedent and was deliberately 'borrowed' from the United States.[2] In 1975 the Equal Pay Act became a Schedule of the Sex Discrimination Act and the task of implementing both was given by the Home Secretary, Roy Jenkins, to a new institution with novel powers, the Equal Opportunities Commission (EOC). His intention was that it would be a clearly visible unit of responsibility like its American counterpart, the Equal Employment Opportunities Commission (EEOC).

One descriptive explanation of social change — the diffusion of innovation theory[3] proposes that such 'borrowing' is a common feature of legislative reform. But its proponents argue that transplanting policies is almost bound to fail because of differences in political environments. The prediction appears to be confounded. Women's pay rose rapidly relative to men's in Britain during a period of voluntary compliance with the Equal Pay Act between 1970 and 1975. Improvement continued after 1975 reaching 75.5 per cent in 1977. Thereafter, a decline set in, so that in 1980 women's pay was 73.5 per cent of men's. The relative pay of American women is much worse than in Britain and, on the whole, the gap has widened since 1963 from just above 60 per cent to just below. The picture, however, is more complicated than is suggested by aggregate figures. The recent downturn in the British figure is partly attributable to inadequacies in the Equal Pay Act. The apparently poor position of American women is, to a certain extent, a consequence of the success of the Civil Rights Act and Executive Orders in increasing the number of women in new jobs; as newcomers at entry-level incomes, they push down the aggregate.[4]

In both countries, however, occupational segregation is a serious difficulty. This may have been increased by a tendency of equal-pay laws to encourage employers to restructure work to ensure that women have no male comparators. This is unlawful under policies to eliminate discrimination in the non-contractual elements of employment. But British employers increasingly explain their differential treatment of women workers by reference to societal values. This sits uneasily with the fact that legislative reform, in part, reflects changing values and sets a seal on them by creating institutions to promote them. In contrast, it is widely believed in the United States that without new legal norms and institutions, the treatment of women by employers would hardly have improved at all.[5] Many British feminists believe that the Equal Employment Opportunities Commission is a much more lively institution that the Equal Opportunities Commission and is, therefore, more effective in ensuring women's rights a place on the political agenda.[6]

If women's equality is taken seriously at an ideological level, it may feed back on the material level by raising expectations, awareness and confidence. There is some evidence of this in the United States, and it is referred to from time to time in this chapter. Consequently, there is some point in considering how institutions in the two countries have gone about implementing equality of opportunity for women and what impact they have made in the process. This exercise, confined to one chapter, cannot be exhaustive. In both countries, departments and agencies other than those explicitly responsible for equality are relevant; for example, the Central Arbitration Committee in Britain and the departments of labour and employment in each. In addition, in the United States, there are whole substructures of state and federally-supervised regional offices responsible for fair employment practices, equal employment opportunities and contract compliance. The next subsections concentrate on the Equal Opportunities Commission and the Equal Employment Opportunities Commission, which play a central role in fleshing out legal norms.

Britain: The Equal Opportunities Commission

When he created the Equal Opportunities Commission, Mr Jenkins thought he had established a powerful body 'to enforce the law in the public interest'.[7] He believed his government's brain-child to be superior to both the older Race Relations Board with its unworkable remedial procedures, and the body proposed by the Conservatives which would have had powers to secure change only through persuasion and conciliation. Mr Jenkins placed long-term strategic responsibilities on the Commission. Enforcement for individuals may, but need not, be part of its responsibilities; individuals also have the right of direct access to tribunals and courts.

The strategic duties of the Commissioners are described in the Act as follows:

(a)   to work towards the elimination of discrimination (that is, in

employment and related matters, education and training and
in the provision of goods, facilities and services)

(b) to promote equality of opportunity between men and women,
generally, and

(c) to keep under review the workings of the Sex Discrimination
Act and the Equal Payment (1970) and, when they are so
required by the Secretary of State or otherwise think it
necessary, draw up and submit to the Secretary of State
proposals for amending them.[8]

A specific task delegated to the Commission is a review of protective
legislation required by the EEC of member states. Social security,
taxation, pensions and nationality were excluded from the Sex Discrimination Act. Nevertheless, the Equal Opportunities Commission is expected
to advise governments about their impact on women.

In order to fulfil its strategic and enforcement responsibilities, the
Commission has a number of powers at its disposal. It has the conventional
authority and resources to undertake its own research. It can also use
other bodies and outside experts to help clarify problems and policy
options. It can undertake informal and formal investigations in almost
any area it chooses, from single firms (or public authorities) to whole
industries or occupations. Informal investigations are something like
research projects and have no immediate legal implications. However,
under the Race Relations Act, the Equal Opportunities Commission
became empowered to issue Codes of Practice for employers. These are
expected to be products of research projects and informal investigations.
If, after being laid before Parliament, no objections to them are
received, the Codes acquire the status of being admissible as evidence
in a court of law. Formal investigations are more like judicial inquiries.
Witnesses and documents can be subpoenaed. If a finding of discrimination is made, a notice backed up by a court injunction can be issued
requiring the discrimination to cease. The Commission may recommend
how this might best be done and it can monitor for five years after
proceedings to ensure that no discrimination continues. The respondent
is protected by various quasi-judicial procedures, including some
relating to right of reply, and by rules about the confidentiality of
information gained in the course of an investigation.

Individuals may, but need not, look to the Equal Opportunities
Commission for help in securing remedies. The Commission may offer
assistance where individual circumstances warrant it or for strategic
reasons; that is, where important principles and precedents are involved.

The assistance may range from straightforward advice, to help with reaching a settlement by conciliation, and providing counsel at a tribunal, in court, in the House of Lords or in the European Court of Justice.

In certain forms of discrimination where there may be no identifiable victim – in cases of advertising, pressure or instructions to discriminate – the EOC and only the EOC may initiate proceedings.

The Commission is financed from a grant-in-aid from the Community Services (Home Office) vote. In 1976/7 this was just under £1 million; for 1977/8 nearly £1½ million, and for 1978/9 just over £1½ million. The 1979/80 grant topped £2 million.[9] The largest amount of expenditure is of staff salaries, followed by rates, rent and maintenance. Commissioners' expenses and the administrative costs account for quite a lot, but for less than research and publicity. Legal services account for almost the smallest portion of its expenditure. Unlike a number of other non-departmental bodies, its accounts are inspected and audited by the Comptroller and Auditor General. To some extent distribution of expenditure reflects the Commission's analysis of its priorities and the appropriate methods for pursuing an equal-opportunity strategy. It also relates to governmental expectations of its main areas of activity.

During 1976, the Commission understandably believed that their most urgent task was to identify as precisely as possible the main problems and the appropriate policy options.[10] Although the Chairman told the Fawcett Society in the middle of that year that the Commission would use its powers and sanctions to the full, other audiences were told that it would not be in the public interest or in the interest of women to rush into using enforcement powers.[11] Although financial allocations in 1979 reflect Conservative preferences for persuasion and co-operation, the opinion in the Commission has shifted to become more in favour of using legal powers and strengthening weaknesses in the law. But the Commission's allocations to research and publicity have increased fivefold since 1976, particularly during Mrs Thatcher's government. Between 1979 and 1980 about £500,000 was spent on these activities, some of it on internal projects. These included surveys of practices in advertising; surveys of five hundred firms and trades unions to discover precisely what forms discrimination takes; how much is known about legal obligations; and how better practices and procedures might be developed. The findings of such surveys were used for guidelines to employers, and, with the fruits of discussion with other bodies, like the Advisory, Conciliation and Arbitration Service, became the basis of a draft Code of Practice.

Research has also been carried out into related areas like child care, pensions, taxation and new technology. The Commission provided evidence for Inquiries into Income Distribution and Wealth, the National Health Service, Legal Services and Appointments to Public Bodies. A good deal of human and financial resources were expended on the controversial issue of protective legislation. Some research for this came from outside the Commission. By 1979 outside bodies and individuals were receiving about three-quarters of the research budget. The London School of Economics, for example, was sponsored by the Commission and the Department of Employment to examine the impact of the Acts in small firms employing mostly women. The Equal Opportunities Commission now has a joint panel with the Social Science Research Council for projects in specific areas like job evaluation, segregation, training opportunities, etc. Individuals receive grants to consider, for example, the training of girls in subjects where boys usually predominate at school and college. A register of research has been established; a research bulletin is published regularly; and the Commission is developing a sophisticated library service. Most of the Commission's research has been published, some in the form of discussion documents, both to inform and to seek out opinion. Large responses were received to its publications on taxation and pensions.

Much less use has been made by the Commission of its legal powers and the use of sanctions. A deliberate decision was made in the beginning not to issue Codes of Practice. The public explanation was that Commissioners were 'very conscious that busy managers and trade union officials have had to come to terms with a great deal of complicated legislation over recent years'.[12] The possibility that private reasons might have been different is discussed later. However, following consultations in 1979, a draft code of good equal-opportunity policies and procedures was published early in 1981 with an invitation for further comments.[13] Another on job-evaluation schemes is in the pipeline. Interest in job evaluation quickened as the Commission came to see occupational segregation as the major impediment to equality. But, although this began seriously in 1978, the job-evaluation committee met infrequently and did not produce a guide until April 1981.[14]

The Commission's record of formal investigations is poorer than was expected by the architects of the Act. Originally, it was hoped that at least one and possibly five investigations would be carried out each year.[15] The first foray was into Tameside Education Authority. The finding that no discrimination was practised was controversial. Whether or not the verdict was an accurate one, difficulties experienced in reaching it spilled over into other areas. This made the commissioners cautious of embarking on other investigations rapidly. Indeed, the Commission's second investigation into Electrolux Ltd was undertaken at the initial instigation of Mr Justice Phillips, Chairman of the Employment Appeals Tribunal, rather than the commissioners. While the investigation got under way, criticisms of the commissioners' choices of general priorities were mounting, inside the Commission and outside. In July 1977 it was reported that staff agreed with outside criticism 'that the EOC [had] dismally failed to make itself known to [or] respected by the public'.[16] Comparisons were drawn with the new Commission for Racial Equality which had initiated two formal investigations in its first six months.[17] Resignations were threatened unless the Commission committed itself to a more rigorous programme of law enforcement, particularly in employment.[18] By the end of 1977 it was clear that commissioners had reassessed their use of powers available to them.[19] During 1978 they decided to investigate the Society of Graphical and Allied Technicians 'in respect of less favourable membership conditions for women and pressure on employers to discriminate'.[20] This was followed in 1979 with decisions to examine certain employment practices in the Leeds Permanent Building Society, the appointment of women in the Sidney Stringer School and Community College in Coventry and the North Gwent College of Further Education.[21] In 1980 two further formal investigations were announced; one into redundancy provisions in the British Steel Corporation at Shotten and the other into the provision of mortgages by the Provincial Building Society.[22]

During the same period, the commissioners also increased their activities in individual cases. After five years of experience of the law and test cases, the Commission has now drawn up a list of proposed amendments to the Equal Pay Act and Sex Discrimination Act. Early in 1981, the Home Secretary was asked to 'find the earliest possible time for placing the proposals before Parliament'.[23] In doing this, the Commission was making suggestions that had been on the agenda of women's groups for a number of years.

The Commission has always taken the view that if discrimination and inequalities are to be eroded, concerted efforts by all government agencies and departments are necessary. This view, coupled with its obligations to advise governments on pensions, taxation and social security, has meant that commissioners have had continuing discussions with, for example, Chancellors of the Exchequer, the Departments of Employment and Health and Social Security, the Home Office, the Manpower Services Commission, the Central Arbitration Committee, and the Advisory, Conciliation and Arbitration Service. The outcomes of approaches to these institutions have varied in the extent to which they have satisfied commissioners. Possible factors contributing to the failure to gain satisfactory responses from, for example, the Treasury, the Manpower Services Commission and the Department of Health and Social Security, will be considered in the final section of this chapter on policy networks. In the meantime it is necessary to outline the powers and activities of the Equal Opportunities Commission's American counterpart.

The United States: The Equal Employment Opportunities Commission

Under Title VII of the Civil Rights Act, the Equal Employment Opportunities Commission was given power only to seek voluntary compliance with the Act. Litigation powers rested with the Department of Justice. Although it was unable to litigate, the Commission could file *amicus curiae* briefs. After 1972, it was granted power of litigation. Enforcing the Act has two aspects: the resolving of individual charges and the eliminating of 'patterns and practices' of discrimination. Cases of the latter type may only be initiated by the Commission. In scope such an undertaking would resemble the British formal investigation. But the EEOC has no 'cease and desist' power like the EOC's authority to issue a non-discrimination notice. If an American investigation revealed widespread non-compliance with the law, the EEOC would need to go to court as in individual or 'class action' cases. Since 1979 the EEOC has assumed responsibility for the Equal Pay Act, once administered by the Wage and Hour Division of the Department of Labor.

Its first budget was $3¼ million based on a prediction of 2,000 cases. The 1978/9 budget was about $94 million. The case-load of individual charges for the preceding year was 87,000. During 1976 about 52 per cent of charges were of racial discrimination, and 31 per cent of sex discrimination. Others were of national origin and religion. The highest share of the budget is spent on the salaries and related expenses of more than 3,000 members of staff.[24] The rest goes on data collection and analysis and investigating charges. Publicity and research about working women not directly related to specific issues or to compliance by particular employers tends to emanate more from the Women's Bureau and other bodies than from the EEOC. The output of the Bureau is prolific, both in the form of published documents and in educative seminars and meetings all over the United States.

The EEOC, like the British counterpart, has been the object of criticism. At first the problem was that low priority was accorded to the sex-discrimination aspects of the Civil Rights Act. Then, in the 1970s, questions were raised about the Commission's administrative efficiency and its division of responsibilities. The more complex system of accountability in the United States revealed these defects and a large backlog of unresolved cases.[25]

Upon taking up the chair in the summer of 1977, Eleanor Holmes Norton immediately instigated a complete overhaul of the institution, bringing in structures and procedures she had used successfully in the New York City Commission on Human Rights. But even before Ms Norton's appointment, the Commission attracted favourable as well as unfavourable comment. Before being able to litigate itself, the Commission's role in the courts was limited but influential. Between 1972 and 1977 it litigated successfully in individual cases also involving other employees. In 1977, thirty-five such class-action cases, each involving more than one thousand employees, were resolved.

The Commission's *amicus curiae* briefs and guidelines are judged to have exercised 'significant' influence on the law.[26] Six hundred such briefs were filed to good effect by 1977. Among these were the briefs and expert evidence submitted by the Commission, from its own investigations and from research commissioned outside, in the inquiry into the American Telephone and Telegraph Corporation. The settlement, the largest ever under civil-rights legislation, covered both racial and sex discrimination.

Comparison of Policy Approaches of the Commissions

Despite upheavals in both institutions, some of which were caused by similar problems, the Equal Employment Opportunities Commission has acquired a reputation for being much 'livelier' than its British counterpart in its approach to policy implementation.[27] By 1968, the EEOC had begun to revise its implementation priorities *vis-à-vis* women as a result of outside pressures and its own learning experience arising from the course of its day-to-day operations. Despite sharing the British problem of uncertainty about the division of responsibilities,

the EEOC has been praised for its activities in the courts, its strict
guidelines about discrimination, and it now enjoys the confidence of
the majority of women's groups. Groups and the EEOC in partnership
are deemed to have turned Title VII into a 'Magna Carta' for working
women'.[28]

British Commissioners argue that the excessive caution attributed to
them stems from a bad press that is no longer a fair reflection of their
approaches and priorities.[29] Like its American counterpart, the Equal
Opportunities Commission has been 'educated' by the process of having
to enforce the law. Having pursued implementation apart from women's
groups, the commissioners have come to share positions developed
earlier by the latter on positive discrimination and necessary amendments to the law. But despite convergence of views about key policy
areas, groups still feel that the Commission's record on the use of its
legal powers to secure desired outcomes is unsatisfactory.[30] In other
words, the Commission still resembles too closely the Conservative
proposal for an advisory body, when a powerful law-enforcement
agency of the type envisaged by Mr Jenkins is thought to be necessary
to launch a serious assault on inequality.

A number of explanations for the different approaches of the two
institutions have been proposed. These include the influences of
different bureaucratic traditions, the systems of interest-group
representation in policy delivery and the relationships of the bodies
concerned to other political institutions. The last will be referred to in
the final section on policy networks. The others, which are closely
related, will be considered next.

Bureaucratic Styles

Baldly put, the British believe in the twin doctrines of ministerial
responsibility and civil service neutrality, and Americans in a politicised
bureaucracy, renewed with each President. Reality, of course, is more
complicated. But even so, the stereotypes do have some reality in the
approaches to policy implementation of the EOC and EEOC.

In the British case, the EOC may be one of the few institutions
which has seriously tried to operationalise the constitutional definition
of the respective tasks of administrators and politicians. The analogy
between the proper roles of EOC staff and commissioners, on the one
hand, and civil servants and ministers, on the other, was once explicitly
made to the EOC staff at a time when there was a good deal of tension

between the two groups about policy directions.[31] The insistence that all policy decisions be left to commissioners has created administrative difficulties. Full Commission meetings take place only once a month. Subcommittees of commissioners are supposed to meet more frequently, but only one of these (Assistance and Monitoring) operated effectively in the Commission's first four years.

Tensions between staff and commissioners arose partly from the difficulties of getting things done and partly because the staff believed in a policy direction more akin to the hard and fast knocks thought by Byrne and Lovenduski to be necessary to bring about real change.[32] During the upheavals, staff were explicitly instructed to behave like administrators, 'leaving their feminist hats at home'. However, the subsequent investigations can be traced to this period and, with changes of personnel on both sides, there appears to be a more realistic appreciation that the evolution of policy involves both administrators and politicians.

The idea that bureaucrats can and should keep public and private hats separate is less well established in the United States. And the wearing of 'feminist hats' in the office has worked to the advantage of women in that country, although the uneasy combination of this behaviour with ideas about meritocracy and neutrality has been evident. Although the EEOC was also wracked with disputes about the proper distribution of policy-making functions, it continued to be regarded as normal that staff on it and related institutions would maintain personal contacts with political groups and co-operate discreetly to stimulate decisions that are favourable to women.[33] Some examples are the activities of some members of the Kennedy Commission on the Status of Women in forming the National Organisation for Women; the discreet encouragement by early EEOC staff members to women to lodge complaints so that they could convince their commissioners that sex discrimination was indeed a real problem; persuasion by senior officials of the Women's Bureau of the Department of Labor of southern female textile workers to join unions and their passing of information to pressure groups about proposals for changes in regulations with an impact on women.

Interest-group Integration into Formal Policy-making Structures

Differences in style reflect and reinforce different patterns of interest-group integration in the two countries through systems of appointment to public bodies. In the United States, within the limits of distribution of appointments to the two main parties, commissioners have to satisfy the civil-rights constituency. Apart from consultations with presidents, there is an opportunity to influence decisions about the chairperson during the process of ratification by Senate. In Britain, appointments to public bodies, in addition to party and region, represent the two sides of industry. Sometimes it is sensible to incorporate expert opinion or to secure acquiescence in this way. But policy content can be eroded by the actions of those delegated to implement it.[34] In the case of the Equal Opportunities Commission, three suggestions for appointees with feminist views were rejected by the Home Office. And there are reasons for speculating that labour, as presently organised, and employers may have a common interest, at least in the short term, in limiting the effects of the Acts.[35]

Because of the rules of confidentiality, it is difficult to ascertain systematically what consequences different styles and systems of appointment have for women. But there are indications of policy consequences which have been advantageous for American women and harmful to the interests of British women. Some specific policy areas where this has been notable are the close involvement of the National Organisation for Women, among others, with the EEOC in the drawing up of guidelines on sex discrimination and the monitoring of settlements. Many groups participated in President Carter's decision to appoint Eleanor Holmes Norton to lead the EEOC and in his proposals to overhaul all civil-rights enforcement institutions. The proposals sent to Congress bear the unmistakable stamp of the preferences of women's groups.[36] Amendments to original thinking reflect the latter's anxieties and were carried against opposition from the Treasury and the American Bankers Association. The President's own Office of Management and Budget orchestrated a campaign to stop opposition in Congress to them.

In Britain, a number of key issues appear to confirm the view that sectional economic interest groups have used their position to 'water down' Cnmmission activities. The difficulty of the workings of the tribunal system could have been mitigated sooner by the early publication of the EOC guide to bringing cases. However, it was delayed three times by TUC representatives who feared that the law and the EOC would undermine incentives for women to join trades unions.[37] Codes of Practice, which have similar standing to that granted by the American courts to EEOC guidelines, have still to be issued. Instead, guidance without legal standing were issued in the first instance. A commissioner, who was also a member of the Confederation of British Industry, wrote to the Confederation, saying he hoped its members realised that it was owing to action by their representatives that they had been saved from the stricter code.[38] Commissioners, although insisting on confidentiality among the staff, apparently routinely refer controversial policy documents to their parent organisations before deciding on what position to adopt at the EOC.[39]

However, it may be that British commissioners, like American ones, are changing their behaviour as a result of having to enforce the law. Despite the delay a Code will be issued. And recently a TUC representative declined to sign a dissenting report on a Commission document on protective legislation which did not coincide with TUC views.[40] But, in her case, the cost was high; the TUC did not allow her to serve for another term on the EOC and withdrew her from her senior post in the TUC.

Part of the 'learning experience' of the British commissioners stems from campaigns against government proposals to limit women's nationality rights and to erode guarantees given to women workers who become pregnant. These issues brought about a recognition that it would be necessary to work more closely with women's groups to secure change. The extent to which this will be as possible in Britain as it is in the United States is considered in the final section on policy networks. In the meantime, however, it is necessary to refer to a policy, fully developed in the United States, but which has only a minimal equivalent in Britain; that is affirmative action. It has been significant in America in promoting the employment of women in new occupations. The brevity of its treatment here is a reflection, not of its importance, but of the limitations of a single chapter which concentrates on institutions at the apex of policy-making.

Contract Compliance and Affirmative Action

The Office of Federal Contract Compliance Programs in the US Department of Labor[41]

The Office administers a policy that is absent in Britain; that is, the requirement placed on government contractors to conform with equal-opportunity policies and to promote the employment of protected groups. Class action and 'pattern practice' charges filed against private employers by the EEOC or Department of Justice may result, too, in affirmative-action plans of the type now being asked for in Britain. But it is the Office of Federal Contract Compliance Programs with the authority of Executive Orders 11246 and 11375 that has developed the typical plan which employers are expected to follow. The sheer size of this aspect of policy and its influence on British pressure groups necessitate some discussion of it.

Executive Orders 11246 and 11375 were promulgated by President Johnson in 1965 and 1967. The first did not cover sex discrimination; the second amended the first to do so and to deal with age discrimination and war veterans. The orders are estimated to affect at least 30 million workers, 325,000 contractors and to involve approximately $50 billion of public funds. In 1976, 3,039 complaints were received by the agency.

Affirmative-action plans to alter the composition of labour forces of government contractors are not supposed to be mere quota systems. These would be unconstitutional, because of the illegality of arbitrary differentiation between individuals and classes of individuals. Plans are supposed to expand the pool of qualified applicants through statistical analyses of suitable recruitment populations and publicity to encourage previously 'absent' groups to apply and train for new occupations. Goals and timetables for increasing minority groups or female employees are laid down. Failure to achieve these could lead to the breaking of contracts.

According to the Department of Labor, improvements in the rate of increase of women entering non-traditional trades are largely due to these plans.[42] But the difficulty of maintaining the distinction between a quota system and a good affirmative-action plan in an unfavourable economic climate has encouraged the growth of opposition to the policy, even among previously sympathetic groups like Jewish liberals.

In Britain, the Labour government deliberately eschewed the full panoply of contract compliance and affirmative action.[43] The argument was that the philosophy of such a policy undermined the foundations of the law. Moreover, it seemed that most government contractors operated in areas of potential high unemployment where the loss of jobs resulting from broken contracts would be intolerable. However, a limited version of affirmative action was permitted in the section of the Act that allows positive discrimination in training. Later, the Home Secretary allowed the Commission for Racial Equality to scrutinise government contractors to ensure that they were not practising unlawful discrimination. The Equal Pay and Opportunities Campaign was told that women would have to await the outcome of the Commission for Racial Equality experiment.[44] The permissive, rather than compulsory, nature of the present British provision means that few employers have taken advantage of it. As a result, pressure is being applied by groups, the National Council for Civil Liberties and the TUC in particular, to encourage voluntary positive discrimination. In addition, one of the Equal Opportunities Commission's proposed amendments to the law is designed to facilitate this.

Creation of Policy Networks to Secure Tangible Benefits

A possible outcome of legislative reform is that, once a law is passed, no real change follows. An early exponent of this view was Edelman.[45] He argues that laws purporting to protect 'victim' groups or extend rights to them may be only symbolic reforms. By the mere passage of laws or the creation of new institutions, governments may be seen to be concerned about 'victims' without necessarily enforcing any material changes. The 'victims' may be satisfied with symbolic success, in which case governments increase their legitimacy at very little cost. But, if tangible benefits are to follow from legal symbols, organisation and collective action are necessary. Organised groups among those protected by the law must take an informed interest in its administration and bargain for benefits.

Edelman's treatment of the administration is mainly concerned with the relationship between enforcement agencies and groups whose activities are supposed to be controlled. This is because his main interest is in why real changes seldom follow legal reforms. In her book on the politics of women's liberation, Freeman is more concerned with the conditions necessary for protected groups to secure the tangible benefits promised in the legal symbols.[46] She grounds her analysis of the politics of women's rights in the literature on social movements. In her account, the following characteristics have to be present for 'victims' to secure both symbolic reforms and tangible benefits. First, there must be a sense of deprivation felt by politically skilled members of the 'victim' group. And there must be a pre-existing communications network of others amenable to being organised. A catalytic event is needed to spur them all into political action to remedy the deprivation. Finally, she also argues that collaboration between interest groups and institutions is necessary to give substance to the law. But she concentrates more than Edelman on positive possibilities. Her analysis shows that the administration may have to do more than react to the demands of already established groups; that is, sympathetic 'insiders' have to help in the creation of coherence out of an amorphous mass of individuals and small groups of 'victims'.

Blumrosen, an academic lawyer and a former senior employee of the EEOC, argues that it is essential for administrators to involve participants from the beneficiary class in order to counteract pressures from the group that is to be regulated and tendencies towards a debilitating 'bland neutrality'.[47] An account by Gelb and Palley of the fates of four policy interests of women's groups makes it clear that a well-rounded network that includes a spread of relevant institutions and groups contributes to success in securing preferred decisions and in monitoring their consequences.[48]

Examples of network orchestration by 'insiders' in the United States have been referred to already in this chapter. When new groups are seen to make gains, the generation of still more is encouraged. *The Mushroom Effect* and *Women Today*, respectively, listed hundreds and thousands of groups in the early 1970s.[49] Such groups not only stimulate better implementation of policy, they also provide exchanges of information about jobs and skills and are sources of mutual moral support. A New York City contract-compliance officer set up one pressure group with these ideas in mind, and a second, composed of eminent New Yorkers, persuaded the US Employment Service Agency to work in tandem with civil-rights institutions.[50] Groups like Wider Opportunities for Women and the Coalition of Labor Union Women co-operate with federal and state government departments in opening up training schemes to equip women with skills.[51] The network also spreads through other institutions, closely connected with, but not directly responsible for, law enforcement.

Blumrosen argues that Congress, too, has facilitated the integration of members of the 'protected' groups into the administrative process by introducing rules about the award of costs in court proceedings during the last ten years which have the effect of 'encouraging private litigation to achieve public purposes'.[52]

In addition the system of accountability and the process of 'advice and consent' for presidential appointments to the Supreme Court and Executive Agencies provide a variety of access points through which groups may initiate or be invited to take part in bargaining for benefits in terms of personnel or policy development.

The lack of interest in the US Employment Service Agency in affirmative action for women in the construction industry, which the New York official responsible for contract compliance had to circumvent, supports the view of British commissioners that, if discrimination is to be eliminated, it has to be attacked by all public agencies.[53] To this end, the EOC has tried to develop fruitful relationships with other governmental bodies. But, at least until 1979, its policy network, unlike that of the EEOC, seems to have concentrated on the upper level rather than the grass roots.

The results of consultations with other government departments and non-departmental bodies have not satisfied commissioners completely. The Committee of Industrial Tribunals rejected the EOC's offer of help in training its members in the provisions of the Acts. Responses by the Manpower Services Commission to initiatives from the Equal Opportunities Commission have proved disappointing. In 1978 the latter was forced to ask the Prime Minister to instruct the Manpower Services Commission to do more about female school-leavers.[54] And, although the EOC is reportedly pleased with relations between the Commission and the Central Arbitration Committee and the Advisory, Conciliation and Arbitration Service, another source gives less reason for optimism in respect of commitment by the conciliation service to enforcing the Sex Discrimination Act.[55] In 1977, the Commission reported that two nationalised industries, despite EOC comment, continued to provide training only at night, hence denying women the possibility of apprenticeships.[56]

Relations between the EOC and central departments and ministers are notable for both failures and modest gains. The Department of Education and Science has been particularly difficult so far as the EOC is concerned, having been suspicious from the start of proposals for a sex-discrimination law.[57] After the passage of legislation, it did little to publicise in its circulars the requirements placed on schools by the Act. Towards the end of 1977 a supposedly confidential report by the Home Office stated that there was no need for an education section in the Commission. Its duties could be split between the Goods, Facilities and Services section of the Equal Opportunities Commission and the Department of Education and Science. The proposed transfer was vigorously opposed by the Commission in discussions with Mrs Shirley Williams.[58] Dr Byrne of the Commission's Education section was dismissed for discussing the matter with the press, although a tribunal later held her sacking to have been unfair.[59]

When Ms Price won her case about age bars in the Civil Service and Civil Service Commissioners were instructed to draw up new conditions of employment, the EOC found them unwilling to consult over the drawing up of new rules.[60] Thirteen departments were criticised by the Commission for not setting an example by seeking qualified women to serve on public bodies.[61]

Commissioners have continually pressed Chancellors of the Exchequer and Secretaries of State for Health and Social Security to end discriminatory tax and social-security regulations.[62] Modest improvements have been made. But, in 1979, social-security benefits still discriminated against women, particularly married women caring for invalid dependants.[63] Initial changes in taxation were regarded as cosmetic by the EOC and a Green Paper published in December 1980 discourages (on grounds of cost) the EOC aim for an early separation of the taxing of wives and husbands. The EOC's proposed amendments to the Sex Discrimination Act, released in January 1981, call for the ending of discrimination in tax and social-security legislation within ten years.

It is not surprising that civil servants and junior ministers might not take the views of the EOC seriously, given that leading politicians do not seem to set the pace. In 1975, there were suspicions that the Sex Discrimination Act, whatever Mr Jenkins's personal commitment, was a 'test-run' for the 1976 Race Relations Act.[64] Later Labour Ministers were evasive in response to questions, suggestions and criticisms.[65] Mrs Thatcher tried to reassure Women in the Media and the Fawcett Society, but she is better known for her general opposition to state intervention in economic and social affairs and her lack of enthusiasm for the women's movement. Unlike American politicians, however, British political leaders have little incentive to espouse the cause of women's rights, because of the less cohesive grass-roots element of the British policy network on equal opportunities.

It is only recently that the Equal Opportunities Commission has begun to take an interest in actively stimulating co-operation with women's groups. To begin with, the Commission invited women to express their views.[66] Subsequent EOC overtures to women's groups were confined to grants to promote research and publicity. In connection with this aspect of EOC relations with feminists, commissioners were at first divided about whether funds should be allocated to radical women's rights groups.[67] In its capacity as a law-enforcement agency (rather than as an advisory or educative body), the EOC has conducted relations with all pressure groups in an 'arm's length' manner. In November 1979, however, a one-day conference with women's groups was held. The most immediate concerns were the pressing issues of the day: possible erosions of the employment conditions of pregnant women workers and the status of women's nationality rights. The Commission acknowledged that if government proposals to narrow existing rights were to be resisted, a concerted campaign was necessary.[68] Since then, although it has stressed its need not to appear like a pressure group, the Commission has tried to instigate a united campaign by pressure groups for its proposed amendments to the Equal Pay Act and Sex Discrimination Act.[69]

But because of different characteristics of the political systems of Britain and the United States, it may be less easy for either the Commission or women themselves to organise a cohesive women's lobby. In summary, the looser party system in the United States – the greater equality between executive and legislature, the importance of the civil-rights constituency in presidential elections between the early 1960s and late 1970s, the more complex system of accountability, Senate ratification of presidential appointments, and greater group involvement in judicial proceedings – all provide opportunities for permeation by groups that formulate demands and carefully avoid the appearance of too much change too quickly. In Britain access points are limited by a more controlled party system that ensures the primacy of class issues on the political agenda, at least at a rhetorical level, and by the dominance of the legislature by the executive. Recent changes and proposals for further reform to increase accountability are probably unlikely to have much impact so long as the other two factors are present and so long as the executive, regardless of its 'colour', places women's equality low on its lists of priorities.

A possible 'joker in the pack' is Britain's membership of the EEC. The covert introduction of some aspects of public law is being accompanied by attempts to create a policy network that resembles that of the United States. According to Hoskyn and others, Community commissioners and officials have 'a much more overt and publicly visible political role'[70] than British civil servants in promoting new proposals:

> They can be heard at consultative meetings openly seeking pressure-group support against recalcitrant national ministries and revealing details of controversial negotiations in a way which would be quite unthinkable in Whitehall.[71]

Hoskyn *et al.*, however, also note that British pressure groups have been slow, especially in the field of social policy, to take up the opportunities allowed by the openness of the EEC.[72] Withdrawal from the EEC by a future Labour government would remove these opportunities.

The EEC apart, institutional arrangements in Britain ensure that the initiative in forming and maintaining a network must come, more than in the United States, from the relatively weak and uninformed grass roots. Difficult though it may be for the women's movement to become a cohesive political constituency, it is important that it does so. The policies of both countries on equal opportunities are based on the assumption of an expanding economy creating more opportunities. Even where there is no significant economic growth, distribution of person-power can be modified where there is a turnover of labour. But, in decline, the policy may become a zero-sum game where those with the least political bargaining power are likely to be the losers. In both countries, opposition to equality for working women has appeared as jobs become scarcer. In the United States, some groups, once in favour of banning sex discrimination, have begun to see women as a threat to the rights of religious and ethnic minorities.[73] In Britain, women's employment rights have hardly secured the status of being a serious issue, but politicians have already revived the notion that married women work for pin-money and are urging the government to take steps to discourage them from the labour-market.[74] Resistance to such notions requires fairly well-established policy networks operating at all major points of access.

Notes

1. The Sex Discrimination Act also covers education and the provision of goods, facilities and services. These are dealt with by separate legislation in the United States. The comparisons in this chapter are made in terms of equality of employment opportunities.

2. The Home Secretary, Roy Jenkins, was already impressed with laws banning racial discrimination in the United States. Between the publications of the White Paper on sex discrimination and the Bill, he and his advisors visited America and discussed the content of British legislation for women. Important changes were made as a result of consultations in the United States. (Interview, July 1977; and House of Commons, *Debates*, Standing Committee B, vol. 388 (1975), col. 46).

3. J. Walker, 'Diffusions of Innovations among American States', *American Journal of Political Science*, vol. 63, no. 3 (September 1969).

4. *1975 Handbook of Women Workers*, US Department of Labor, pp. 92, 125.

5. *New York Times*, 12 September 1976; *US News and World Report*, 4 September 1978; and *Wall Street Journal*, 7 August 1978.

6. For example, A. Coote, 'Equality and the Curse of the Quango', *New Statesman* (December 1978); and *Guardian*, 17 December 1976.

7. House of Commons, *Debates*, vol. 889 (1975), col. 522.

8. Sex Discrimination Act (1975).

9. Equal Opportunities Commission, *Third Annual Report, 1978* (1979); *Fourth Annual Report, 1979* (1980); and *Fifth Annual Report, 1980* (1981).

10. Equal Opportunities Commission, *First Annual Report, 1976* (1977), pp. 4-5, 12-13, 37.

11. Equal Opportunities Commission press notice 12 June 1976; and *First Annual Report, 1976* (1977), p. 5.

12. Equal Opportunities Commission, *First Annual Report, 1976* (1977), para. 2.

13. Equal Opportunities Commission, 'Code of Practice for the Elimination of Sex Discrimination and the Promotion of Equality of Opportunity in Employment', consultative draft (January 1981).

14. Equal Opportunities Commission, press notice, M 60, 21 April 1981.

15. Interview, July 1977.

16. *Guardian*, 11 July 1977.

17. *The Times*, 30 December 1977.

18. *Guardian*, 11 July 1977.

19. *The Times*, 30 December 1977.

20. Equal Opportunities Commission, *Third Annual Report, 1978* (1979), p. 16.

21. Equal Opportunities Commission, *Fourth Annual Report, 1979* (1980), p. 10.

22. Equal Opportunities Commission, *Fifth Annual Report, 1980* (1981), pp. 7-8.

23. Equal Opportunities Commission, press briefing 16 January 1981. The list was long. Proposals are intended to eliminate the inadequacies of the 'Equal Pay Act', clarify the relationship between it and the Sex Discrimination Act, to strengthen both by incorporating aspects of European law, and to facilitate positive discrimination.

24. Interview Office of Policy and Program Implementations, Equal Employment Opportunities Commission, Washington, May 1978.

25. Civil Rights Commission, *Federal Civil Rights Enforcement Effort* (1977), ch. 4; and Report to Congress, Controller and Auditor General, September 1976; and Oversight Hearings by House Subcommittee on Equal Employment Opportunities, December 1976, July 1977.

26. Civil Rights Commission, *Federal Civil Rights Enforcement Effort*, p. 201.

27. For example, Anna Coote, *Guardian*, 17 December 1976.

28. D. Robinson, 'Two Movements in Pursuit of Equal Employment Opportunity', *Signs*, vol. 4, no. 3 (Spring 1974), p. 427.

29. Fawcett Society Newsletter, June 1981.

30. Fawcett Society Newsletter, June 1981.

31. Interview, July 1977.

32. P. Byrne and J. Lovenduski, 'The Equal Opportunities Commission', *Women's Studies International Quarterly*, vol. 1 (1978).

33. Examples are provided by: J. Freeman, *The Politics of Women's Liberation* (1975); and J. Gelb and M. Palley, 'Women and Interest Group Policies: A Comparative Analysis of Federal Decision Making', *Journal of Politics*, vol. 41 (1979).

34. A full argument about this process is provided by J. Richardson and G. Jordan, *Governing under Pressure* (1979).

35. Psychological reasons for male resistance are suggested by M. Best and W. Connolly, *The Politicized Economy* (1976). Economic reasons for resistance by both sides are part of segmented labour-market theories. See R. Barron and D. Norris, 'Sexual Divisions and the Dual Labour Market' in D. Barker and S. Allen (eds.), *Dependence and Exploitation in Marriage* (1976).

36. Interviews, Office of Management and Budget, Washington, May 1978.

37. A. Coote, *The Guardian*, 17 December 1976; and Justice for Women, *New Society*, 13 January 1977.

38. L. Mackie, *Guardian*, 23 March 1977.

39. Interviews, February 1978 and September 1980.

40. P. Toynbee, *Guardian*, 10 March 1980.

41. Department of Labor, *1975 Handbook on Women Workers*. Civil Rights Commission, *Civil Rights Enforcement Effort*.

42. Interview, Office of Federal Contract Compliance Programs, Washington, May 1978.

43. House of Commons, *Debates*, vol. 893 (1975), cols. 1447-515.

44. Equal Pay and Opportunities Campaign, Newsletter, December 1978.

45. M. Edelman, *The Symbolic Uses of Politics* (1964), esp. pp. 22-9.

46. J. Freeman, *The Politics of Women's Liberation* (1975), pp. 12-43, 48-9, 54-5, 230-7.

47. A. Blumrosen, 'Toward Effective Administration of New Regulatory Statutes, Parts I and II', *Administrative Law Review* (Winter and Spring 1977), pp. 102, 209-14.

48. Gelb and Palley, 'Women and Interest Group Politics: A Comparative Analysis of Federal Decision Making', pp. 383, 389.

49. Freeman, *Politics of Women's Liberation*, p. 147; and J.M. Col, 'Women's Support Networks: Strategies for Development', unpublished paper, IPSA Round Table, Essex, August 1979.

50. Interview, New York City Central Compliance Office, April 1978.

51. Proceedings of Conference on Equal Pay and Opportunity, Wellsley College, April/May 1978.

52. Blumrosen, 'Toward Effective Administration of New Regulatory Statutes, Parts I and II', p. 98.

53. Equal Opportunities Commission, *First Annual Report, 1976* (1977), p. 8.

54. G. Linscott, *Guardian*, 26 April 1978.

55. J. Gregory, 'The Great Conciliation Fraud', *New Statesman* (3 July 1981).

56. Lady Lockwood, 'Protective Legislation: Who Benefits—Men or Women?', speech to Society of Occupational Medicine, 28 October 1977.

57. C. Callender, 'The Development of the Sex Discrimination Act 1971-75', unpublished dissertation, University of Bristol (October 1978).

58. *Times Educational Supplement*, 4 November 1977.

59. *Guardian*, 31 December 1977 and 11 January 1978.

60. Interview, 1979.

61. G. Linscott, *Guardian*, 26 April 1978.

62. Equal Opportunities Commission, *Second Annual Report, 1977* (1978), pp. 35-6; *Third Annual Report, 1978* (1979), pp. 28-31; *Fourth Annual Report, 1979* (1980), pp. 25-7.

63. Equal Opportunities Commission, *Fourth Annual Report, 1979* (1980), p. 26; and M. Benn, 'Women Denied Equal Treatment under the new Social Security Legislation', *Rights* (National Council for Civil Liberties, September-October 1980).

64. Misgivings were felt by both those against a strong race-relations act (*Daily Telegraph*, 13 November 1975) and those who hoped that sex-discrimination legislation would be taken seriously but feared that it would not if the Sex Discrimination Act was merely a model for the Race Relations Act. Comments that this was 'the real purpose of the Act' have been made in private to the author. That it was consciously used as a model for the Race Relations Act has been confirmed (without the implications of the private comments) by M. Rendel, 'Legislating for Equal Pay and Opportunity for Women in Britain', *Signs*, vol. 3 (Summer 1978).

65. P. Byrne and J. Lovenduski, 'Sex Equality and the Law in Britain', *British*

Journal of Law and Society, vol. 5, no. 2 (1978), pp. 161-2. An example is the reply from the Secretary of State for Employment to Mr Ashley, MP on 20 February 1979 that the operations of the Equal Opportunities Commission were for it to decide. House of Commons, *Debates*, 962/63 (1979), col. 99.

66. Equal Opportunities Commission, press notice, 7 July 1976.

67. Ashdown-Sharp, *Sunday Times*, 27 February 1977.

68. Equal Opportunities Commission, *Fourth Annual Report, 1979* (1980), p. 29.

69. Equal Pay and Opportunities Campaign, newsletter, May 1981.

70. C. Hoskyn, J. Keiner, A. Wickham, V. Hall-Smith and M. Suringar in the Rights of Women Group, 'The EEC and Women—a case study of British and European Legislation on Equal Pay', unpublished paper presented at Conference of the Political Studies Association, Women and Politics Group, Bedford College, 27 September 1980, pp. 3-4.

71. Ibid., p. 3.

72. Ibid., p. 4.

73. Freeman, *Politics of Women's Liberation*, pp. 201-2.

74. For example, Lord Spens, reported in *The Guardian*, 28 July 1979. And he has sympathisers in both Houses. Such sentiments miss the point that, despite the Sex Discrimination Act, women and men still largely work in different labour-markets. Even if the ethical premiss were accepted, the desired outcome would happen, in present circumstances, only if the effects of recession were appropriately distributed and if men were prepared to accept low-paid part-time work.

I am grateful to people who granted me interviews and groups, cited in this chapter, where I was given access to papers.

9 THE NEW RIGHT, SEX EDUCATION AND SOCIAL POLICY: TOWARDS A NEW MORAL ECONOMY IN BRITAIN AND THE USA[1]

Miriam E. David

The question of sex is now firmly on the public agenda, rather than being hidden and private. It is even considered as a topic for schools. How sex is to be part of education is very specific. It is raised as an issue within the context of the debate about how to develop family policies, or rather policies for the family. At present, the dominant tendencies in these political debates are rather conservative. Sex education as a subject within the school curriculum is now demanded by some as a way of preventing the further decline in social order and moral values by reasserting old values about the relations between men and women and their essence. This use contrasts markedly with the tendency over the previous couple of decades to address the question of sex explicitly, in order to change the social structure and break down the fact and ideology of the sexual division of labour in social and economic life. Indeed, I shall argue that the rise of this approach to sex and family life is, in part, a reaction to the, albeit slender, developments in dealing with sex discrimination.

Sex, and I use that term advisedly, rather than the now more conventional sociological term 'gender', is what is at issue. It is the term used in political circles to cover questions of both social sex roles (in other words, gender) in access to, and treatment in, schooling and also sexuality or biological sex roles. Indeed these two apparently analytically separable questions are now, in politics, being used inseparably. In particular, it is argued that social sex roles are based upon biological sex roles and it is in the family and/or sexual relation-ships that sex difference should be reinforced.

The shifts in approaches to the family and sex and their place in education are occurring in both Britain and the USA. In this paper, I want to compare how the shifts are taking place and raise some questions about the future. The shifts, in both countries, concern the political rationales for the uses of education for both the economy and social structure and relate to a breakdown in the political consensus. The main evidence I want to use is from the state's debates about education and its effect on the socio-economic system. In particular, I will focus on national politics, looking at what the British government, through its Department of Education and Science, has discussed and, in the USA, the way this issue has entered the agenda of the federal government both in Congress and in presidential initiatives.

I will not look at the evidence in local communities or individual schools because of lack of space. I do not think, however, that this evidence would contradict my thesis that a shift is beginning to occur, however thinly veiled and contradictory some aspects of it are.

Breakdown in Political Consensus and Rise of the New Right

The shifts in rationales about education are occurring in both Britain and the USA because of recent changes in national political complexions towards more right-wing governments, bolstered up by particular, conservative political pressure groups. In this context, both the British Prime Minister, Mrs Thatcher, and the American President, Mr Reagan, hold broadly similar views on the role of the state in relation to the economy and especially on state policies in the area of domestic policy. I do not want to argue that Thatcher and Reagan hold the same political views, that they represent the same interests, that their economic policies are the same or, most importantly, that their policies when implemented would have the same impacts, since the two socio-economic systems and demographic contexts are rather different. Nevertheless, there are certain crucial similarities that make comparison relevant. Both Britain and the USA are advanced capitalist societies experiencing serious economic recessions. Reagan and Thatcher hold similar views as to how to manage recession, especially on how the state should respond. In particular, they raise explicitly the question of the relationship not only between the public and private sectors, but of the family and the economy and the use of education in mediating these various relationships. These merit further examination.

On both the left and the right politically and in academic circles, it is now commonplace to argue that there has been a breakdown in the political consensus that has prevailed since at least the Second World War on the role of the state within the economy. Thatcherism for Britain and Reaganism for USA are cited as the main evidence of these shifts, and arguments are presented about them both separately and together.

In the case of Britain, Bob Rowthorn, writing in a recent article

whose title neatly encapsulates the theme, 'The Past Strikes Back', argues
that 'the process of disintegration (of the consensus) is rather complex
. . . within the two main political parties – Tory and Labour – there have
emerged powerful radical currents which reject the consensus approach
as a failure and seek a fundamental shift in the balance of power in
society . . .'[2] His general argument is that Thatcherism represents a
real break not only with the Social Democratic tradition but with
established Conservatism in the post-war period, or what has been called
Butskellism. It is posed as a return to a brand of nineteenth-century
Toryism, spiced with *laissez-faire* Liberalism.

Peter Taylor-Gooby, writing in *Critical Social Policy*, argues that
Thatcherism is not simple and needs to be analysed at two levels, which
then should be linked:

> The phenomenon of the growth of right-wing politics has to be
> analysed at two levels: the structural level of the functional
> imperatives of the developing crisis of capitalism and the super-
> structural level of the capacity of ruling groups to construct the
> appropriate mass ideology – authoritarian populism.[3]

He goes on to argue that 'a number of impressive accounts of the
shifts in British political life that culminate in the return to office of a
radical right government are available', but points out that choosing
between them must be on the basis of what Rowthorn terms 'a
materialist account of changes in ideology'.[4] In other words, he asks
why there has been popular acceptance of the construction of New
Right ideology, or what Hall calls 'authoritarian populism'.[5] He argues
that lived experience corresponds more to the individualism in new
right thought than to state collectivism. The rise of the New Right is
due to the failure of social democracy to create an acceptance of
collectivism and especially of the welfare state. He goes on:

> It has often been argued that the failure of the welfare state to meet
> needs could be accounted for by its insertion in the straightjacket of
> a capitalist, patriarchal society. The contradiction of the capitalist
> welfare state is likely to be experienced by many people as a failure
> of that institution. As such it promotes the kind of separation of
> interest that lays the groundwork for individualism.[6]

But he also adds that Thatcherism may be unstable: he suggests that
there is 'a fragility to new right hegemony'. So, although he draws

attention to the radical political shifts and some of their causes, he is not very certain about their future impact.

Chantalle Mouffe also attempts to understand the rise of the New Right by comparing Britain, the USA and France. She claims:

> Through the redefinition of a series of fundamental notions like liberty, equality and democracy, and their rearticulation in a discourse whose central principle is the affirmation of 'individual freedom' as 'the ultimate goal in judging social arrangements' (Friedman, 1962), liberal democratic ideology is being severed of its links with the defence of democracy and social justice and is being turned into a 'New Individualism' spreading the old gospel of self-help, thrift and individual responsibility. The aim of that ideological offensive is to transform the existing common-sense articulated around social-democratic values so as to reduce the expectations of the people, to destroy their sense of solidarity and responsibility towards the under-privileged and to prepare them for the more authoritarian type of society which is already being installed in many places. That process is beginning to bear its fruits and a new definition of reality has emerged according to which ideas considered as unacceptable ten years ago seem today almost taken for granted. Such a shift in attitudes has certainly played an important part in the rise to power of a new brand of conservatism in Britain and the United States.[7]

She also claims that the characteristics of the New Right in the US and Britain are 'remarkably similar'. She goes on:

> The battle is launched on two main fronts, the attack on 'big government' is combined with a forceful reassertion of the traditional values of the family, role of women, abortion, homosexuality and other social questions. Indeed one of the most striking characteristics of this movement is that it tries to unite people across party lines and class divisions on the basis of social and moral issues.[8]

The arguments about Reaganism in the USA, even without the parallels to Britain, have a similar flavour. Reagan, himself, in his election campaigns, argued that he was to provide America with a New Deal, likened, in its radical approach to state policies, to that of F.D. Roosevelt.[9] The difference was to be in content: Reagan would uncouple the state from the economy. David Plotke, for instance, has argued that:

The present moment is marked by a dramatic political fragmentation, the shattering of traditional positions and alignments, and diverse (often inchoate) efforts to form new ones . . . central economic, social and political features of the US in the last eighty years (from the late nineteenth century) are on the verge of (and in some cases well into) far-reaching changes.[10]

Plotke, however, does not argue that the breakdown of the consensus will necessarily lead to a shift to the far right. He is more equivocal:

For now, the predominant force in the new administration certainly seems to be traditional conservative Republicanism, which moved even further to the right in the 1970s, but still remains tied to the dominant post-war Liberal consensus . . . Their perspective is un-ambiguously stamped by the interests of the largest corporate groups, tinged very little by the semi-populist themes of the Reagan campaign.[11]

Plotke's optimism is refreshing, if not convincing, for much of the rest of his evidence relates to the breakdown in the consensus in certain critical areas: 'One possible scenario is for the administration to acquiesce in far right initiatives on "social" issues. The likely immediate issues are busing and abortion'.[12]

Certainly, other more recent analysts of Reaganism have been less equivocal in their interpretation of its radical nature, although all agree on its possible unstable future. Both Mike Davis and Alan Wolfe[13] agree with Plotke that there has been a shift to the right, but they argue that the shift constitutes a dramatic breakdown in the political consensus. Wolfe starts his article boldly: 'Ronald Reagan is the first American president of the twentieth century whose political origins do not lie in the broad consensual centre of American politics.'[14] He goes on to review sociological evidence and analyse the growth of the radical right in America and locates it in relation to liberalism. He argues:

In retrospect, the political success of American conservatives is not only related to, but dependent on, the failure of American Liberals . . . Yet if American conservatism was strengthened by the failure of American liberalism, the fact that the right was an alternative path of political and economic development in the post-war years would also become a source of weakness . . .

The right assumes power as ideology and utopia at the same time, a blueprint to maintain privilege and a reaction against the privilege it seeks to maintain . . . the American right is a force for rapid change and a defence of tradition at the same time.[15]

Mike Davis is equally sure of the shifts:

Like the beast of the apocalypse, Reaganism has slouched out of the Sunbelt, devouring liberal senators and Great Society programmes in its path . . . Public discourse has been commandeered by multitudes of 'post-liberals', 'neo-conservatives' and 'new rightists' who offer the grotesque ideological inversion of positive discrimination for the middle classes and welfare for the corporations. Indisputably a seismic shift rightwards is taking place at every level of American politics with grim implications for the future of minorities, women and the labour movement.[16]

He also sees a direct comparison between Reaganism and Thatcherism, although noting crucial differences:

Thatcherism represents far more of a tough-minded and politically coherent partisan bloc than Reagan's loaded deck of New Rightists, cold-war vigilantes and uneasy members of the Eastern Establishment . . . Reaganism . . . is a popular front against the depreciation of inefficient fixed capital or the deflation of speculative equity.
    In abstract terms, both Thatcherism and Reaganism imply strategies of 'super-exploitation' . . . but they pursue these goals in different contexts and under different constraints . . .[17]

    All three — Plotke, Wolfe and Davis — draw attention to the rise of the 'social' as crucial to the breakdown of the political consensus in the United States. Plotke, for example, states:

In the US, anti-feminism has seemingly played a greater role in building the Right in the last few years than in most countries . . . perhaps it has to do with the particular manner in which family-related issues have intersected those involving the expansion of the State.[18]

Wolfe is equally certain that social issues played a large part:

Much of the success of the American right in building a popular base

for its economic and foreign policy programs is tied to its mobil-
ization of sentiments concerned with cultural and familial issues. As
Rosalind Petchesky has emphasized, 'The politics of the family,
sexuality, and reproduction – and most directly, of abortion – became
a primary vehicle through which right-wing politicians achieved their
ascent to state power in the late 1970s and the 1980 elections'.[19]

Davis also adds the same points:

> The New Right scavenged much of its identity from the growing
> backlash against the civil rights movement . . .
>   Simultaneously the sustained, systematic expansion of single-issue
> movements under right-wing control was creating an unprecedented
> panoply of inter-locking organisations and constituencies, ranging
> from 'law and order' interest groups (Americans for Effective Law
> Enforcement, National Rifle Association, etc.) to 'new cold war'
> lobbies (American Security Council) or politicized fundamentalism
> (Rev. Jerry Falwell's Moral Majority). The largest and most effective
> category of single-issue groups, however, were those devoted to the
> defence of the sanctity of white suburban family life, including
> dozens of mass anti-busing movements, Phyllis Schafly's anti-ERA
> Eagle Forum, Anita Bryant's anti-gay-rights campaign, and – largest
> of all – the 'Right to Life' crusade. Significantly, several of these
> single-issue blocs – the pro-cold war, anti-busing and anti-abortion
> movements in particular – mobilized widespread support from
> classical New Deal blue-collar constituencies, thus demonstrating
> that social conservatism, racism and patriotism provided powerful
> entrees for New Right politics where Goldwaterite economic
> conservatism has dismally failed.[20]

Piven and Cloward, writing about the recent attacks on social welfare
and Reagan's attempts to dismantle the welfare state or the New Deal,
argue that:

> the concerted attack on social welfare is an attack on developments
> that have altered the basic outlines of American economic and
> political institutions. And we will conclude that the outcome of
> the inevitable conflict over social welfare spending is central to the
> future course of the American political economy as well.[21]

They coin a new phrase, 'the moral economy', to indicate the extent to

which social welfare has become, since the New Deal, accepted as part
of the functions of the state. They cite a lot of evidence, from opinion
polls and popular journals, to indicate how social welfare is now viewed
as political entitlement rather than privilege and that, significantly, the
state's spending on social welfare is not puny. Equally it has potentially
empowered the working classes. They argue that Reagan's axe is an
attack on these now established notions, but they take a rather
optimistic approach to the future, concluding:

> But what conservatives view with despair as the crisis of democracy
> might also be viewed as an opportunity, precisely because it is a
> challenge to an unfettered capitalism. We are at a new juncture in
> the evolution of the institutional forms of the democratic and
> capitalist state, and the question is whether capitalism will be
> restrained, can be restrained by democratic demands . . . The moral
> economy of the welfare state suggests the possibility of widespread
> popular support for new solutions.[22]

What is clearly now a central theme in the rise of the New Right in
both the USA and Britain is not only the attack on the role of the state
in the economy but the exploitation of ideas about social organisation
and the role of the family in particular. What is less commonly referred
to is the theme I want to address: the breakdown of the political
consensus about the uses of education for both the economy and the
family *and* the rise of the New Right's approach here in particular. I
would argue that the breakdown of the political consensus has affected
arguments about education and, in particular, that the New Right has
begun to promulgate a new notion about education which is profoundly
moral. Not only is it developing an overall new approach to schooling,
but also advocating new subjects in attempts to transform education.
The new subject is moral education: to include variously sex education,
or rather family-life education, education for parenthood, health
education, religious education, social and life skills, and personal values
or what, in the USA, is known as values clarification.

Although there is no necessary unanimity in the aims and content
of these subjects, what is significant, at this juncture, is the way in
which these subjects have been put together as a new curricular package
and are being promoted together. Indeed, it could be argued that any
one of these subjects alone is both radical and progressive. Certainly, in
the past, the main proponents of sex education have been progressives.
In this instance, however, the New Right have colonised sex education

with the professed aim of using it to promote strict values about
family behaviour and responsibility: hence also its links with moral
education rather than with biology, its usual associate.

Equality of Educational Opportunity Consensus

It is now well-established that in the post-war period, in both Britain
and the USA, a broad political consensus has obtained on using
education as an economic and social investment to serve economic
growth, by means of the principle, at least, of equality of educational
opportunity. I do not want to argue that the political pursuit of this
principle did not, in fact, serve in the reproduction of the socio-
economic system, but rather to acknowledge the strength of the
political arguments, strategies and educational policies linked to
achieving equality of educational opportunity in government circles.
Indeed, it has been argued that the academic study of education in the
1950s was begun by attempts to help politicians with this objective.[23]
More recently sociologists of education have attacked that paradigm
and have tried to analyse the underlying, conservative nature of such a
set of strategies.[24]

The way the principle has been enunciated and applied has varied in
time and place, between Britain and the USA. But in both countries the
position and claims of three social categories have been addressed in
implementing the principle: social class, ethnicity and, most recently,
sex (or rather gender). As a result of major socio-economic changes,
economic growth and some feminist political action, both the USA and
Britain have tried to reduce sex differences in access to, and treatment
within, the education system.[25] I would argue that the USA has
developed a stronger legal framework than Britain, with a longer
history, and one that has resulted in more legal and political action to
acquire the entitlements created through the legislation.

Recent US initiatives to reduce sex discrimination in public and
economic life specifically started with the Civil Rights Act of 1965,
although there is now much academic controversy about the origins of
this. The major object of the legislation was to reduce discrimination
against certain ethnic minorities, especially the blacks. Jo Freeman,
amongst others, has argued that the inclusion of women as a category
in one of the 'titles' or clauses of the Act was an 'accident'.[26] However,
prior to 1965, recognition in the polity of women's exclusion was
noted and a Committee on the Status of Women had been established

in 1961 by President Kennedy. For whatever reason, progress in implementing the Act's provisions for women was limited. Between 1965 and 1967, shifts occurred in policy implementation for ethnic minorities, especially over whether individuals or groups should be covered. By 1965, the President, through a traditional mechanism of issuing Executive Orders, initiated a strategy of what quickly became known as Affirmative Action, similar to what is also known as positive discrimination – taking steps to ensure that categories of people, rather than individuals alone, were not discriminated against. As affirmative action was pursued, the techniques developed for achieving equal treatment in jobs, housing, education were the setting of quotas for ethnic minorities in relation to their presence in the population. Glazer has called this the method of 'statistical parity'.[27] It has also been referred to as reverse discrimination.[28] Gradually, this technique has been applied to the question of sex discrimination in education. It was applied to all institutions with federal contracts, and this policy was strengthened through the Educational Amendments of 1972. Title IX specifically prohibits discrimination on the basis of sex in elementary and secondary schools, colleges and universities. It states:

> No person in the USA shall, on the basis of sex, be excluded from participation in, be denied the benefits of, or be subjected to discrimination under any education program or activity receiving federal financial assistance . . .[29]

At the same time, the body set up to monitor and enforce the civil-rights legislation – the Equal Employment Opportunities Commission (EEOC) – was given stronger and tighter powers. Two years later Congress enacted the Women's Educational Equity Act (1974) specifically to achieve more equality of opportunity in the education profession. It dealt with discrimination in teachers' pay, the question of maternity leave for teachers and finances to schools for particular subjects, courses, testing procedures, and also guidance and counselling. By 1975 a huge complex legal framework had been created to deal with what Davidson, Ginsburg and Kay call 'sex-based discrimination',[30] and many cases were brought to test the limits of this legislation, including a wide range on education.

British strategies to provide equal educational opportunities for men and women, boys and girls have a much shorter pedigree. Essentially, the only provision here is through the Sex Discrimination Act 1975. Although Her Majesty's Inspectors had taken the initiative to study 'Curricular

Differences between Boys and Girls' in the two years prior to the
passing of the Act, their findings did not weigh heavily in the development of a legislative framework for education.[31] Education, too, was
treated differently from other policy areas, such as housing and
employment, with responsibility for implementation being placed with
the Department of Education and Science or individual acts of litigation,
rather than the Equal Opportunities Commission. It should be noted,
however, that contrary to the USA, teachers' conditions in Britain were
more equitable. Women teachers, after a fifty-year campaign, achieved
equal pay by 1961. Moreover, maternity leave and benefit (established
only in 1978, through the Pregnancy Disability Law,[32] as an entitlement
for teachers in the USA) had been granted in Britain after the Second
World War.[33] Moreover, some local education authorities, notably the
London County Council, had developed their own system of maternity
allowances, as a strategy to employ women teachers, in the early decades
of the twentieth century. It cannot be argued that the USA has been
more committed to achieving equal educational opportunities for men
and women. The question depends upon whether it is the treatment of
students and pupils alone or the organisation, structure of and access
to education that is addressed. Both Britain and the USA have, in
different ways, developed a complex legal apparatus for tackling the
thorny issue of sex discrimination in schooling and in the related area
of the organisation of employment. It is important to note that the
principle of equality of opportunity was applied to those areas of
economic and social life that are traditionally seen as public. The
wider question of the division between public and private life was not
addressed. The sexual division of labour in the family, as it affects
both the structure of schooling and the economy, was not on the
political agenda. In other words, the political consensus about equality
of opportunity was very specific: it was about the structure or rather
the *form* (to use Bowles and Gintis's terms)[34] of schooling, in terms of
access to and type of educational institution. The content of schooling
and, more specifically, the general *curriculum* were not really at issue.
At the national or federal political level, non-intervention in the
curriculum was a very deliberate policy.

In Britain, although central government has, since the Second World
War, had strong powers over the organisation of education, through the
Ministry and later the Department of Education, it has quite consciously
eschewed involvement in the curriculum, maintaining a strong separation
of powers. Local education authorities were given the duty, in the
1944 Education Act, to 'contribute towards the spiritual, moral, mental

and physical development of the community', although these were not detailed. The only subject that was specified for the curriculum in law was religious instruction, allied to the statutory requirement to hold a religious assembly regularly. This was written into educational legislation as a concession to the religious authorities who agreed to more state control as an exchange, notwithstanding the settlement between Church and local authorities being reached in a way in which the latter did not win wide powers over the religious voluntary organisations running schools. The partnership remained relatively unequal. Equality of opportunity between religious affiliations has not been a subject for educational legislation in Britain.

In the USA, equality of opportunity between religious groups has been achieved through constitutional means – the separation of Church and state. Hence religious instruction is declared unconstitutional in schools which are publicly supported. Religious schools have been denied public support or funding. A Supreme Court ruling of 1922 legitimised the dual nature of public and denominational schools. Although all schools receiving public funds are to be completely secular, the state does not lay down the subjects/courses to be taught in schools. It outlaws courses which are deemed to be religious rather than scientific.

Breakdown of the Educational Consensus

This political consensus that the object of education is to achieve equality of opportunity between social groups, be they on the basis of class, race, ethnicity or sex, is beginning to break down. The shift away from this principle is not fully or well articulated and vestiges of the commitment to it still remain. Nevertheless, I think that the shifts are highly significant and may, eventually, affect the whole nature of schooling. The shifts are profoundly *moral*: they are about entitlements to schooling and about what schooling itself gives, or should give, in adult life. The shift towards a concern with the content of schooling – the school curriculum – rather than the social organisation of schools, reflects a new or a revived concern with social order and social values. In other words, attempts are being made to ensure that schooling confirms the legitimacy of the present inegalitarian socio-economic system. Children are to be taught to accept a future in which employment may not be guaranteed. It is also, I believe, the first time in the history of compulsory schooling that such an explicit effort has been made to use the school curriculum to teach the virtues of patriarchal social organisation, family patterns and especially relationships between men and women. I do not want to argue that such ideas have not permeated the school curriculum before. Indeed, they have been fundamental to school organisation and to the relations between schooling and the family since modern education was established.[35] But hitherto the patriarchal order was the essence of the *hidden* curriculum. The shifts are partly new and partly a reversal. The methods of achieving old ends are new. It seems to me that this is the first time a concerted effort has been made to teach such subjects as moral education or family-life education. Such issues were seen before as private, taboo and not an area in which the state should intervene. If they were an issue at all, they were a subject for the family, to be taught by parents to their children. So what is new is the state's desire to take over parental responsibility to ensure that these ideas are taught. The curious contradiction is that what is to be taught are old, apparently traditional values of family privacy and duty and personal liberty.

These shifts towards moral education and away from sex equality in education are not only about ideas or ideology but also about material circumstances. They are both about the legitimacy of the present inegalitarian social and sexual order, its work ethic and ethic of familialism. But they are also, equally importantly, about how best to prepare children for their real roles in the social and sexual division of labour.

These shifts in the rationales about education may too (as with the breakdown of the general political consensus) be analysed as reactions to the failure of social democracy in Britain and liberalism in the USA to deal with the economic recession of this last decade. Education is part of the political armoury for coping with recession as well as growth. Indeed, it has frequently been argued, for Britain at least, that 'education has been scapegoated for our economic ills'.[36] Liberal or Social Democratic schooling had failed to deliver the goods: equality of educational opportunity did not exploit talents which would ensure the participation of the most able in the jobs for which they were best suited. A meritocracy in social terms would not work. Education could, happily, be returned to its initial elite system of selection and social control, since neither the strong nor the weak definitions of equality of educational opportunity had achieved what was hoped.[37]

However, more important is the reaction of the New Right to the failure of Social Democracy or Liberalism to contain the breakdown of family life. On the one hand, it wants to reverse this demographic tidal wave and, on the other, it accuses, by implication, particular radical tendencies for creating and/or condoning this breakdown. The demographic trends which are a cause of major concern are the increase in divorce; the growth of what we in Britain refer to rather oddly, I always feel, as one-parent families and what the Americans call much more appropriately, if pompously, female-headed households; and within this category perhaps most politically significant, especially in the USA, teenage pregnancy, particularly out-of-wedlock, schoolgirl mothers. Finally, the phenomenon of 'working mothers' causes a good deal of political conflict. There is little doubt or disagreement about these demographic trends in either Britain or the USA.[38] The political conflict is over whether the trends should be reversed, consolidated or stabilised. The New Right wants to stem this tide and believes that its main enemy is feminism. Feminists are blamed for creating both the demographic trends and applying political pressure to obtain social policies that reinforce these tendencies. The policies that are now under attack are equal-rights legislation, especially for women and mothers at work, and, in the USA, the attempt to add an amendment to the US constitution (the Equal Rights Amendment), social benefits to mothers alone with children, child-care policies and abortion policy. Indeed, in the USA what arouses the most ire from elements of the New Right – it is what Jerry Falwell, leader of the Moral Majority described as 'America's biological holocaust' – is abortion policy. Indeed, all the popular weekly magazines such as *Time*, *Newsweek* and *US News and World Report* have claimed that the two key domestic issues on the political agenda are 'abortion and school-prayer'.

It is the case that not only are certain domestic policies already enacted under attack but there is also an attempt to replace such policies with new, more right-wing policies. Whether these attempts will be successful must remain, for the moment, a matter for conjecture. In the USA, it has been claimed that the political alliances creating the New Right are inherently unstable.[39] In Britain, although these attempts to rescind supposedly feminist social policies are much more veiled, none the less they remain potent.[40] In particular, the arguments of the New Right, especially about social policy, are politically appealing because of the psychological and social threats posed by the rapid social, familial and demographic changes that Britain and the USA have witnessed in the last couple of decades. Although it is unlikely that the New Right's domestic policies will reverse demographic patterns such as female or rather maternal employment or the rate of divorce; they will not confirm or consolidate such developments and they will feed people's (both men and women's) anxieties about changing patterns of sexuality and the social, familial roles attendant upon them. In other words, women will be forced to shoulder the double burden of employment and motherhood without respite, help or condolence from the state.

What evidence is there, then, of the New Right's new moralism and positive, rather than negative, policies to change family policies in education?

New Politics of the School Curriculum

In Britain, the breakdown of the political consensus about equality of educational opportunity began under the Labour government in the 1970s. That government committed itself to transforming the educational system, in order to tie it more clearly to the needs of the economy. Several policies were developed to that end, including setting in train a review of school curricula. This approach, however, remained within the political consensus, however much it diverged from previous Labour policies. Hall has argued that 'the Tories gained territory without having to take power', and most of his evidence is drawn from the changes in strategies on education.[41] In *Unpopular Education* (1981), further concrete examples of this shift towards vocationalism and training are presented.[42] The Tories, on taking power, have, however, further shifted the terrain of educational debate, although drawing on Labour initiatives such as in *Education in Schools: A Consultative Document.*[43]

Their discussion about future schools policy has centred upon the question of the school curriculum, and three major policy statements have been produced on this issue in the last two years. The fact that they have produced three major pieces of educational legislation must not be ignored. These three Education Acts, however, bolster my contention that there has been a shift in political orientation. All three reinforce parental rights in education, in which individual parental choice weighs more heavily than ensuring that equality of opportunity between children of different parental, social backgrounds is enforced. Although the past legislation on educational opportunities is not technically rescinded, the Education Acts go a long way to reversing them in practice. The 1979 Education Act, for instance, reneges on the commitment to comprehensive secondary schooling. This is confirmed by the current Secretary of State for Education's policy on sixth forms in schools—retaining those of 'proven worth'—rather than pursuing a policy of equal opportunities for children above the minimum school-leaving age. It is also reinforced by the policy on assisted places, reviving the direct-grant scheme in an individualistic form. The 1980 Education Act, drawing on a Bill drafted by the Labour administration, also legislated for parental choice, both by requiring local education authorities to provide school prospectuses on which parents could make 'informed' decisions about their own children's schooling, and also by allowing for the representation of a parent on a school's governing body. This form of parental representation, as I have argued elsewhere,[44] will not make for more parental participation and does not, in essence, transform school governance. The change is symbolic rather than real; towards the rhetoric rather than the fact of parental control. Governing bodies are not afforded greater powers over the running of schools than hitherto. The shift in the treatment of 'special educational needs', through the Education Act 1981, is also likely to be away from creating equal opportunities. The emphasis is on educational integration and the treatment of special needs within so-called normal schools, rather than in special educational institutions. Parents, again, are afforded individually more rights over type of school and are given the right of appeal or redress over local education authority decisions. Given the individualistic nature of these rights, differences between children are extolled, rather than similarity of treatment.

Most significant, however, to my mind, of the shifts in educational policy are the official pronouncements on the school curriculum, set out in three documents—*A Framework for the School Curriculum* (January 1980); *The School Curriculum* (March 1981); and Circular 6/81 of 1 October 1981.[45] This is the first time since the Second World War that official government statements have been made on the *content* rather than the form of schooling, although some attempts have been made to alter the system of school examinations. Perhaps it is the case that the government itself was not fully aware of the important step it was taking:

> The legal responsibility for the curriculum is laid down in broad terms in the Education Acts. The Secretaries of State believe that these statutory provisions are sound and do not intend to change them. But there is an accumulation of evidence . . . that there is a need to review the way these responsibilities are exercised.[46]

In fact, the recommendations went further than judging responsibilities.

The Department of Education and Science finally made pronouncements on the subjects to be taught in schools and argued the case for the introduction of *new* academic areas:

> There are frequently demands, for which a good case can be made, for new subjects to be taught in schools and for new areas to be covered within the rubric of traditional subjects. New claims are always being made – for example, for the development of economic understanding, environmental education, *preparation for parenthood*, education for international understanding, *political and social education* and consumer affairs. [My italics] [47]

So, even in the government's own terms the review of the school curriculum was not only to ensure its adequate teaching but its adequacy in terms of coverage and subject-matter. Although the concern, in the reviews, was with the key, traditional subjects in the curriculum such as mathematics and English, and the development of a core, or a common curriculum, consisting of at minimum these two subjects, a major focus of the review was to ensure the emphasis on moral values and their specific inclusion. In other words, I would argue that the government was less concerned to ensure that, through schools, children were imbued with the correct skills (especially vocational) to participate in employment and more that they developed, to use Ted Benton's phraseology, the right dispositions. [48]

Although the documents do not (and cannot, within the present terms of the Education Acts) have the force of law, the Department of Education and Science fully and seriously *intends* there to be a change of practice on this score, and suggests how the new responsibilities of teachers, headteachers, governing bodies and local education authorities should be exercised. *The School Curriculum* spells out in great detail the aims and *content* of education in all schools supported financially by central and local government together. Although initially a broad ideological frame is given for the aims of schooling (which, in fact, closely conforms to those spelled out in the Labour government's discussion document) most of the document is framed with a concern for *subjects* to be taught in order to acquire skills or areas of experience. It is argued, though, that:

> What is taught in schools, and the way it is taught, must appropriately reflect *fundamental values* in our society . . . Three . . . issues deserve special mention. First, our society has become

multi-cultural . . . Second, the effect of technology on employment patterns sets a new premium on *adaptability, self-reliance* and other *personal qualities.* Third, the equal treatment of men and women embodied in our law needs to be supported in the curriculum. It is essential to ensure that *equal curricular opportunity* is genuinely available to both boys and girls. [My italics] [49]

Despite this apparent commitment to equality of opportunity between the sexes, the preference of the Department of Education and Science is clearly for the reinforcement of sexual differentiation, especially in the family. It now claims that certain new subjects are necessary to the curriculum:

There are also some essential constituents of the school curriculum which are often identified as subjects but which are as likely to feature in a variety of courses and programmes and may be more effectively covered if they are distributed *across* the curriculum. These concern personal and social development, and can conveniently be grouped under the headings of *moral education, health education* (including *sex education*) and *preparation for parenthood and family life.* [My italics] [50]

In defining what constitutes these various topics, it is stated that 'preparation for parenthood and family life should help pupils to recognise the importance of those human relationships which sustain, and are sustained by, family life, and the demands and duties that fall on parents'.[51] The Department of Education and Science now clearly acknowledges that family life is not entirely a private matter, but is circumscribed by public laws and state policies. It accepts its own duty to clarify to children what the state believes is entailed in being a parent. Nevertheless, the extent to which parenthood (and its corollary sexuality) is legitimately a matter for state intervention, especially for schools, is hedged. It is not yet treated as synonymous with other school subjects or topics. The Department continues to regard it as a partly private, personal issue, and elevates it to a special status in the curriculum:

Sex education is one of the most sensitive parts of broad programmes of health education, and the fullest consultation and cooperation with parents are necessary before it is embarked upon.[52]

Moreover, to that end, regulations have been given legal status, through the 1980 Education Act, which 'require LEAs to inform parents of the ways and contexts in which sex education is provided'.[53] Sex education is clearly viewed as a grey area of public and private concern and, to the extent that it is still treated as private and hidden, it is not available for public-policy change. Hence, the social roles that are predicated upon supposed biological sex roles being partly hidden within the family are not the subject of policies to achieve equality of opportunity. In other words, the social roles of motherhood and fatherhood (which stem from the biological fact of being a woman or a man) are not available for social-policy change. Moves to modify the sexual division of labour in the economy can only be of limited relevance, if no parallel moves are taken to modify family roles and they remain hidden and private. Thus, the commitment in the rest of the document to sexual equality of opportunity is limited. It is clearly only about public opportunities, although the Department of Education and Science veils this by referring only to *adult life*, rather . than to its original broader concept of adult and work life. Nevertheless, adulthood is now apparently a synonym for economic life, since the whole emphasis is on the links between education and the economy, especially to industry and to the development of careers. Lip-service is therefore paid to using schools to promote sexual equality in job opportunities:

> It is essential that career opportunities should be kept equally open to boys and to girls. The obstacles to equal employment opportunities for women are deeply rooted in attitudes in the home and in society. Schools can do much to diminish these obstacles through the content of the curriculum.[54]

The commitment is quite evidently towards equality between men and women who have no maternal responsibilities. Otherwise, this pious wish to eradicate sex differences in curricular offerings would run directly counter to its efforts to ensure the teaching of a broad spectrum of moral education, emphasising parental responsibilities in society. The root notion of the family to be used in these subjects is that of patriarchy; sexual relations are unequal – fathers rule in the family and women are subordinate. Woman's main roles, through marriage, are those of economic dependant on her husband and as housewife, caring for both husband and children. In this family model, women are, by virtue of their work within the family as both wives and mothers, effectively excluded from equal participation in the labour force.

This patriarchal notion of the family is not on the political agenda to be changed. Rather, it is now to be reinforced not only through changes in the school curriculum towards the teaching of parenthood but also through other moves to dismantle aspects of the welfare state and return mothering to its proper place in the family. For instance, another feature of the 1980 Education Act which bears heavily on this issue is the removal of the legal responsibility on local education authorities to provide nursery education for children aged between 3 and 5 years old. In a recent clarificatory circular it is clear that there is no obligation on local education authorities to provide nursery-school sessions that bear any relation to compulsory schooling.[55] Indeed, it is recommended that nursery teachers effectively work a 'double-shift', teaching in two schools each week. The net effect of these policy changes will be to increase the burden on mothers of early child care. This becomes even more obvious when it is seen that the other traditional governmental partner in child-care provision — the Department of Health and Social Security — has stated categorically that child-care arrangements for both pre-school children and school-age children after the school day or in the holidays are not a state responsibility, but one entirely for parents.[56] No attempts are being made by this government to support working mothers by improving their conditions of service to provide statutory parental rights to leave for sick children, let alone benefits. Indeed, maternal rights in employment have been severely curtailed.[57]

The Thatcher government has an absolutely clear notion of the family and parental responsibility. The state has to enforce the notion that mothers should not shirk, and will not be assisted by state policies in abrogating their child-care obligations. To this end, the government is dismantling those parts of the welfare state which allow the family to abrogate responsibility for child care and child-rearing. More importantly, it is beginning to use schools explicitly to reinforce notions of family, especially maternal, responsibility.

Although it can be argued that sex education is not necessarily conservative and, indeed, there is much evidence to suggest that previous attempts to get it included in school curricula were very progressive, at this juncture it seems to me that it is to be used to bolster the patriarchal family. For instance, the Festival of Light, a very reactionary pressure group welcomed the Department of Education and Science's initiatives on sex education, but demanded that more thorough guidelines be sent to local education authorities.[58] It wanted the guidelines to state that sex education should be on the basis of 'chastity before marriage and fidelity within it . . . We suggest that in reviewing sex education schemes, the DES should emphasize the crucial importance of the married partnership as the only adequate basis for family life.' Indeed, its call for a sex-education review is because, in the last decade, there has been a dramatic rise in teenage pregnancy and one-parent families which its members attribute to the growth of secular sex-education programmes. Interestingly, and significantly, they do not demand an end to such programmes but their transformation into a religious commitment to the family. Sex education can act as both an incentive to as well as a prevention from promiscuity. It clearly depends upon context.

Politics of Family Protection through Schools

In the USA, the shifts away from the principle of equality of opportunity in education began under the ostensibly liberal Carter administration, although, as for Britain, it could be argued that they were prompted by New Right political pressure.[59] For instance, Carter tried to convert the well-established decennial White House Conference on Children into one on the family. But he failed to achieve any policy outcomes, because he vacillated over definitions of the family. In so doing, he initiated what has been called 'the war over the family'.[60] Under the Reagan administration, the New Right pressure has been accepted unquestioningly and forms the basis for changes in educational policy. It takes a simple and uncomplicated moral stance, aiming to return responsibility to the family, the model being the white suburban middle-class, heterosexual, nuclear family.[61] In this, the hundred-year-old tradition, or ideal, of community, public secular education is to be destroyed and replaced by parental and religious control of schools. The key way in which this is all to be enacted is through the Family Protection Act, currently going through Congress.[62] Its main provisions are educational, although it also deals with tax laws and other principles affecting the family. It aims both to rescind much of the recent equal-opportunities legislation for race and sex and to replace it with traditional moral and familial education. Thus, federal aid, which is now considerable, will be withdrawn from schools which prohibit either voluntary school prayer or sex segregation in 'sports or school-related activities' on affirmative-action grounds; or which provide 'any program which produces or promotes courses of instruction or curriculum seeking to inculcate values or modes of behaviour which contradict the demonstrated beliefs and values of the community', or any programme which supports 'educational materials or studies . . . [which] would tend to denigrate, diminish or deny role differences between the sexes as it [*sic*] has been historically understood in the United States'.[63] Moreover, parents are to be entitled to preview, or rather *censor*, textbooks prior to their use. In other words, the whole focus of the school curriculum is to be transformed to one in which traditional moral and especially religious values play a greater part. Here, sex differentiation is to be applauded. Moreover, the belief that the religious family is the repository of all that is good underpins other dramatic policy changes, namely tax concessions for parents whose children attend private or parochial schools and also the removal of federal control over discrimination in private schools. Racial, sexual and religious segregation is promoted by endorsing parental or 'Christian' schools, and removing tax penalties. The Act, in sum, 'protects' the traditional family, and especially women, by endorsing moral and religious notions and reversing policies seeking to promote racial and sexual equality. The abolition of the federal Department of Education—part of the policy of 'New Federalism'—confirms the idea that the family should be responsible, rather than the state, for education and the inculcation of values. The values to be upheld are religious; confirmed, at another level, by the various efforts in the state Supreme Courts to allow the teaching of 'creationism' as a 'scientific' rather than religious theory.[64]

Thus the shift in political ideologies about education is even more explicit in the USA than in Great Britain. Not only are all educational attempts at equal opportunities to be reversed, but the religious patriarchal family is to suffuse both the curriculum and educational organisation if the Moral Majority (the Chairman of whom introduced the Family Protection Act) has its way. Reagan, although supporting reductions in 'big government' and hence federal interference in cases of school discrimination, has not yet endorsed the Family Protection Act. The Act does present a curious contradiction: federal and local enforcement of the preaching and teaching of private, familial values.

The New Moral Economy

In conclusion, I suggest that in the last several years in both Britain and the USA political ideologies about education have shifted towards a concern with 'fundamental values' about social organisation. These ideologies are, in fact, a reversal of the post-war political consensus on equality of educational opportunity. They are all part of an attempt to return social and economic organisation back to the *status quo* before the Second World War. In particular, the focus is upon family life in its myriad forms. Five changes in sexual patterns prompt concern. They are the rise in teenage, out-of-wedlock pregnancy and parenthood; the growth of one-parent families; the increase in divorce; the phenomenon of working mothers, especially with very young children; and finally the development of abortion policy. All are essentially about women's place in society and women's rights. The present desire is to stem these changes and, if possible, reverse them and bring back the family form of a nuclear, two-parent family with a male breadwinner and dependent housewife, caring for the children.

However, it is the method of achieving these traditional ends that is new and significant. The aim is to use both moral exhortation and special teaching of moral or religious education. What cannot be achieved privately by social constraints and fiscal and financial policies, which give support to the patriarchal family, is to be produced publicly in the education system. This overt shift to the public domain to preach family privacy and responsibility is a curious contradiction. Although the subject-matter of education remains in harmony with the New Right's initiatives to reduce 'big government' and to dismantle the welfare state, by returning responsibility to the family itself, and its womenfolk in particular, the method adopted of using education to instil these private, familial values is at odds with this strategy. For instance, Pelham has claimed that 'there is no firm estimate yet of what the Family Protection Act would cost the Treasury in terms of lost revenues, but the figure would be in the billions'.[65] Neither has the implementation of England's *School Curriculum* been publicly costed but, clearly, it could not be achieved without considerable additional public expenditure. Perhaps we should not, then, fear this new rationale for schooling, but rather take it at its face value. It is moral exhortation from right-wing pressure groups who, in all likelihood, fear feminism more realistically than we should fear them. Their stand in respect of education is obviously defensive and is, in all probability, impossible to implement fully. Nevertheless, it is significant that they have captured the political terrain to espouse their position and so forcefully to reassert the virtues particularly of patriarchal motherhood.[66] Even if the curricular package of moral and sex education is not incorporated into most schools, the other elements of the agenda undoubtedly will be achieved in the short run — the reversal of anti-discrimination policies and returning welfare responsibilities to the family — for these are already set in train.

What, then, can be done to counter such tendencies? Is it possible to take back the political terrain and recover sex and moral education for a more progressive stance? Zillah Eisenstein has persuasively argued that although liberalism alone is not essentially radical, there are still radical possibilities in liberal feminism.[67] Can feminists and socialists regain the arena of state education and transform it into popular, radical ideology? Given the contradictions in the New Right's scenarios and the claims made by other academic commentators of the instability of this 'authoritarian populism', the outlook is probably not as bleak as I have indicated. Neither sex education nor the family are in and of themselves entirely reactionary forces. They can be used to develop a more radical strategy to counter the state's attempts to keep women in their place.

Notes

1. An earlier version of this paper was given at the Sociology of Education Conference at Westhill College, Birmingham (1982) and will appear in S. Walker and L. Barton (eds.), *Gender, Class and Education* (1982).

2. B. Rowthorn, 'The Past Strikes Back', *Marxism Today* (January 1982), p. 13.

3. P. Taylor-Gooby, 'The New Right and Social Policy', *Critical Social Policy*, vol. 1 (1981), p. 18.

4. Rowthorn, 'The Past Strikes Back', p. 24.

5. S. Hall, 'The Great Moving Right Show', *Marxism Today* (January 1979), p. 1.

6. Ibid., p. 29.

7. Chantalle Mouffe, 'Democracy and the New Right', *Politics and Power*, vol. 4 (1981), p. 239.

8. Ibid., p. 231.

9. S.M. Miller, 'Reagan, Reaganism and the Real World', *New Society* (15 January 1981), p. 91.

10. D. Plotke, 'Reaganism: Is it as Bad as it Sounds?', *Marxism Today* (2 February 1981), p. 9.

11. Ibid., p. 7.

12. Ibid., p. 11.

13. M. Davis, 'The New Right's Road to Power', *New Left Review*, vol. 128 (1981); A. Wolfe, 'Sociology, Liberalism and the Radical Right', *New Left Review*, vol. 128 (1981).

14. Wolfe, 'Sociology, Liberalism and the Radical Right', p. 3.

15. Ibid., p. 22.

16. Davis, 'The New Right's Road to Power', p. 28.

17. Ibid., p. 47.

18. Plotke, 'Reaganism', p. 12.

19. Wolfe, 'Sociology, Liberalism and the Radical Right', p. 14.

20. Davis, 'The New Right's Road to Power', pp. 35 and 38-9.

21. F.F. Piven and R. Cloward, 'Moral Economy and the Welfare State', paper presented to the Annual Conference of the British Sociological Association (9 April 1981), p. 2.

22. Piven and Cloward, 'Moral Economy', p. 26.

23. D. Finn, N. Grant and R. Johnson, 'Social Democracy, Education and the Crisis', *On Ideology, Cultural Studies*, vol. 10 (1977).

24. J. Demaine, *Contemporary Theories in the Sociology of Education* (1981); and M. Young and G. Whitty, *Society, State and Schooling* (1977).

25. J. Fishel and A. Pottker, *National Politics and Sex Discrimination in Education* (1978).

26. J. Freeman, *The Politics of Women's Liberation* (1975).

27. N. Glazer, *Affirmative Discrimination* (1976).

28. R. Dworkin, *Taking Rights Seriously* (1977).

29. 'Women in Education', *Harvard Education Review*, vol. 49 (Winter and Spring 1980).

30. K.M. Davidson, R.B. Ginsburg and H. Kay, *Sex-Based Discrimination Texts, Cases and Materials* (1978).

31. HM Inspectors of Schools, *Curricular Differences between Boys and Girls* (1975).

32. C.T. Adams and K.T. Winston, *Mothers at Work* (1980), p. 33.

33. M.E. David, *The State, the Family and Education* (1980).

34. S. Bowles and H. Gintis, *Schooling in Capitalist America* (1976).

35. David, *State, Family and Education*.

36. H. Silver, 'Education and Social Policy', *New Society* (30 November 1978).

37. A.H. Halsey, *Educational Priority*, Vol. 1 (1973).

38. R.E. Smith (ed.), *The Subtle Revolution* (1980).

39. Davis, 'The New Right's Road to Power'.

40. T. Davis and C. Hall, 'The Forward Face of Feminism', *Marxism Today*, (October 1980), pp. 14-19.

41. Hall, 'The Great Moving Right Show'.

42. Centre for Contemporary Cultural Studies, *Unpopular Education* (1981).

43. Department of Education and Science, *Education in Schools: A Consultative Document*, Cmnd 6869 (1977).

44. David, *State, Family and Education*.

45. Department of Education and Science, *A Framework for the School Curriculum* (1980); *The School Curriculum* (1981); and Department of Education and Science and Welsh Office, *The School Curriculum*, Circular 6/81 (1981).

46. Department of Education and Science, *Framework for the School Curriculum*, para. 1.

47. Department of Education and Science, *School Curriculum*, para. 13.

48. Ted Benton, 'Education and Politics' in D. Holly (ed.), *Education or Domination?* (1974).

49. Department of Education and Science, *School Curriculum*, para. 22.

50. Ibid., para. 23.

51. Ibid., para. 25.

52. Ibid., para. 26.

53. Ibid.

54. Ibid., para. 54.

55. Department of Education and Science, *Nursery Education*, Circular 7/81 (1981).

218 The New Right, Sex, Education and Social Policy

56. Speech by Geoffrey Finsberg, Under-Secretary of State, House of Commons *Debates*, no. 56 (4 November 1981), cols. 106-9.

57. A. Coote and J. Coussins, *The Family in the Firing Line* (1981).

58. 'Sex Education Review', *Times Educational Supplement*, 30 December 1981.

59. G. Steiner, *The Futility of Family Policy* (1980).

60. B. Berger, 'The War against the Family', *The Public Interest* vol. 62 (Winter 1981), pp. 113-14.

61. R.P. Petchesky, 'Antiabortion, Antifeminism and the Rise of the New Right', *Feminist Studies*, no. 7 (1981).

62. *Congressional Quarterly*, vol. 39, no. 410 (3 October 1981), p. 1916.

63. Ibid.

64. D. Dickson, 'Adam and Eve and Darwin', *New Society* (26 February 1981), p. 954.

65. A. Pelham, in *Congressional Quarterly*, vol. 39, no. 410, (3 October 1981), p. 191.

66. L. Gordon and A. Hunter, 'Sex, Family and the New Right', *Radical America*, vol. 11 (1977-8).

67. Z. Eisenstein, *The Radical Future of Liberal Feminism* (1980).

CONTRIBUTORS

Brian Abel-Smith has been Professor of Social Administration at the London School of Economics since 1967. He is the author or co-author of some 22 books and has acted as special advisor to four secretaries of state in the UK, as well as serving as a consultant to the ILO, ISSA, OECD and WHO.

Irene Bruegel is an active feminist and member of the Conference of Socialist Economists Sex and Class Group. Many of the ideas she presents in the book were developed through teaching a course on the Economics of Sex Discrimination at the North East London Polytechnic, where she lectured until recently. She is currently working on a study of the entry of young people into the labour-market.

Miriam E. David has been involved in the women's movement in both Britain and the USA. She is the author of several books including: *The State, the Family and Education* (1980), *School Rule in the USA* (1975), and co-author of *Half the Sky: An Introduction to Women's Studies* (1979). She teaches social administration at the University of Bristol, and is currently working on a book with Caroline Freeman about the theory and practice of child care.

Dulcie Groves is a Lecturer in Social Administration at the University of Lancaster. She is currently doing research on women and occupational pensions and, with Dr Janet Finch, is editing a book on the implications for women of current policies on community care.

Hilary Land is a Reader in Social Administration at the University of Bristol. One of her main interests is the impact of state social policies on the family, and her publications include: *Large Families in London* (1969); *Change, Choice and Conflict in Social Policy* (with P. Hall, R. Parker and A. Webb) (1975); 'Who Cares for the Family?', *Journal of Social Policy* (1978); and 'The Family Wage', Eleanor Rathbone Memorial Lecture (1979). She is a feminist, and has been active in campaigns to change the tax and income-maintenance systems. She lives in Bristol and London with her small daughter.

Jane Lewis is a historian teaching in the Department of Social Science and Administration at the London School of Economics. She is the author of *The Politics of Motherhood: Child and Maternal Welfare in England, 1900-39* (1980), and is currently preparing a textbook on women's social history.

Elizabeth Meehan lectures in politics at the University of Bath. She took her first degree at Sussex University, where she carried out research on working-class liberalism. The subject of her DPhil thesis at Oxford is a comparison of equal-opportunity policies for women in Britain and America, and her main teaching interests are British, American and comparative politics.

Ann Oakley is a feminist, sociologist and mother. Her major publications are: *Sex, Gender and Society* (1972); *The Sociology of Housework* (1974); *Housewife* (1974); *Becoming a Mother* (1979); *Women Confined* (1980); and *Subject Women* (1981). She is the Wellcome Research Fellow at the National Perinatal Epidemiology Unit, Radcliffe Infirmary, Oxford, and Honorary Research Officer, Department of Sociology, Bedford College. She is currently working on the history of antenatal care.

INDEX